POLAND'S POLITICIZED ARMY

Communists in Uniform

by George C. Malcher

PRAEGER

PRAEGER SPECIAL STUDIES • PRAEGER SCIENTIFIC

New York • Philadelphia • Eastbourne, UK
Toronto • Hong Kong • Tokyo • Sydney

Library of Congress Cataloging in Publication Data

Malcher, George Charles.
    Poland's politicized army.

    Bibliography: p.
    1. Poland. Wojsko Polskie. 2. Poland. Wojsko Polskie
—Political activity. 3. Poland—Politics and government
—1980-   . I. Title.
UA829.P7M26   1984   322'.5'09438   84-6894
ISBN 0-03-071736-1 [alk. paper]

Published in 1984 by Praeger Publishers
CBS Educational and Professional Publishing,
a Division of CBS Inc.
521 Fifth Avenue, New York, NY 10175 USA

Printed in the United States of America
on acid-free paper

Contents

iii

List of Acronyms

AK	Armia Krajowa (Home Army, anti-Communist resistance up to 1948)
AL	Armia Ludowa (People's Army Communist underground up to 1945)
ASG	Akademia Sztabu Generalnego (General Staff Academy, Warsaw)
ASW	Akademia Spraw Wewnetrznych (Academy of Internal Affairs)
ATK	Akademia Teologii Katolickiej (Academy of Catholic Theology, Warsaw)
BCh	Bataljony Chlopskie (Peasant Battalions, anti-Communist resistance linked to AK)
BIB	Board for International Broadcasting
BWW	Biblioteka Wiedzy Wojskowej (Military Knowledge Library)
CAW	Centralne Archiwum Wojskowe (Central Army Archives)
CBW	Centralna Biblioteka Wojskowa (Central Army Library)
CDO	Centrum Doskonalenia Oficerow (Center of Advanced Officer Training)
CGO	Centralna Grupa Operacyjna (Central Operation Group)
ChSS	Chrzescijanskie Stowarzyszenie Spoleczne (Christian Social Association)
CKKP	Centralna Komisja Kontroli Partyjnej (Central Party Control Commission)
CKR	Centralna Komisja Rewizyjna (Central Audit Commission of the PUWP)
CKW	Centralny Kolportaz Wojskowy (Military Publications Distribution)
CMTO	Centralne Manewry Techniczno-Obronne (Central Paramilitary Exercises)
COM DWP	Centralny Osrodek Metodyczny Domu Wojska Polskiego (Methods Center at Polish Army House)
CONIW	Centralny Osrodek Naukowej Informacji Wojskowej (Center of Military Scientific Information)
CPP	Centralna Pracownia Psychologiczna (Central Psychological Laboratory, of Central Medical Comm. of the Army)
CPSP	Cykl Przedmiotow Spoleczno-Politycznych (Sociopolitical subjects as part of curriculum at military schools)

CSOP	Centrum Szkolenia Oficerow Politycznych (Training Center for Political Officers at Lodz)
CSSMW	Centrum Szkolenia Specjalistow Marynarki Wojennej (Center for Training Navy Specialists)
CZA	Centralny Zespol Artystyczny (Central Army Ensemble)
DIP	Doswiadczenie i Przyszlosc (Experience and Future discussion group)
FJN	Front Jednosci Narodu (Front of National Unity)
GKO	Garnizonowy Klub Officerski (Officer's Club of garrison town)
GOP	Grupy Ochronno-propagandowe (military-political groups in 1947 elections)
GP	Grupa Partyjna (smallest cell in the PUWP)
GPHP	Garnizonowa Poradnia Higieny Psychicznej (psychological clinic of garrison)
GPK WOP	Graniczny Punkt Kontrolny WOP (frontier crossing post)
GZP WP	Glowny Zarzad Polityczny Wojska Polskiego (Chief Political Directorate of the Polish Army)
HKCZ	Honorowa Ksiega Czynow Zolnierskich (Army Book of Honor)
IBS WAP	Instytut Badan Spolecznych WAP (Institute of Social Studies of the Military Political Academy)
ICA	International Communication Agency
IC MON	Instytucje Centralne MON (Central Institutions of the Ministry of Defense)
IOCK	Inspektorat Obrony Cywilnej Kraju (Inspectorate of Civil Defense)
IPP M-L	Instytut Podstawowych Problemow Marksizmu-Leninizmu (Institute of Basic Marxism-Leninism)
IPS	Indywidualne Programy Studiow (individual study programs)
JW	Jednostka Wojskowa (larger self-managed army unit)
KBW	Korpus Bezpieczenstwa Wewnetrznego (Internal Security Corps)
KIK	Kluby Inteligencji Katolickiej (Clubs for Catholic Intellectuals)
KKP WP	Komisja Kontroli Partyjnej Wojska Polskiego (Party Control Commission of the Army)
KMPiK	Klub Miedzynarodowej Prasy i Ksiazki (International Book and Press Club)
KMW	Kola Mlodziezy Wojskowej (Army Youth Circles)
KO	Kultura i Oswiata (culture and education facilities)
KOK	Komitet Obrony Kraju (National Defense Committee)

KOR LOK	Kluby Oficerow Rezerwy w LOK (Reserve Officer Clubs, part of Defense League)
KOS	Kola Oporu Spolecznego (social resistance groups, part of Solidarity Underground)
KPJ	Komitet Partyjny Jednostki (Party Committee of Army Unit, Regiment)
KPN	Konfederacja Polski Niepodleglej (Confederation of Independent Poland)
KPOP	Kursy Przekwalifikowania Oficerow Politycznych (Conversion Courses for Political Officers)
KSN	Kongres Solidarnosci Narodu (National Solidarity, an opposition group)
KSS-KOR	Komitet Samoobrony Spolecznej —Komitet Obrony Robotnikow (Committee of Social Defense—Workers' Defense Committee)
KUL	Katolicki Uniwersytet Lubelski (Catholic University, Lublin)
KW PZPR	Komitet Wojewodzki PZPR (Regional Party Committee of the PUWP)
KWoP	Kola Wiedzy o Partji (party knowledge circles)
KWW	Kola Wiedzy Wojskowej (military knowledge circles)
KZ PZPR	Komitet Zakladowy PZPR (Works Party Committee of the PUWP)
LOK	Liga Obrony Kraju (Defense League, a paramilitary organization)
LWP	Ludowe Wojsko Polskie (Polish People's Army)
MKiS	Ministerstwo Kultury i Sztuki (Ministry of Culture and Arts)
MKO	Miedzyregionalny Komitet Obrony (Interregional Committees of Solidarity Underground)
MO	Milicja Obywatelska (Citizens' Militia)
MON	Ministerstwo Obrony Narodowej (Ministry of Defense, Poland)
MOiW	Ministerstwo Oswiaty i Wychowania (Ministry of Education)
MSW	Ministerstwo Spraw Wewnetrznych (Ministry of Internal Affairs)
MTGO	Miejskie Terenowe Grupy Operacyjne (Urban Operation Groups in towns)
NIK	Najwyzsza Izba Kontroli (Supreme Chamber of Control)
NJW MSW	Nadwislanskie Jednostki Wojskowe MSW (Vistula Security Troops of the Ministry of Internal Affairs)
NKP	Naukowe Kola Podchorazych (Study Circles in Officer Schools)
NRK	Narodowa Rada Kultury (National Council for Culture)

NSZZ	Niezalezne Samorzadne Zwiazki Zawodowe (prefix of Free Trade Union, Solidarity and others)
OCK	Obrona Cywilna Kraju (National Civil Defense)
OGO	Okregowa Grupa Operacyjna (Military District Operation Groups)
OHP	Ochotnicze Hufce Pracy (Voluntary Labor Youth Organizations)
OKI	Osrodek Ksztalcenia Ideologicznego (Center for Ideological Training)
OKO	Okregowy Klub Oficerski (Officer Club for a Military District)
OKON	Obywatelski Komitel Ocalenia Narodowejo (Civic Committees of National Salvation)
OKOR	Ogolnopolski Komitet Oporu Rolnikow (All-Poland Resistance Committee of Farmers)
ONSiW	Osrodek Nauk Spolecznych i Wojskowych (Center for Sociological and Military Studies
OOP	Oddzialowa Organizacja Partyjna (party cell below Party Primary Unit)
OPI	Osrodek Przetwarzania Informacji (Data Processing Center)
ORW	Organizacja Rodzin Wojskowych (Dependents of Regular Army Personnel)
ORMO	Ochotnicza Rezerwa Milicji Obywatelskiej (Voluntary Militia Reserve)
OSH	Oficerski Sad Honorowy (Officers' Court of Honor)
OSP	Ochotnicza Straz Pozarna (Voluntary Fire-Fighting Units)
OTK	Obrona Terytorialna Kraju (Defense of National Territory)
OW	Okreg Wojskowy (Military District)
PAN	Polska Academia Nauk (Polish Academy of Sciences)
PCK	Polski Czerwony Krzyz (Polish Red Cross)
PGWAR	Polnocna Grupa Wojsk Armii Radzieckiej (Northern Group of Soviet Forces)
PK	Przeglad Kadrowy (review of personnel)
PO	Przysposobienie Obronne (Defense training in schools)
POP	Podstawowa Organizacja Partyjna (Party Primary Unit)
POW	Pomorski Okreg Wojskowy (Pomeranian Military District)
PPA	Polish People's Army
PRL	Polska Republika Ludowa (Polish People's Republic, PPR)
PRiTW	Polskie Radio i Telewizja (Polish Radio and Television)

PRON	Patriotyczny Ruch Ocalenia Narodowego (Patriotic Movement of National Revival)
PUWP	Polish United Workers Party
PZKS	Polski Zwiazek Katolicko-Spoleczny (Polish Lay Catholics Organization)
PZPR	Polska Zjednoczona Partia Robotnicza (Polish United Workers Party-PUWP)
RKK	Regionalna Komisja Koordynacyjna (Regional Coordination Commission of Solidarity Underground)
RM	Rada Mlodziezowa (councils for youth matters in the army)
RMP	Ruch Mlodej Polski (Poland's Youth Movement, pre-Solidarity opposition organization)
ROMO	Rezerwa Ochotnicza Milicji Obywatelskiej (type of militia reserve)
ROPCiO	Ruch Obrony Praw Czlowieka i Obywatela (Movement for the Defense of Human and Civil Rights)
RPZ	Rada Podoficerow Zawodowych (Council of Regular NCOs)
RSZ	Rodzaj Sil Zbrojnych (Arm of Service: Army, Navy, Air Force, Air Defense)
RUSW	Rejonowy Urzad Spraw Wewnetrznych (District Office of Internal Affairs, security)
RW	Rada Wojskowa (Military Councils, at higher command levels)
RWE	Radio Wolna Europa (Radio Free Europe)
SB	Sluzba Bezpieczenstwa (Security Service)
SD	Stronnictwo Demokratyczne (Democratic Party, linked with the PUWP)
SINTO	System Informacji Naukowej, Technicznej i Organizacyjnej (Scientific, Technical, Organizational Information System)
SKS	Studencki Komitet Solidarnosci (student support for Solidarity)
SOR	Szkola Oficerow Rezerwy (School for Reserve Officers, now SPR)
SOS	Specjalne Oddzialy Samoobrony (Specialized Self-defense Subunits)
SOW	Slaski Okreg Wojskowy (Silesian Military District)
SPR	Szkola Podchorazych Rezerwy (School for Reserve Officers)
SU	Soviet Union
SZMW	Socjalistyczny Zwiazek Mlodziezy Wojskowej (Socialist Union of Army Youth)

TGO	Terenowe Grupy Operacyjne (Field Operation Groups)
TKK	Tymczasowa Komisja Koordynacyjna (Provisional Coordination Commission of Solidarity Underground)
TKKS	Towarzystwo Krzewienia Kultury Laickiej (Association propagating a secular outlook)
TKN-LU	Towarzystwo Kursow Naukowych-Latajace Uniwersytety (Association of Mobile Universities)
TKZ	Tajne Komisje Zakladowe (Factory Commissions of Solidarity Underground)
TOIP	Terytorialny Osrodek Informacji Politycznej (Territorial Center of Political Information)
TOOC	Terytorialny Oddzial Obrony Cywilnej (Civil Defense Unit based on locality)
TOS	Terenowe Oddzialy Samoobrony (Locality Self-defense subunits)
TPPR	Towarzystwo Przyjazni Polsko-Radzieckiej (Polish-Soviet Friendship Society)
TSD	Techniczne Srodki Dydaktyczne (technical teaching aids)
TWO	Towarzystwo Wiedzy Obronnej (Defense Knowledge Association)
UB	Urzad Bezpieczenstwa (State Security Organization)
URM	Urzad Rady Ministrow (Office of the Council of Ministers)
UW	Uklad Warszawski (Warsaw Pact)
WAM	Wojskowa Akademia Medyczna (Military Medical Academy)
WAP	Wojskowa Akademia Polityczna (Military Political Academy)
WAT	Wojskowa Akademia Techniczna (Military Technical (Academy)
WDW	Wojskowy Dom Wypoczynkowy (Army Rest Home)
WGO-K	Wojskowe Grupy Operacyjno-Kontrolne (Military Operation-Inspection Groups)
WIH	Wojskowy Instytut Historyczny (Military Historical Institute)
WIOC	Wojewodzki Inspektorat Obrony Cjwilnej (Regional Inspectorate of Civil Defense)
WKDO	Wyzszy Kurs Doskonalenia Oficerow (advanced officer training, higher level)
WKO	Wojewodzki Komitet Obrony (Regional Defense Committees)
WKU	Wojskowa Komisja Uzupelnien (Army Recruiting Commission)
WOP	Wojska Ochrony Pogranicza (Frontier Guard Troops)

WOPK	Wojska Obrony Powietrznej Kraju (Air Defense Troops)
WOSL	Wyzsza Oficerska Szkola Lotnicza (Air Force Officer School)
WOSR	Wyzsza Oficerska Szkola Radiotechniczna (Radio-Technical Officer School)
WOSS	Wyzsza Oficerska Szkola Samochodowa (Motor Transport Officer School)
WOW	Warszawski Okreg Wojskowy (Warsaw Military District)
WOWewn	Wojska Obrony Wewnetrznej (Internal Defense Troops)
WRON	Wojskowa Rada Ocalenia Narodowego (Military Council of National Salvation)
WSMW	Wyzsza Szkola Marynarki Wojennej (Higher School of the Navy, academy level)
WSNS	Wyzsza Szkola Nauk Spolecznych (Higher School for Social Sciences of the Central Committee PUWP)
WSO	Wyzsza Szkola Oficerska (Officer School)
WSOPW	Wyzsza Szkola Oficerow Polityczno-Wychowawczych (Higher School for Political-Education Officers)
WSOSK	WSO Sluzb Kwatermistrzowskich (Quartermaster Service Officer School)
WSOWCh	WSO Wojsk Chemicznych (Officer School for Chemical Troops)
WSOWI	WSO Wojsk Inzynieryjnych (Officer School for Engineer Troops)
WSOWL	WSO Wojsk Lacznosci (Officer School for Signal Troops)
WSOWOPl	WSO Wojsk Obrony Przeciwlotniczej (Air Defense Officer School)
WSOWP	WSO Wojsk Pancernych (Officer School for Armored Troops)
WSOWRiA	WSO Wojsk Rakietowych i Artylerii (Officer School for Rocket and Artillery Troops)
WSOWZmech	WSO Wojsk Zmechanizowanych (Officer School for Mechanized Troops)
WSW	Wojskowa Sluzba Wewnetrzna (Army Security Service)
WSzW	Wojewodzkie Sztaby Wojskowe (Regional Military Staff)
WUML	Wieczorny Uniwersytet Marksizma-Leninizma (Evening Universities of Marxism-Leninism)
WUSW	Wojewodzki Urzad Spraw Wewnetrznych (Regional Office of Internal Affairs)
ZBoWiD	Zwiazek Bojownikow o Wolnosc i Demokracje (Union of Fighters for Freedom and Democracy)
ZBZZ	Zwiazek Bylych Zolnierzy Zawodowych (Union of ex-Regular Army Soldiers)

ZDK	Zasady Dzialania Kadrowego (Principles of Personnel Management)
ZG	Zarzad Glowny (main board, of an organization)
ZHP	Zwiazek Harcerstwa Polskiego (Polish Scouts Association)
ZMP	Zwiazek Mlodziezy Polskiej (Union of Polish Youth)
ZOMO	Zmotoryzowane Odwody Milicji Obywatelskiej (Militia Motorized Reserve)
ZOOC	Zakladowy Oddzial Obrony Cywilnej (Factory Civil Defense Unit)
ZOS	Zakladowy Oddzial Samoobrony (Factory Self-Defense Subunits)
ZOSP	Zwiazek Ochotniczych Strazy Pozarnych (Union of Voluntary Firefighting units)
ZSL	Zjednoczone Stronnictwo Ludowe (United Peasant Party, linked with PUWP)
ZSMP	Zwiazek Socjalistycznej Mlodziezy Polskiej (Union of Polish Socialist Youth)
ZSZ UW	Zjednoczone Sily Zbrojne Ukladu Warszawskiego (Warsaw Pact United Armed Forces)
ZT	Zwiazek Taktyczny (Division level Army Unit)
ZZP	Zwiazek Patriotow Polskich (Union of Polish Patriots)
ZZPW	Zwiazek Zawodowy Pracownikow Wojska (Trade Union of Army Civilian Employees)

Every officer a trained Marxist

Every officer an expert in military
and political matters

—W. Jaruzelski

Introduction

For some 16 months between August 1980 and December 1981 the emergence and unparalleled expansion of the Solidarity trade union movement in Poland were the subject of intense interest to people and governments in the West. This was due partly to Western mass media having access to information on developments in Poland—unprecedented, for a Soviet bloc country—but mainly to the enormous sympathy that the cause of "Solidarnosc" has evoked practically everywhere. For it was the protest of a whole people repeatedly the victim of the expansionist designs of its powerful neighbors, frequently defeated but never subdued; it was the revolt of industrial workers against the inefficiency and corruption of an alien economic system; it was a determined stand against the enforced atheist ideology and the denial of basic political and human rights.

Unfortunately, Solidarity was a challenge not only to the Polish Communist Party and its puppet government but also to Soviet imperialism in Eastern Europe. Consequently, in the West two questions were increasingly asked: When will the Soviet Union invade? and What would be the attitude of the Polish Army? In December 1981 both questions were answered by one action: The Polish Army itself stepped in and saved the situation for Moscow. This came as a complete surprise to the West, to Solidarity leaders, to the church, and to the Polish people.

It is the purpose of this book to explain how the Polish Army had the will and the means to destroy the organizational structure of Solidarity, curb the nation's aspirations to freedom, and reimpose Soviet tutelage. It is a story of an army within an army, a political Army within a conventional fighting army, an instrument of a committed nucleus of politicians in uniform led by General Jaruzelski. It will be shown that over more than a decade General Jaruzelski and his associates used their high positions in the army to build up a political army at the expense of a fighting army. This involved a big expansion of the political apparatus of the army and an extension of its normal internal army role to the whole of the civilian sector. In this way the Political Officer Corps was turned into a political elite active in and outside the army. At the same time "line" officers, that is, commanders of army units, were made to join the party, accept party discipline, and with it subservience to the leadership of the political army.

Further, it will be explained why many of the in-built features of Poland's defense system could be exploited in the pursuance of the political army's objectives and how the concept of the universal defense obligation opened all the doors to the political military. It will be seen that from the early 1970s the political army was systematically penetrating all spheres of Polish life under the guise of defense requirements taken in the widest meaning of the term. Regular army and noncommissioned officers were appointed to full-time civilian posts or worked in civilian organizations on an unpaid basis. Similar posts were found for personnel retired from the army on health or age grounds. Toward the end of the decade the weak and hard-pressed Communist Party officially agreed to share with the army political control at regional and lower levels.

If this process of smooth and unobtrusive infiltration had continued the political party would, by the mid-1980s, have taken the place of the Communist Party and ruled Poland, not so much in the name of Marxism-Leninism but as a protector of the "Polish reason of state" subordinated to the overriding Soviet interest. The economic crisis and the emergence of Solidarity interrupted the evolutionary process. The army was forced to intervene by imposing martial law in December 1981.

Chapters 7 and 8 of this book explain the inordinate delay in taking action against Solidarity, which had developed into a national freedom movement and made a profound impact not only on the ruling party but also on the army, including the political army. This complicated preparations for martial law, which in the end contained measures directed against the political opposition in the country and against dissenters within the ranks of the party and the army.

Above all martial law was designed to create conditions and provide an excuse for new legislation, institutions, and procedures that have given the political military virtual control over the state administration and key sectors of the national economy. The objectives for the mid-1980s have been brought forward by a few years.

The ending chapters highlight some of the problems that are either already blocking the road to absolute political power or making it very problematic, thus confirming a very old Polish proverb: "Man fires but God carries the bullets."

Factual information, with very few exceptions, comes from the press and periodicals and books published by or under the auspices of the Polish Ministry of Defense, in Polish. This is official source material presented in quotation or paraphrased form. The most authoritative among these sources is Wojsko Ludowe, a monthly publication of the Chief Political Directorate (GZP) of the Polish Army, which functions as a kind of general staff for the political army.

1
Army Leadership and Defense System

The imposition of the state of martial law on December 13, 1981, amounted to an invasion of Poland, not as was feared by the Soviet Army but by Poland's own Polish People's Army (PPA). The totally unexpected intervention and assumption of political power was the work of a well-organized informal political faction in the army, which for easy reference may be called the "political military" or "the political army" as opposed to a normal fighting army. On December 13, 1981, the leaders of that faction brought forward a formal and official Military Council of National Salvation (WRON), which consisted of 17 top army generals and five colonels. Every member of WRON held at the time a key position in the army or administration (see Appendix A) and was able to make a major contribution to the imposition and operation of martial law.

They had been in these posts long enough to know how to make full use of various features of Poland's defense system, which had greatly facilitated the development of the political army, its management, and finally its use. They had the opportunity and the means to build up a personal following. It is fair to say that the official leaders of the PPA constitute the core of the leadership of the political army. The latter group contains a number of officers who are no longer in active service. They all have a common background, which may be called "Soviet roots."

The comprehensive composition of WRON was also meant to prove that all parts of the Polish Army, that is, the whole of the Polish Army, intervened to save the Com-

munist system in Poland. In fact it merely proves that
the political military were well placed for taking and implementing important decisions. True active support in the
army was rather limited. It came mainly from the political apparatus of the army, which consists of full-time
professional political officers. Together with activists
of the Communist Party organization in the army who
are mostly regular army officers they secured an essentially passive support from serving conscripts. The political army is numerically small. Its strength lies in its
political organization capacity and skills. The fact that
relatively small numbers managed to arrest a huge freedom movement and assume effective control of the affairs
of Poland for the foreseeable future is the best proof that
we deal here not with a normal military but a new type of
political-military force.

POLITICAL MILITARY LEADERS: THEIR BACKGROUND

The polish military press and other official sources maintain
that three things constitute the roots of the postwar Polish Army and
form its basic tradition: service with the Polish Army formed in the
Soviet Union (1943/44), brotherhood-of-arms with the Red Army
(1944/45), and suppression of the armed Polish anti-Communist
underground (1945-48). The better-known political military leaders
experienced all of this in their early military careers, and these
experiences formed a type of school-tie bond among them. In addition
they have had development training at Soviet military academies,
maintained regular official and personal contacts with high-ranking
officers of the Soviet Army, and must have earned the Soviet Army
blessing that is required before appointment to higher posts in the
Polish Army.

All these factors taken together are the makeup of the political
military leaders, their Soviet roots. No wonder that as a group and
as individuals they are fully committed to the defense of the Soviet-
Socialist system in Poland, to which they owe absolutely everything.

It should also be noted that most of them were born between
1922 and 1926, which means that they are rapidly approaching retirement from army service. It is no coincidence that the system of government they have introduced guarantees to all of them first-class
second careers.

Polish Army in the Soviet Union

In accordance with a Stalin-Sikorski agreement of December 4, 1941, General Anders formed a Polish Army from among the population deported from Soviet-occupied Poland. In 1942, at the time of rapid German advance, this totally unequipped army was allowed to leave the Soviet Union to join the Western Allies. Early in 1943, when the fortunes of war began to change, Stalin conceived the idea that a Polish Army marching into Poland alongside the Red Army could be a military as well as a political asset. A band of Polish communists who had fled deep into the Soviet Union before the advancing German armies was organized into a Union of Polish Patriots (ZZP) and ordered to spread the idea among Poles who for one reason or another did not manage or did not want to join the Anders army.

ZZP propaganda and Red Army recruiting centers instructed accordingly produced the human material that allowed Red Army organizers to form on Soviet territory the 1st Polish Division named after Kosciuszko, in early summer 1943, the 1st Polish Corps in August 1943, and the 1st Polish Army in March 1944.

Shortage of officers was from the beginning the main problem. It was partly overcome by secondment of Red Army officers (11,500 by October 1944 and more later) and partly by rapid training of new Polish officers (about 18,000 up to the end of the war). The problem here was the low level of education of candidates for officer schools who came mainly from rural areas of Eastern Poland. This was reflected in the quality of the young officer corps of that period. A well-known military publicist wrote that there were no illiterates among them but the level of education was less than mediocre. He went on to say:"We developed the complex of being insufficiently educated, of lacking the knowledge of basic facts of history, geography, not to mention mathematics, physics and chemistry. . . . "[1]

The Polish Army (SU) in the Soviet Union became the Polish People's Army in July 1944 when it entered Poland (by then already deprived of its Eastern provinces) and was amalgamated with left-wing anti-German resistance groups known as the People's Army (AL). The Polish Army in the Soviet Union was Polish only in name, that is, it had some trappings of Polishness. In essential matters it had nothing in common with Polish armies of the past, especially the prewar Polish Army and its successor, the Polish Army that fought on the side of the Western Allies in World War II.

Regarding its role, organization and structure, rules and regulations, equipment, and everything else that makes an army, the Polish Army was a miniature copy of the Red Army. To be more exact, it could have been a copy had it been possible to apply even the reduced Red Army standards dictated by war. The average young officer in the

Polish Army had only primary school education and was sent to front-line units after a course at an officer school lasting only three months.[2]

That would have been quite unacceptable in the Red Army. The disparity of standards and the resulting difference in caliber were one of the reasons why in dealings with the Russians, officers of the Polish Army were seriously handicapped.

In copying the Red Army model the Polish Army adopted the institution called the political apparatus of the army staffed with full-time political officers. This had a profound influence on the future development of the Polish People's Army. It turned the latter into a political army with ambitions to rule the country. It can be said categorically that a Polish Army without the political apparatus would not have been able to intervene in the way it did in December 1981.

Political officers of the Polish Army had before them the daunting tasks of indoctrinating the troops, especially young officers, along Communist lines and getting them to accept the alliance and friendship with the Soviet Union, when the latter had already decided to annex Polish territories in which they had been born. One senior political officer wrote about that much later:

> Polish citizens were joining Polish Army units mainly because they wanted to return to Poland, fight for its liberation. Political integration, acceptance of the ideological platform of the Union of Polish Patriots, came later as a result of a lengthy process that was full of conflict. It was the job of political officers to fight for the control of Polish souls.[3]

That perhaps was the reason why large numbers of political officers were needed. At the end of the War (May 1, 1945) 25 percent of the Polish officers in the Polish People's Army were political officers.[4]

Indoctrination worked. At less than 21 years of age one is at an impressionable age. Most young officers of the Polish Army in the Soviet Union were born between 1922 and 1926, which would make them less than 21 in 1943. At any rate, members of the Polish Army took an oath that runs as follows: "I swear to be faithful to the Soviet Union, our ally, who gave me the weapons to fight against our common enemy and I swear to safeguard the brotherhood-of-arms with the Red Army."[5] Apart from that, whatever reservations Poles might have had about that Polish Army were quickly set aside. All were well aware that once the Anders army had gone, those who were left behind had no chance of leaving the USSR except on Soviet terms.

Brotherhood-of-Arms with the Red Army

Poles of the Polish Army in the Soviet Union simply could not avoid this brotherhood-of-arms. Red Army officers were present at all low, medium, and higher command levels. In the 1st Division they represented 66 percent of the officer complement and in the 2nd Division, named after Dabrowski, in which Jaruzelski has served as commander of a reconaissance unit, 76 percent. The remainder were prewar Polish Army and newly trained officers. It was openly admitted that this did create integration problems. A breakthrough came when the 1st Division underwent its baptism of fire in the battle at Lenino in October 1943. This was allegedly the beginning of the brotherhood-of-arms, which grew and developed as Polish units fought their way alongside the Red Army from Western Russia to Berlin.

The brotherhood was severely tested all the way. Poles of the Polish Army saw first of all that the eastern border of Poland had been moved some 200 miles to the west. Then, on the territory of the new Poland, into the areas already "liberated," the party machine and security troops moved in to install the Soviet system. Finally, there was the Warsaw rising. According to an entry in the General Polish Encyclopedia:

> By August the 8th the Command of the 1st Byelorussian
> Front had worked out a plan for the attack on Warsaw.
> The 8th Stalingrad Guards Army and the Polish 1st Army
> and others were assigned to this operation. The plan,
> scheduled to come into operation at the end of August,
> was submitted to Stalin who did not approve it for strategic
> as well as political reasons.[6]

Stalin's political reasons were that by refusing to come to the aid of Warsaw he was able to deal a fatal blow to the whole West-oriented resistance movement in Poland and thus further his cause of Poland's sovietization. For this reason the Polish 1st Army had to stand idly by and watch Warsaw burn and bleed to death when it could have been saved.

Leaving aside such wider issues, there can be no doubt that on the personal level, in the course of fighting a common enemy, close links and bonds had been established between some Polish and Red Army officers. These were maintained in the postwar period.

For the great majority of Poles, brotherhood-of-arms with the Soviet Army has a totally hollow ring. For Jaruzelski and his type of Polish military it is an article of faith that needs to be reaffirmed on all occasions. In his address to the 6th Party Congress (December 1971) Jaruzelski said:

> Brotherhood-of-arms with the Soviet Army, which has
> been built on common ideology, on blood shed together,
> and which has stood the test of many years of cooperation
> finds today its expression in working together as allies.
> This friendship is our great achievement. We shall de-
> velop and continue to enrich it with new and deep-rooted
> values.[7]

This did not go unnoticed by the Soviets. On the occasion of the
30th anniversary of the PPA, Marshal Grechko, the architect of Soviet
military power, then minister of defense of the USSR, said: "The military achievements of the Polish Army demonstrate clearly the skillful
and energetic leadership exercised by the Political Bureau Member,
Minister of Defense, General Comrade Jaruzelski, our great friend
and comrade-in-arms."[8]

Suppression of the Anti-Communist Opposition (1945-48)

For many officers and men of the PPA, victory over Germany
did not mean an end to fighting. Enemy No. 1 was replaced by enemy
No. 2, the great majority of the Polish people who opposed and re-
sisted the introduction of the Soviet-sponsored system. According to
official data, in July 1944, that is, just before the arrival of the Red
Army and Polish Army on Polish territory, the strength of the so-
called London camp (home army, peasant battalions, and others) was
about 500,000 against an estimated strength of 20-50,000 in the Communist camp, which made a ratio of 10:1 in favor of the right-wing
anti-German resistance.[9]

The Militia and Security Service and even the 30,000-strong
Internal Security Corps (KBW), formed in 1945 by converting selected
army units into security troops, could not cope with the situation. The
army was called in. In an all-out drive that begun in March 1946, four
army infantry divisions working together with the above-mentioned
security forces and a newly formed Voluntary Militia Reserve (ORMO)
crushed what was by then called "the armed reactionary underground"
or sometimes simply the "London underground."[10]

General Jaruzelski, who had taken part in the operations, made
the following comment in a glossy publication, 20 Years of People's
Rule: "The initial hope that the underground would wane and disinte-
grate as result of the political achievements of the people's rule did
not materialize. Thus it became necessary to fight it out, to replace
the force of logic with the logic of force."[11] This now has a very
familiar ring and speaks for itself.

Apart from these military operations, the army also took part

in what was officially described as "large-scale political operations."
Here the army assisted the provisional Soviet-sponsored government
in the implementation of the agrarian reform (breaking up estates of
the landed gentry), transferring Poles from territory annexed by the
Soviets to the lands taken from the Germans. The army also won for
the Democratic Bloc of Parties a decisive victory in what were to be
the first free elections in postwar Poland (January 19, 1947). There
was a real danger that they would be won by the Polish Peasant Party
of Stanislaw Mikolajczyk, which had the support of most Poles and of
the West. A special technique was used: On order of the minister of
defense (November 4, 1946) the army formed special "protection and
propaganda groups." In the first phase of the operation (December 5-
21, 1946), 2,229 groups totalling 45,239 military personnel (30 percent of the total army manpower) organized 25,635 political meetings
that were attended by 2.5 million people. In phase two (December 28,
1946-January 21, 1947), 2,614 groups totalling 61,466 army personnel
(about 41 percent of the total) organized 42,608 political meetings that
were attended by over 4 million people. The army's official role was
to protect the polling stations and the voting procedures.[12]

The result was a foregone conclusion. On election day, the people "followed the call" and voted, mainly openly, for the Democratic
Bloc. The election gave 394 seats to the Democratic Bloc and only 28
seats to the Polish Peasant Party. In this way Poland acquired a Soviet-
sponsored government that was duly recognized by the Western Allies
as the first "legitimate" postwar Polish government.

The 1945-48 confrontation is normally referred to as "consolidation of the people's rule." Only recently came the admission that it
was in fact a civil war that cost 30,000 Polish lives.[13] This revelation
was to convey the idea that the imposition of martial law prevented a
repetition of this tragedy.

A biographical note on a member of the Jaruzelski group would
normally include the stereotype formula: "has participated in the struggle to free Poland from German occupation and in consolidating the
people's rule." This period also counts as war service for pension
rights. It is now planned to erect a memorial for those who fell in the
struggle.

There are certain analogies between the 1945-48 and the post-
1981 situations. Official army propaganda exploits them in various
ways but mainly to carry the message that the army would never fail
the nation.

General Jaruzelski: The Undisputed Leader

Biographical data: Jaruzelski, Wojciech, general of the army,
chairman of the National Defense Committee and supreme commander

of the Polish Armed Forces (since November 1983), prime minister (since February 1981), first secretary of the Polish United Workers Party (since October 1981).

Born July 6, 1923 in Kurow, Poland. Graduate of the General Staff Academy, Warsaw, and of the Voroshilov General Staff Academy, Moscow. In the Polish army since 1943 (Infantry Officer School, Ryazan, USSR), during World War II he was commander of reconnaissance unit of 5th Regiment, 2nd Polish Division, and went on to fight the anti-Communist underground in Poland (1945-47). His career continued as follows: deputy head of Directorate of Combat Training (1947-57), commander of 12th Mechanized Division, Szczecin (1957-60), head of Chief Political Directorate of the Polish People's Army (1960-65), chief of General Staff (1965-68), deputy minister of Defense (1962-68), minister of Defense (1968-83). Successively Maj.-Gen., 1956, Lt.-Gen., 1960, General, 1968, General of the Army, 1973, member of PUWP since 1948, member of Central Committee, PUWP, since 1964, alternate member of Political Bureau (1970-71), full member of Political Bureau since 1971, member of Seym since 1961, Chairman of the Military Council of National Salvation (December 13, 1981-July 22, 1983).

However, there is more than that to General Jaruzelski's career. One official biographical note on Jaruzelski, published in Poland in 1982, describes the general as "political functionary," which is a literal translation of the Polish term "politician."[14] This description is helpful in that it confirms what has been known for a long time. Jaruzelski is not a general or army man in the Western meaning of the word. He is simply a prominent member of a social group in Poland that describes itself as "Communists in uniform."

But is Jaruzelski a politician? The most normal feature in the career of a politician, be it east or west or south of the Iron Curtain, is that his fortunes are subject to ups and downs. Politics are full of pitfalls and no politician can avoid them all the time. There were no such fluctuations in the career of General Jaruzelski. His is a steady climb to the top with no falls or even slips. Yet there were occasions when he should have fallen, as did his close associates Gomulka in 1970 and Gierek and Jaroszewicz in 1980. At the 6th Plenum of the Party Central Committee in September 1980, immediately after the emergence of Solidarity, Jaruzelski even admitted that like the others he had been responsible for the mistakes that led to the 1980 crisis. It did not do him any harm. On the contrary, as the crisis deepened his position and influence grew. To his post as minister of defense he added that of prime minister (February 1981), first secretary of the party (October 1981), "savior" of Poland as chairman of the Military Council of National Salvation (December 1981), supreme ruler of

Poland (November 1983) and "savior of the world." The latter is an inference to be drawn from his speech in February 1982 when he tried to justify the imposition of martial law: "History may prove one day that while World War II started about Poland, World War III did not start thanks to Poland."[15]

Jaruzelski is not a politician; but he is a functionary, an obedient servant of a system in which this kind of animal is known as "aparatchik." The system that Jaruzelski serves is easily identified.

In all official biographical notes on Jaruzelski his Polish Army career starts with the Infantry Officer School at Ryazan (1943). He is said to have a distinguished war and postwar record as a "line" officer. There is no mention of his basic political officer training at any of the political officer schools of the Polish Army. That could mean that he had such training in the Red Army before he joined the Polish Army. He also must have performed political officer functions before 1960, when he was made head of the Chief Political Directorate of the Polish Army. A rank outsider could not have been appointed to that key post.

As could be expected, Jaruzelski's progress was fast. At 33 he was the youngest general in the Polish Army. After five years at the Chief Political Directorate he was made chief of the General Staff (1965). His appointment in April 1968 at the age of 45 as minister of defense was most certainly connected with the planned invasion of Czechoslovakia. He replaced Marshal Spychalski, who had a record of disobedience to the orthdox line. The Polish contingent in the invasion was under the command of General Siwicki, Jaruzelski's close friend.

In the 1970s Jaruzelski's mission was to ensure the political reliability of the Polish Army as a component of the Warsaw Pact. Directly linked with that was the need to prepare the army for an internal role, for a defense of the system should the Communist Party lose control during one of the recurring Polish crises. To facilitate this Jaruzelski was made full member of the Political Bureau (1971). At the 8th Party Congress (February 1980), when signs of the approaching political and economic crisis were already visible, Jaruzelski declared that the army would fulfill its duty to the party, the nation, and the Socialist fatherland and also that the Polish-Soviet friendship and brotherhood-of-arms were inviolable. A few months later Jaruzelski was "launched" in the Soviet Union when the main party organ Kommunist in its issue No. 7 (May 1980) published his contribution on 25 years of the Warsaw Pact. There is also Jaruzelski's declaration in his speech of December 13, 1981, which accompanied the imposition of martial law: "The Polish-Soviet alliance is and will remain the cornerstone of the Polish reason of state, a guarantee of our frontiers. Poland is and will remain a firm link of the Warsaw Pact, a reliable member of the Socialist community of nations."[16]

In the tradition of Communist leaders General Jaruzelski enjoys making long speeches. A book containing 36 speeches made in 1981-82 (11 at Party Central Committee meetings and 9 in the Seym [Parliament]) was published early in 1983. The 1983 record is even more impressive. Jaruzelski did not develop this gift after he introduced martial law, yet before that time a legend was built around him, according to which he owed his rapid advancement to his excellent record and impressive talents as a soldier. He is said to have kept the army out of politics because as a true Polish patriot he would not allow it to be used against the Polish people. After December 1981 the legend died very quickly in Poland but is dying much more slowly in the West. Again, this cannot harm Jaruzelski. He can rely on his hand-picked political elite because since 1968 he has been signing all the promotion orders and was countersigning them even earlier as head of the Chief Political Directorate.

DEFENSE SYSTEM WITH IN-BUILT POLITICAL FACILITIES

The building of the political army was greatly helped by certain aspects of the Defense Doctrine and Structure (see Figure 1). In the area of doctrine there is first of all the concept of universal and obligatory defense dictated by the character of a future war, especially if it were to be nuclear. Then there is the in-built political role of the army in a Soviet-Socialist state based on the premise that the army as an instrument of revolution has helped to establish the system and has the sacred duty to preserve and defend it against both internal and external enemies.

Universal Defense Obligation

The all-pervading aspect of the universal defense obligation was described by General Jaruzelski far back in 1964 when as head of the GZP he wrote:

> The issues of defense must penetrate all spheres of life of the country—economic, social, and political. The armed forces form the basis of defense but their activity covers only a part of the defense tasks. The remaining tasks, especially those connected with territorial defense require organization, material, and training for a large number of our citizens and for all units of our administrative, economic, and social organization. Defense of the country is as never before a vital matter to the whole nation and affects every citizen in a most direct way.[17]

FIGURE 1: Poland's Defense System (pre-November 1983)

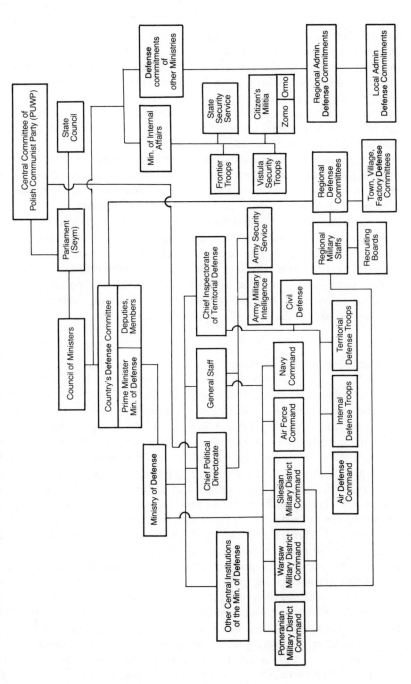

The idea was enshrined in the law on universal defense obligations that came into force in Poland in November 1967 following a very similar law in the Soviet Union in April 1967. Article 1 of the law states that defense of the Fatherland and of Socialist achievements of the Polish nation is the concern and duty of every citizen; Article 2, that this obligation applies also to all organizations, institutions, enterprises, cooperatives, and civilian associations. Article 3 points out that the armed forces protect the sovereignty and independence of the nation, while Article 4 lists various military and paramilitary defense obligations of citizens. [18]

An efficient registration and mustering system operated jointly by army and state administration bodies ensures that a Polish citizen is enlisted into the system at an early age and remains in it, his dossier passing from one defense organization to the next.

The fact that all individuals and corporate bodies in Poland are compelled to discharge their defense obligations and need guidance from professionals on how to do it gives the military access to all areas of activity and, through this, unique opportunities to influence and exert pressure in favor of the army's political objectives. The political army made full use of this facility for the penetration of the civilian sector by the army (see Chapter 6).

National Defense Committee

The National Defense Committee (KOK) played a major part under martial law and after a suitable up-grading (November 1983) is now used by the political military for running the whole country (see Chapter 12). Until then, under the law on universal defense obligations (1967), responsibility for defense was vested in the Council of Ministers' National Defense Committee. This was the supreme organ of the state in defense matters. It decided defense policy and monitored its implementation. It laid down guidelines for the armed forces and Civil Defense and co-ordinated the activities of central and regional authorities in the field of defense. [19] The latter meant that the committee controlled the contribution of the civilian sector to the defense of the country, which in the interpretation of the political military included fighting internal opposition to the existing rule.

The ex-officio chairman of the KOK was the prime minister himself, under whose name and authority committee decisions were issued. But his time was limited, therefore in practice the committee was run by the minister of defense who was ex-officio deputy chairman. Other deputy chairmen and members of the committee were appointed by the Council of Ministers. [20] For a full decade up to August 1980, Poland's defense was in the hands of Piotr Jaroszewicz (prime minister) and

General Jaruzelski (minister of defense). Although both men were equally responsible for the allocation of the country's resources as between military and civilian needs and therefore contributed equally to the latest crises, only Jaroszewicz paid for the mistakes of the "former leadership." Jaruzelski was safe, even made prime minister, presumably because "he put all his money" on training the political army. In addition, as prime minister and minister of defense he had the KOK all to himself during the crucial ten months before he imposed martial law.

Under the national (central) KOK there is a whole hierarchy of defense committees at regional (voyevodship) and local levels and in large enterprises. In each of Poland's 49 regions there is a Regional Defense Committee (WKO) as a directing organ in defense matters. It consists of people in key positions who are appointed by the national KOK. The head of the regional authority is normally chairman of the regional committee. The same applies to local authorities and enterprises with the heads and directors chairing the local defense committees. This arrangement makes for the closest possible tie between management of the local administration and economy and the defense commitment for the area. Regional and local defense committees are given professional assistance by Regional Military Staffs (WSzW), who are regular army personnel subordinated to commands of military districts. About 30 in number per region, they are commanded by a colonel, which is an indication of their importance. They provide a direct link between the civilian authorities and the army. Their permanent presence in the civilian sector is an obvious asset to the political military.

Ministry of Defense

Like the minister of defense himself, the Ministry of Defense occupies a privileged position in the state hierarchy. According to the Small Military Encyclopedia it is the organ of state administration responsible for the implementation of the decisions of the KOK and of the Council of Ministers relating to defense. Its main functions are direction of the armed forces, coordination of defense measures undertaken by other ministries, and implementation of international military obligations. Among the more important sections of the ministry are the General Staff, the Chief Political Directorate, Chief Quartermaster, Personnel Department, Finance Department, Chief Inspectorate of the Territorial Defense, and the Inspectorate of Training. They are known as Central Institutions of the Ministry of Defense (IC MON). Their relative importance is denoted by the fact that some are headed by deputy ministers of defense.

The minister of defense, in addition to his position as deputy chairman of the KOK responsible for the armed forces and strategic defense planning, is commander of the armed forces. He commands through the chief of general staff, the commanders of military districts (Pomerania, Silesia, Warsaw), the commanders of arms of service (air force, air defense, navy) and through the chiefs of other troops and support services.[21]

Professor J. Muszynski of the Military Political Academy wrote in Wojsko Ludowe (in 1983) that the question of supreme authority had not been decided either in the Polish Constitution or the law on universal defense obligations. The Council of State, Council of Ministers, prime minister, KOK, minister of defense, and minister of internal affairs all had some direct competences in respect to the armed forces but not supreme authority. Yet in his view state and military supreme authority was an extremely important matter if the armed forces were to fulfill properly the internal and external roles, especially in as complex a situation as the present one in Poland. Professor Muszynski proposed to overcome the difficulties by creating the post of president of the Polish People's Republic.[21]

This was one of the first indications that General Jaruzelski would be prepared to trade his three present posts for a presidency. Many commentators thought that General Jaruzelski was after a marshal's of Poland baton. Three of his predecessors in the post, M. Rola-Zymierski (1945-49), K. Rokossowski (1949-56), and M. Spychalski (1956-68), had been marshals of Poland. But Jaruzelski is different: His predecessors had to leave the post in connection with a major upheaval in Poland while he survived December 1970 and August 1980; each one also at one time or other spent some years in prison for having strayed from the official line.

Defense of National Territory (OTK)

The development of the political capacity of the Polish Army was helped by the fact that Poland's defense system consists of two subsystems: one concerned with external defense commitments, the other with internal defense. The first is made up of operational forces (land, sea, and air) earmarked for operations within the framework of the Warsaw Pact against an external enemy. The second consists of forces designed to protect the homeland against enemy action and subversion, to maintain essential services, and to protect the civilian population against the results of weapons of mass destruction. According to one definition the range of military and civil defense tasks is carried out jointly by political, military, administrative, and law enforcement authorities.[23] The military authority in question is the Chief Inspec-

2
The Politically Active
Officer Cadre

The capacity of the political army depends almost entirely
on the quality of the officer component of the regular army
cadre. Regular junior and senior noncommissioned officers
(NCOs) are in the main employed in technical jobs and are
seldom politically active. The term of service of conscripts
is too short to allow them to play more than a passive role.

Among officers, only political officers are full-time
political workers. They form the core of the political army,
a kind of elite of political leaders and organizers. A major
part of a political officer's career is in the political apparatus of the army. Many move on to other important posts
in the army or are seconded for duties outside the army.
The latter was normal practice long before the political
army grabbed many civilian posts under the cover of martial law. All political officers belong to the one and only
Political Officer Corps.

Most officers belong to the Communist Party organization in the army but a much smaller number are politically active. They are those who at the time hold party
office—for example, members of party committees and
those army unit commanders who see in political work with
the troops a sure means of professional advancement.

OFFICER CADRE AS A WHOLE

The quality of the politically active officer cadre can to some
extent be gauged from information on the officer cadre as a whole. It
is fair to say that prior to 1958 the Polish People's Army had no offi-

cer corps worthy of that name. This was largely due to low education standards at entry to officer schools. Since then there has been a steady improvement in the caliber of the officer cadre, although in the 1970s the "improvement" was geared largely to political objectives.

Professional Cadre at the End of the 1970s

The International Institute of Strategic Studies gives the following figures for the Polish Armed Forces in 1981:[1]

	Regulars	Conscripts	Total	Percent Regulars
Army	53,000	154,000	207,000	25.60
Navy	16,000	6,000	22,000	72.73
Air Force	61,000	27,000	88,000	69.32
Total	130,000	187,000	317,000	41.01

The higher proportion of regulars in the navy and the air force is due to the relatively larger amount of technical equipment in these forces.

It is not possible to get reliable figures of the breakdown of regulars into officers and NCOs. However, if one accepts Western estimates that in the Soviet Army 20 percent are officers and applies this ratio to Poland, one gets an officer component of some 64,000 and an NCO component of about 66,000.

Speaking generally about the relative importance of the political role played by the three main elements in the forces one might say:

- The conscript service (two years, except in the navy, missile, and signal units where it is three years) does not allow one to assume an active role.
- Regular NCOs of all grades have primarily technical functions and their general education is insufficient for political activities.
- Officers are politically very active either as political officers or to a lesser extent as unit commanders responsible for the political reliability of troops and as staff officers.

The constant praise showered on the professional army cadre by the civilian and military mass media is in fact intended for the officer element of the cadre. One may cite two passages by General Jaruzelski:

The military cadre is a section of the people's intelligentsia known for its deep patriotism and readiness to self-sacrifice; it is a body of party activists who many times in the past have proved to be ideologically strong and reliable.[2]

> The professional cadre plays the main and leading role [in the army]. It has been created by the party and party membership among the cadre is very high. The cadre represents a section of Polish Socialist intelligentsia dedicated to the nation, to the party, and to the people's rule and acting according to a firm Marxist-Leninist ideology. [3]

Further proof is <u>Wojsko Ludowe</u>, which deals mainly with matters concerning the officer class, although it is supposed to be a monthly journal for the whole regular cadre.

Personnel of the regular army belong to one of three basic corps with differing requirements of general education at entry to the respective military schools: grammar school (university entry) level, for officer schools; secondary/trade school level, for warrant officer schools; and primary school level, for NCOs. This is another reason why the political army is based on the officer corps.

It appears that figures on the rank structure of the Officer Corps of the Polish Army have not been published. According to a Western source the Polish Officer Corps is dominated numerically by majors, lieutenant-colonels, and colonels. Colonels alone are estimated to number about 3,500 and generals about 200. [4]

There are many indications that most of the colonels are political officers. It is not uncommon to find a lieutenant in the post of company or even battalion commander.

Officer Schools and Military Academies

The professional cadre of the army is the product of an extensive network of military schools, which consists of four categories of schools: schools for NCOs, schools for warrant officers, officer schools, and military academies. Only the latter two categories are relevant to the political army issue.

There are five military academies and eleven officer schools. The academies rank as university level establishments and the officer schools only as higher level professional schools. The academies prepare certain high-class specialists for all parts of the army and carry out scientific research in their respective fields:

General Staff Academy (ASG), Warsaw
Military Political Academy (WAP), named after F. Dzierzhinskij, Warsaw
Military Technical Academy (WAT), Warsaw
Higher Naval School (WSMW), Gdynia
Military Medical Academy (WAM), Lodz

The first two take officers with relevant service experience mainly for postgraduate or other advanced level studies. The Technical and Medical Academies and the Higher Naval School take candidates with grammar school education to become engineers, doctors, and naval officers. After a five- to six-year course of specialist studies, graduates from the three academies obtain qualifications that give the same rights as those obtained at civilian universities. This facilitates work interchange with the civilian sector and helps the political army in its penetration of certain civilian areas. The contribution of the Military Technical Academy to Poland's technological progress is continually publicized in the military press and publications.

All the academies have postgraduate study facilities and the right to grant degrees of doctor habilitatus, doctor, master, and master engineer. Graduates of the General Staff Academy are given the title of diplomaed officer, which is equivalent to the degree of master, master engineer, doctor of medicine, and also of doctor habilitatus of military sciences.

Officers for the various types of troops and services of the army are trained at 11 officer schools known since 1967 as Higher Officer Schools (WSOs), because from that time a higher professional education was provided in a four-year course of study. They are in fact normal not "higher" officer schools. Graduates are promoted to the lowest rank of officer and get the engineer-commander qualification, which is not equivalent to a university degree and denotes the main function as a commander of an army unit with a technical bias (which all of them have).

List of officer schools
(speciality, named after, location)

Mechanized Troops	Kosciuszko	Wroclaw
Armored Troops	Czarnecki	Poznan
Rocket and Artillery Troops	Bem	Torun
Air Defense	Kalinowski	Koszalin
Engineer Troops	Jasinski	Wroclaw
Signal Troops	Kowalski	Zegrze
Air Force	Krasicki	Deblin
Radio-Technical Troops	Bartosik	Jelenia Gora
Motor Transport	Waszkiewicz	Pila
Chemical Troops	Ziaja	Cracow
Quartermaster Service	Buczek	Poznan

In 1969 at the first seven of these schools and at the Higher Naval School, in addition to the main command-technical direction of studies, a political stream (department or faculty) was introduced where cadet

officers train for careers in the political apparatus of the armed
forces on separate four-year courses with an extensive range of sociopolitical subjects.[5] In 1983 or perhaps earlier the Radio-Technical
Troops school was added to the above list. Graduates from the political stream of WSOs are given a "diploma of higher studies in sociopolitical sciences," which is not equivalent to a normal university
degree. This development marked the beginning of the politicization
of the officer corps of the PPA.

According to the same source, training is carried out on three
planes: in a program of instruction, through practical experience in
military units, and social and political work outside official hours.
The instruction program consists of subprograms: sociopolitical,
general military, general education, and military specialist. The
sociopolitical program includes Marxist philosophy, political economy,
scientific Communism, military pedagogy, history and principles of
party-political education work in the army. The aim of officer training
is to produce a highly qualified military man who is at the same time
a well-qualified and dedicated social and political activist. In General
Jaruzelski's words a regular officer is not only a trained military man
but above all a fighter for the Socialist cause.

The central army weekly wrote in 1979 that military academies
and officer schools began to overtake civilian universities as regards
methods of education and modern facilities.[6] This is not surprising
because General Jaruzelski is especially keen on improving the quality
of the officer corps. He admitted in 1973 that Soviet Army specialists
helped to lay the foundations of the Polish Army military schools and
that the Polish Army had been using continuously the facilities of Soviet
schools to prepare highly qualified officer cadres.[7]

The Model of a Polish Army Officer
Has a Strong Political Bias

In 1972 the Ministry of Defense issued a "Postulated model of
an officer of the Polish People's Army." The desired qualities were
listed under five headings: ideological attitude, professional attitude,
intellectual qualities, capacity for organization and leadership, and
qualities for specific job.[8] As always, ideology comes first and is
described in full detail, whereas the components of the remaining
attributes are merely enumerated. Ideology covers the concepts of
commitment to Socialism, socialist patriotism, proletarian internationalism, and scientific-humanist world outlook.

The same attributes are expected from a good Polish communist.
That is why General Jaruzelski could say that by becoming an officer
a person has not only chosen a profession but also made a political

declaration, has joined one of the leading deeply idealistic bodies of the people's intelligentsia.[9] He is also the author of two often-quoted slogans "Every officer a trained Marxist" and "Every officer an expert in political-military matters."

Achievement of the desired model may not be easy in view of the motivation of candidates for regular officer careers. This was a subject of a number of poll-type investigations in the 1970s whose results were fairly consistent. One, carried out in 1977/78 with cadet officers of all four years at three officer schools (Air Force, Armored Troops, Rocket and Artillery Troops), has shown that nearly 70 percent were motivated by positive factors (attractive profession, 42.6 percent; service in a chosen arm, 11.5 percent) but over 30 percent by negative factors like failure to get a place at a civilian university, accommodation prospects ("shortest way to an apartment"), good living conditions, and so on. Asked whether they would repeat the choice of career, 45.5 percent replied that they would choose studies at a civilian university and only 22.7 percent of those with good and very good grammar school certificates would repeat the choice.[10] The above is confirmed by another source that says that 75 percent of candidates to officer schools came from population centers that have no university level schools or where such schools provided inadequate civilian study facilities.[11]

In this situation it is not surprising that the drop-out rate in officer schools is considerable. Early in the 1970s it was almost 30 percent. A 1982 source said that in recent years the number of those who completed the first year but did not graduate had been growing. He blamed poor or total absence of motivation. It was found that many have deliberately chosen to go to an officer school in order to discharge the conscript service obligation at the school rather than in a normal army unit.[12]

Officer schools suffer from a chronic shortage of candidates in spite of intensive annual recruitment drives accompanied by excursions and free entry passes to army establishments and schools. One notable exception is the Quartermaster Service Officer School. Graduates obtain a degree in economics, which is considered a "practical" qualification. Also, quartermaster officers control the flow of supplies in the army. This could be another reason for the school's popularity.

At one time Wojsko Ludowe devoted much space to a discussion of whether being an officer was a profession or a vocation. The view that prevailed was that it was a profession but a very noble one. A high-ranking political officer argued that the profession has a high social standing because nomination to the first (lowest) officer grade is made by the Council of State, as in the case of ambassadors, university professors, and judges.[13]

Young Officers of the Pre-1958 Period

The present leadership of the political army consists in the main of officers who started their military careers before 1958 when there was no Polish officer corps worthy of that name. Until 1956, when the bulk of Soviet Army officers left the Polish Army and returned to the Soviet Union, most positions of responsibility were held by them. There was no need for highly qualified Polish officers and they were not produced.

Training standards for young Polish officers were deplorably low. There were three main reasons that, one might say, went hand in hand. First, the rapid increase in the number of officers needed because the Cold War made it necessary to reduce the officer courses during 1949-55 to one year or even several months.[14] Second, educational requirements for admission to officer schools were lowered with the result that, for example, in infantry schools 60-70 percent of cadet officers had only primary school education. For that reason 15-20 percent of the course time had to be devoted to teaching general knowledge subjects.[15] Visible proof of the low status of officer schools of that period was that graduates were considered to have reached the educational standard equivalent to "technician" normally attained at a civilian trade school. The third reason was the class origin criteria for admission to officer schools. According to Wojsko Ludowe, from the academic year 1948/49 onward the criterion of class origin was given priority in the selection of candidates for officer schools. The principle was established whereby 60 percent of future cadet officers were to be of working class origin, 30 percent of peasant origin, and only 10 percent were to come from the working intelligentsia. These criteria were strictly adhered to during the first half of the 1950s. "Ensuring the class character of the officer corps provided and continued to provide a guarantee of lasting links with the working class and of permanency of socialist changes."[16]

The application of the class origin rule meant that bonus points were given to candidates of working class and peasant origin in order to outweigh the preference gained in entrance examinations by academically better qualified candidates from the intelligentsia. In this way intellectual capacity was sacrificed to secure political reliability.

The year 1958 marks the beginning of a new Polish Army Officer Corps. In December 1957 a law on conditions of service of army officers was passed. This, it was said, together with other legal acts, did a great deal to "stabilize" the profession. Full grammar school education was made a condition for entry to officer schools. A network of full-time and evening courses was established to help officers achieve the new minimum education standard. As a result, by 1968 only 2.5 percent of officers did not have a general education of grammar school level, whereas in 1956 the percentage was 71.4.[17]

As could be expected, raising the educational level meant gradual relaxation of the class origin rules. In the late 1970s candidates to officer schools were 36-43 percent of working class origin, 20-22 percent of peasant origin, 36-40 percent from the intelligentsia, and 1-4 percent from artisans. In the intelligentsia group were 10-15 percent sons of regular army personnel.[18] The very different backgrounds of officers of the early postwar vintage and of the 1960s and 1970s account for the existence of a kind of generation gap within the officer corps. There is considerable evidence of animosity between the two groups, which may have a bearing on the current situation. It is claimed that in 1983, in a group of commanders and specialists, 75 percent of officers had higher (than grammar school) education.

DEVELOPMENT OF THE NEW POLITICAL OFFICER CORPS

The buildup of the political army began with a striking change in terms of quantity and quality in the training of new political officers introduced in 1969. The majority of new political officers go through a ten-year training program before they are fully qualified and obtain the Degree of Master, which at a civilian university is given after four years of study. The program consists of a four-year course at the political faculty of an officer school, three years of practical political work in army units, and a three-year postgraduate course at the Military Political Academy. There was no need for that caliber of political officers in their normal role of ensuring political reliability of the troops. It was clearly a part of the bid for political power in the country.

Training of Political Officers before 1970

Of several political officer schools that had trained 5,396 political officers by the end of World War II, only the largest of them, the Central School for Political-Education Officers at Lodz, remained to continue training of new political officers. On courses of less than one year's duration the Lodz school produced 1,446 political officers in 1945 and 1,347 in 1946. Two-year courses that began in January 1947 resulted in about 300 graduates in 1948 and 1949 taken together.[19]

This sharp fall in the number of graduates was due to a fall in demand following the deletion late in 1946 of the post of political deputy company commander from the establishment of units. Even so it was found that at the end of 1949 only 58 percent of the established political

officer posts were manned. In January 1951, in connection with the
Cold War, the political deputy company commander post was rein-
troduced. In 1952 only 50 percent of political officer posts were filled.
A crash program of training was introduced to correct the situation.[20]

As a result of this program over 5,000 political officers graduated from the Lodz school in the years 1950-56, in 11 separate graduation ceremonies. Under such conditions political safeguards were
all-important. As regards class origin, 60-75 percent were of working class and 25-40 percent of peasant origin. Candidates were volun-
teers or recommended by party or party youth organizations and the
political apparatus of the army itself. A three-stage selection process
consisted of interviews with the recruiting officers, medical and psychological examination at the school combined with entry examinations
in general and sociopolitical knowledge, and finally assessment by
superiors made during the time from entry to taking the military oath.

The end of the Cold War brought a partial reduction of the armed
forces (November 1955). The post of political deputy commander was
again eliminated, causing a drastic fall in demand for political officers.
The Lodz school was officially closed and in its place a center for
career development training of political officers was established. A
year later that center also ceased to exist and the training facility
became one of four army centers of general education. In the years
1957-64 the Military Center for General Education, named after L.
Warynski, helped over 2,000 officers to obtain secondary education,
which had become the minimum education standard for the officer
corps. In 1964 the General Education Center became once more a
political training establishment, known as the Training Center for
Political Officers (OSOP, and later CSOP). The new center did not
train new political officers from scratch, as did its predecessor
before 1956, but was limited to career development of existing political officers and to conversion of "line" officers to political officers.[21]

It is important to note that in the years 1957-69 there were no
facilities for basic training of new political officers and therefore
there was no regular increase in the total number of political officers
in the Polish Army. Conversion training was the only source of new
officers during that period. For this reason the introduction in 1969
of a political faculty ("stream") at eight WSOs with the first intake
in 1970 were of the greatest significance to the future Political Officer
Corps. It can be said without exaggeration that when in 1974 the first
graduates left the political conveyor belt of the WSO, the Political
Officer Corps was practically reborn and the army itself was launched
on a political path of development. An early sign of this was the introduction (in 1975) of a hybrid post combining political duties with those
of a commander. It was decided that in all units the commander of the
first platoon in a company would at the same time be a nonestablished

political deputy company commander. This post was officially reserved for graduates of the political stream of WSO and held by them for at least one year after graduation.[22]

This measure served several purposes. First, some definite political duties were now officially paid for by the military side of the army. Second, immediate and suitable use was found for the large numbers of graduates of the WSO political stream. Third, it substantiated to some extent the claim that a political officer is able to function also as a military commander and that his political officer qualifications were not the only means of livelihood.

Political Training at Higher Officer Schools

The decision not to have one large political officer school but to distribute basic training of new political officers over eight schools, which hitherto trained only officers of the command-technical profile, was a deliberate move aimed at hiding the vast expansion of political officer training and reducing the gulf between these two categories of officers. The first step was gradual integration of study programs of both streams, with sociopolitical studies forming the overlap between them.

In the academic year 1976/77 new programs of study were introduced at all the WSOs. They are described here in detail because it was stated at the time that "cadet officers trained under the new programs would acquire knowledge, skills, convictions, and habits that they will need during the period of active professional life from the early 1980s to the early years of the 21st century."[23]

According to that source many central institutions of the Ministry of Defense and military schools had taken part in evolving the new program and the work had been a matter of special interest to General Jaruzelski himself. The aim of the new programs is to produce an officer of high ideological and moral values, professional qualifications, and personal culture. Graduates would have a large volume of sociopolitical, general, military-technical, and pedagogical knowledge as well as didactic and instruction skills. At all officer schools sociopolitical subjects represent the most important group. Its content is based on the experience gained in teaching these subjects in the years 1970-76 and on two basic documents: "Principles of training of cadet officers at WSOs," which concerns ideological and political training of commanding and of party-political cadres of the Polish Army, and "Principles of cadre management in the Polish Armed Forces." From all these, separate study programs have been developed, one for the "command stream (faculty)" and another for the "political stream," where one exists at a WSO.

Sociopolitical subjects form the backbone of the study program in the political stream of a WSO. Their scope and total number of teaching periods is four times bigger than in the command-technical stream. In the latter, specialist-military and military-technical subjects are allotted four times more time than sociopolitical subjects. The program in the political stream is geared to producing a political officer who is a party-political organizer. The teaching of military subjects in that stream is intended to produce an officer who would be able to command a military unit of the given service, for example, a political graduate from the Higher Officer School of Armored Troops would know how to command a tank unit.

The fact that sociopolitical subjects are the basis for the whole course of studies is heavily stressed. Success or failure in this area decides the course result. This is partly due to the fact that pedagogy, which is in that group of subjects, plays such a crucial part in preparing the cadet officers for their future trahining and education role.

The new study programs have become more compact by linking sociopolitical subjects that hang together into subject blocks. Three such subject blocks have been introduced in the command-technical stream and six in the political-stream:

Command Technical Stream

1. Fundamentals of Marxism-Leninism
2. History
3. Fundamentals of military training and party political work

Political Stream

1. Marxism-Leninism
2. Fundamentals of political sciences
3. History
4. Psychological, sociological, and pedagogical basis of military training
5. Party-political work in the army
6. Selected problems of culture

In the field of sociopolitical sciences the number of lectures was decreased in favor of exercises and seminars. Therefore, in the political stream there are 910 hours of lectures and 830 hours of exercises and seminars, in the command-technical stream 254 and 216 hours, respectively. This change created better conditions for discussing ideological, world-outlook, sociopolitical, pedagogical, and cultural questions. It provided more opportunities for independent thinking and for analyzing from the Marxist-Leninist standpoint the events and processes, ideological-political and socioeconomic, that take place in the world and in Poland. It helped to develop debating skills and to draw proper conclusions and to make decisions. The change also gave the teaching staff better chances to shape the personality and intellect

of cadet officers, activate their interest, and check to what extent
the prescribed literature was being absorbed.

In the group of sociopolitical subjects for the political stream
of studies, 65 percent of the time is assigned to problems of Marxism-
Leninism, fundamentals of political sciences, and history. Identical
proportions are maintained in the command-technical stream. The
subject "selected problems of culture" was a new addition to the program. Cadet officers are given the Marxist interpretation of the function of culture and its role in developing one's personality. They learn
about contemporary trends in literature and arts and about Poland's
contribution to world culture. They are also subjected to cultural education in accordance with a program evolved by the Directorate of
Culture and Education of the GZP. The latter program links the cultural education of cadet officers with activities of civilian centers of
popular culture and regional centers of creative cultural activity.

In addition, offshoots of the National Study Center for Adult
Education and Culture have been established at the seven WSOs that
have a political stream. They help cadet officers to complete special
correspondence courses and obtain a diploma that gives the right to
work professionally in the field of culture popularization. [24] This has
a bearing on the cultural penetration of society described in Chapter
5.

There have been changes in the programs of WSOs since 1976,
but the sociopolitical group of subjects remained unchanged. There
are still three subject blocks in the commanding stream with 650
class periods and six subject blocks in the political stream with 2,000
class periods. [25]

The number of political officers is uncertain. The only useful
figure ever published was that in 1952 the establishment for political
officers was 15 percent of the total number of officers. Assuming that
this percentage still applies, the current political officer establishment would be 9,600. It is very likely that before 1974, when the output of the political faculties of the WSOs began, it was difficult to
match actual strength with establishment figures. The actual number
might have been only about 8,000. This deficiency was soon made up
because the WSOs have produced hundreds of political officers every
year since 1974. This estimate is based on the assumption that the
political stream of a WSO is of company or battalion strength, depending on the size of school. To this one must add the output of the conversion courses from the Lodz Training Center. The political apparatus of the army could not have absorbed these large numbers of new
political officers, even if it had been possible to increase the establishment, which is unlikely. I hazard a guess that seasoned political
officers were all the time posted out into the civilian sector where
they were part of the army personnel who were on detached duties

outside the army. It is very likely that the number of political officers in the latter category exceeds the number of those in the army (see Chapters 5 and 6).

Military Political Academy, Warsaw

The quality of training of political officers at the Lodz school was inadequate for higher posts in the political apparatus of the army. Therefore in May 1945 the Higher School for Political-Education Officers (WSOPW) was created at Rembertow, near Warsaw. Two-year courses that combined theoretical studies with practical work in military units, and at one time also played an active part in the confrontation with the right-wing political opposition, helped to prepare better-qualified political officers—but not many, because in the years 1945-51, only 247 political officers were trained there. In 1951 the WSOPW was the basis for forming the Military Political Academy (WAP).[26] Prior to that some political and technical officers destined for higher posts were trained at academies in the USSR and Czechoslovakia. The total number of officers trained abroad in the years 1945-49 was 419.

General Wladyslaw Polanski, commander of WAP since 1972, writing in connection with the 30th anniversary of WAP, stated that soon after its formation the academy was named after F. Dzierzhinskij by a decree of the Council of Ministers. He added that this was symbolic and denoted the ideological orientation of the new academy.[27] (See F. Dzierzhinskij profile in Appendix D.)

According to Polanski, in the years 1951-57 it was not possible to organize academic level teaching and research because the academy lacked suitably qualified teaching staff. The situation began to improve slowly after 1954, when some of the academy's own graduates after a three-year course decided to continue their military-scientific careers at the academy. They were at that time acquiring higher qualifications at civilian universities and establishments. Polanski had the Polish personnel in mind because elsewhere in the article he said that from the very beginning the Political Military Academy named after Lenin in Moscow had provided assistance with cadres and programs.

It appears that the level of teaching capacity was matched by the learning capacity of the students of that period. Polanski said explicitly that the majority, although handicapped as regards general education, had a great deal of war and postwar army service experience and brought with them party zeal and an honest will to learn. According to Polanski, many who studied at the academy in those years were now in top-level posts in the political apparatus of the Polish Army.

In the years 1957-77 WAP established its profile of studies and its structure of three faculties (pedagogy, history, and economics). In

1957 a four-year program of studies leading to a master's degree was introduced in the pedagogy and history faculties. In 1966 the economy faculty was added. During that time, postgraduate studies were also expanded, including extramural courses. There were also shorter lower-level political officer courses.

During the first part of this period (until 1967) students were in the main political officers who did crash courses at the Lodz Political Officer School before it closed in 1956. Polanski said that after studies at the WAP they distinguished themselves through ideological-education work in military units and became excellent leaders of the troops and that they now represented the core of the senior cadre of political officers. [28] During the period 1967-77, students were mostly officers who had converted from line to political officer duties. One can guess that one of the reasons for this conversion was the desire to escape the demands arising from the technical complexity of modern arms. Line officers of the pre-1957 vintage often found it easier to reach the prescribed secondary school level standard by choosing arts rather than science subjects.

An important new chapter in the life of the academy began in 1977 when it became part of the integrated system of political officer training, which consists of three stages: a four-year course of studies at one of the eight Higher Officer Schools already described, three years of service in a political post in military units, and a three-year course of study at the academy. In connection with the new tasks WAP was reorganized. The four-year master's degree course was reduced to three years and most programs were changed and modernized.

In 1976 Polanski wrote that the needs of political officers for greater knowledge of social sciences have grown rapidly. This called for a widening of studies on the methodology of sociological research. Economic and especially socioeconomic studies needed to be expanded. In the existing programs subjects related to data processing, theory of management, praxeology, and so on, were not adequately covered. There was a need to develop theoretical studies on state and legal systems, sociology of the army, sociology of political systems, and so on.

Polanski said that in 1977 several hundred political officers, graduates of the political stream of WSOs who had three-year practical experience as commanders and political officers in army units, would enroll for the new courses. The latter will also be open to graduates of the command-technical stream who had converted to political officer careers. This would mean that the number of students would be greater than was provided for in the establishment. The first year would be used for "leveling out" the knowledge of students with different backgrounds. Only the best would be admitted to second-year studies. Those who did not make the grade would receive a cer-

tificate of completing a higher development course (WKDO). They had
the right to apply again later when they filled the gaps in their knowledge and obtained good results in service.[29] The end products of the
three-year courses are political officers, military economists, and
specialists in defense planning. Though courses are geared to obtaining a master's degree in pedagogy, political science or history, and
economics, 65 percent of the time in each faculty is taken up for
raising pedagogical qualifications and practical abilities to direct
party-political work in army units. Thus in spite of the specialization
the academy succeeds to produce a uniform type of political officer.
In the 30 years of existence of WAP, nearly 9,000 political officers
have completed postgraduate and other courses.

The idea that WAP is training political officers for use inside
the army cannot be taken at face value. It is difficult to visualize how
the army can absorb and employ the hundreds of political officers produced by the academy every year. One must bear in mind that these
officers had spent a full ten years on high-level political training. The
only acceptable explanation is that they were being prepared for a
political role outside the army. In addition to the teaching role WAP
always had substantial research commitments. These are described
in Chapter 5.

Training Center for Political Officers at Lodz

While the WSOs together with WAP form a kind of conveyor belt
for the mass production of the high-powered new model of political
officers, the Training Center for Political Officers at Lodz (CSOP)
appears to be engaged in small-series production of special types and
on other nonstandard jobs. This is reflected in the structure of the
CSOP, which currently has several different training facilities:
Development Courses (higher level) for Political Officers (WKDO),
Conversion Courses for Political Officers (KPOP), School for Political Reserve Officers (SPR), School for Political Warrant Officers,
and Foreign Languages Study Center.[30]

CSOP is one of the best-known army training establishments for
political officers and has the longest tradition. Its commandant stated
that in the years 1944-81 (with a break in 1957-64) about 29,000 political officers attended various courses. He added that graduates had
always been in the first line of the ideological front and were examples
of idealistic, patriotic, and internationalist attitudes. Many were now
in leading positions in the army, the national economy, and state administration, and were active as politicians, scientists, writers, and
so on. In the early postwar years they fought to establish the People's
Democracy, which they were now defending.[31]

About 30 percent of students are graduates of civilian universities or WSOs. This is because the School for Political Reserve Officers, which takes only university graduates, represents the biggest unit of the CSOP. The school for Political Reserve Officers is interesting if only because it is the only departure from the principle that jobs in the political apparatus of the army are reserved for career personnel. When in 1973, in accordance with the law on universal defence obligation, Reserve Officer Schools (SOR) were formed, it was decided to establish also a School for Political Reserve Officers within the Training Center at Lodz. The one-year training at SOR counts for one year of conscript service, which a university graduate is obliged to undertake. Four months of that time is spent at the school and the remaining months on duties in units. These duties are the same as those discharged by political officers after graduation from a four-year course in the political stream of a WSO.

Four months of political training for eight months' political work in the army would not be cost effective if the system did not offer some longer-term advantages to the political military. There are indications that political reserve officers are destined to play a role in the ideological and political struggle in Poland. A very strong hint of that is given in an article that appeared in Wojsko Ludowe in 1977. Describing the training process at the Lodz School for Political Reserve Officers, the author gives an example of a right kind of initiative by a cadet officer at the school, a master of sociology in civilian life. He used his first one-day pass to visit a large Lodz factory to discuss with the director a scheme of cooperation between a group of his colleagues and the factory management. The result was a series of meetings with the labor force and regular lectures at the "factory school of education in citizenship."[32]

In this connection it is necessary to refer to a resolution of the Council of Ministers (1973), which says that the time of army service in an SOR counts for seniority in a civilian post and the character assessment issued on leaving the army is taken into account by future employers when making appointments. The assessment covers such virtues as self-discipline, organizing ability, conscientiousness, and sociopolitical attitudes.[33] But another source says that only those who distinguished themselves during army service would be given an assessment with a special recommendation, which in the new place of work would help materially in shortening the waiting time for an apartment, in appointments for jobs, and in counting seniority.[34]

However, one good turn calls for another. The reserve political officer concerned is in this way effectively handed over to the party organization in the place of work. From then on he is obliged to serve the system faithfully, something he might have never done had he not been made to do his conscript service in a school for reserve political officers.

The Lodz School for Reserve Political Officers is given a great deal of publicity in military and other publications. This could be a sign that it is planned to expand this type of training facilities.

Portrait of a Political Officer

In 1974 at the Military Political Academy a conference in which the leading political cadre of the army also took part was devoted wholly to the subject of "personality of a political officer." The conference was a kind of summing up of a debate among political officers that has been going on for years. The view that emerged was that at various times different demands were put on political officers but ideological fervor and strict implementation of the party line had always been the principal requirements. Other characteristics stem from the special position of a political officer as a superior in the military hierarchy and as a party organizer with a mission in society, among the troops. He must demand iron but conscious discipline, fortify the "sole commander" principle and at the same time act as a spokesman for the troops, advise them not only in political and social but also in personal matters. [35] A 1976 source stated that Marxist-Leninist knowledge is one of the essential attributes of a political officer and that he could not carry out his duties without it. His professional attributes were also important:

- He should be the most active officer among the cadre who educate the citizen-soldier.
- He should know how to organize the political training process and be keenly involved in it.
- He should have the skill to conduct party-political work in the widest sense of the word, that is, ensure that the troops get to know all the binding instructions issued by the party, state authorities, and the army and that they are made aware of the political reasons for all forms of military training; he must inspire party and party youth activities in the unit, conduct cultural-education work, and maintain the links between the army and society at large. [36]

General Sawczuk, as head of the GZP, defined a political officer as a party worker who subordinates all his life and work to the cause of Socialism, is ready to commit himself fully and defend its values. The effect of his work depends on a thorough knowledge of Marxism-Leninism and the ability to practice it in daily life. In addition to the knowledge of general Marxist theory—that is, philosophy, political economy, scientific Communism, and methodology—he must know well some social sciences and the theory of culture. He must himself be a highly cultured person.[37]

Political officers of the Polish Army are often told that during the Russian Revolution Voroshilov, Gamarnik, Stalin, and Mikoyan were directing political work in the Red Army as Brezhnev, Bulganin, Yepishev, Suslow, and other leaders of the Soviet Communist Party did during World War II.

Political officers wear the uniform of the units in which they serve. There are no insignia or badges to denote the special character of their service. This is probably a deliberate departure from standard practice that a separate corps has its own insignia. But a senior political officer can be spotted by his styling "Lt. Colonel MA" or "Colonel Dr." (Podpulkownik Mgr., Pulkownik Dr.).

3
Political Organizations of the Army

The duty to defend the Soviet-Socialist system against
external and internal enemies stipulates that the Polish
Army cannot be apolitical and is endowed with organizations and institutions that enable it to exercise a political
role. Before the army's intervention in December 1981
the norm was that all elements of state authority, including the army, accepted the civilian party's "leading
role." This meant that the political apparatus of the
civilian Communist Party controlled the political apparatus of the army, the party organization of the army,
and the army's personnel policy and could in this way
ensure that all army activities conformed to the party
line.

The party line on defense was based on two premises: (1) in the nuclear era defense is the responsibility
of the nation as a whole and not of the armed forces alone;
(2) Poland's defense depends on the joint effort of all the
countries of the Soviet bloc and of the Soviet Union in particular. It is easy to see that both premises provided the
conditions and environment in which the political army
could be created and developed to reach its strong position in the country. That is why the political army supported the leading role of the civilian party to the full,
even when the whole nation questioned the principle or
its interpretation. Until 1981/82, when the political
army assumed control over the civilian party, the former
remained an example of unqualified obedience to the latter.

The three political organizations in the army are the
political apparatus, the party organization, and the party

37

youth organization. Because all members of the political apparatus are also members of the party organization, it is possible to refer to both organizations together as the military party.

THE MILITARY COMMUNIST PARTY

The military Communist Party (see Figure 2) is an integral part of the civilian Communist Party and is governed by the party statute. This means that party members serving in the army can play a full part in the life of the civilian party. At the same time the military party enjoys semiautonomy because it has its own political apparatus of full-time functionaries (political officers) who are responsible for planning, direction, organization, and coordination of political work in the army. They are assisted by members of the party organization who as a rule are spare-time voluntary political workers organized in party primary units, which are the lowest party unit. Members of the party organization form their party committees at various command levels, from regiment up to and including the Ministry of Defense. The committees compare to area and factory party committees of the civilian Communist Party. They are elected for a term of two years.

From the regiment level upward, party committees together with the part of the political apparatus attached to the given level form a single party-political organ of that level. The aim is to provide harmony between the professional and the voluntary element among political workers. This has never been achieved and the political officers have dominated the stage. It was one of the causes of trouble within the military Communist Party during the Solidarity era (see Chapter 7).

How the two parts of the military party are meant to complement one another is described by General Sawczuk:

We have in the army a full-time political apparatus with a considerable number of well-trained party organizers. These people devote every day all their work, abilities, efforts, and enthusiasm to the implementation of the party line, of party resolutions and instructions and in this way build the morale and combat readiness of troops. We also have huge numbers of party activists in various service posts who to a large extent participate in the propagation of our ideas, who win people over, and mobilize them for the cause of Socialism.[1]

FIGURE 2: Military Party (Army's Political Set-up)

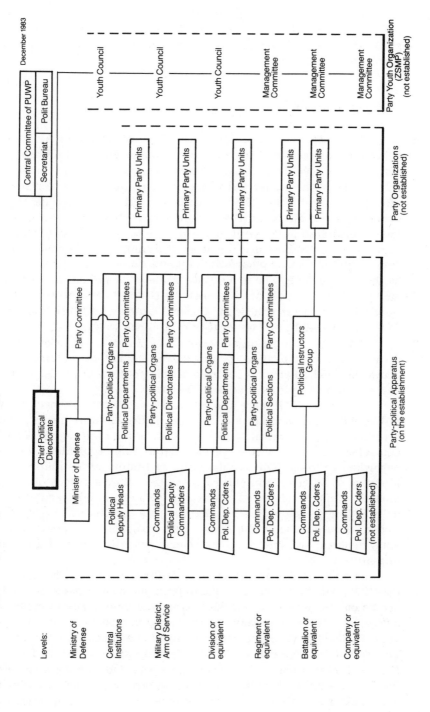

Thus the division of labor between the two groups is that the political apparatus has the "officers" who plan, organize, and direct political operations and the party organization provides the "troops" who help to carry them out.

Political Apparatus of the Army

The Chief Political Directorate (GZP) of the Polish Army is subordinated directly to the Minister of Defense but is guided by directives of the Party Central Committee. As one of the central institutions of the ministry it is always listed in the second place after the General Staff. The GZP in fact functions as a sui generis general staff of the political army and now probably ranks higher than the General Staff as a result of the army's newest political role. It is in the army's protocol that whenever the minister of defense visits army units or attends other official functions he is always accompanied by the head of GZP, who is a deputy minister of defense and a three-star general. The post has been held by General Jaruzelski (1960-65), General Urbanowicz (1965-71), General Czapla (1971-72), General Sawczuk (1972-80), and General Baryla (since 1980).

The GZP is a big organization, with a number of functional directorates (organization, propaganda and agitation, culture and education, and others). It controls all the political activities of army personnel in as well as outside of the army.

Under the GZP there are political directorates for each of the military districts and arms of service, political departments for each division or its equivalent, political sections for each regiment or equivalent, and subsections for each battalion or equivalent. Directly subordinated to the GZP are the Military Historical Institute, the Ministry of Defense Publishing House, the editor's offices of the monthly Wojsko Ludowe, of the weekly Zolnierz Polski, and of the daily Zolnierz Wolnosci. The GZP controls the ZSMP through the Youth Council of the Polish Army. Regional press, officer clubs, study centers, and artistic groups come under the political directorate of a military district.[2]

In addition to working downwards through its own channels, the GZP uses its central position to organize conferences, teach-ins, and so on, for top people working in certain fields. For example, at a three-day teach-in organized for leading personnel of the political apparatus and party organization at division and equivalent level the head of the GZP described the implementation of the 6th Party Congress resolution and outlined tasks connected with the elections to the Seym. Many such horizontal meetings are organized periodically, e.g., before and after party congresses—or annually—a meeting for "leading workers of the ideological front. These meetings are often attended by important personalities of the civilian party.

A favored form of work is preparing guidelines on various subjects through which the party line and instructions of the Ministry of Defense are translated into concrete tasks for the political apparatus, party, and party youth organizations. They are proof that the GZP is concerned with every aspect of life in the armed forces. It is assumed, it seems, that without the right kind of political motivation no job can be done properly. A good example is the "Guidelines on Party-Political Work in Air Force Training" issued in May 1979, which stresses the need for improving military and flying discipline. Both are to be achieved by "forming attitudes of active commitment" on the part of flying and ground personnel. During a meeting with air force personnel the head of the GZP launched the slogan "Every flight is a combat flight." The Political Directorate of the air force came out against "could-not-care-less attitudes." To do this effectively political officers were given a short course in psychology and medicine. The tasks and recommendations contained in the guidelines were included in the monthly and annual programs of the party-political and ideological education in all air force and air defense units. [3]

Safety of flying, admittedly an important matter, can be achieved without involving political officers. In the Polish Air Force this is probably one more justification for the existence of large numbers of political officers.

Interesting light is shed on the scope and methods of work of the Political Department of a division in an article describing its activities during tactical exercises. An abridged version is given in Appendix B.

The duties of the political apparatus on a lower level and their respective priorities are described in an instruction for young political officers. [4] The first group of duties is clearly defined as deepening and founding the patriotic and internationalist (that is, anti-imperialist) awareness of soldiers, the strengthening of ideological and brotherhood with the Soviet Army, and developing the soldiers' pride that Poland is a member of the Warsaw Pact.

The second group of tasks, not so well defined, refers to promotion of all those processes that unite the army environment around the objectives that the party and government have put before the nation and its soldiers. This includes all the efforts that support the commanders in their military training programs.

In a third group are education and other means aiming at the development of Socialist staff relations that are based on mutual trust and respect and on principles of military ethics and custom. Here belong the improvement of military discipline and order, observance by all soldiers of the equal rights and duties principle, maintaining regular contacts between cadre and troops, taking note of their feelings and worries.

Finally, in the fourth group are propagation of culture in all areas of army life and various measures that help to maintain and deepen regular contacts between the army and the people, especially the working class, and links with organs of state authority, with science and arts circles.

The above calls for comment. The earlier concept of brotherhood-of-arms with the Soviet Army has been extended to include ideological brotherhood. The army environment (in the second group) covers the army itself but also the families of regular soldiers, army pensioners, civilian employees, and personnel on permanent detached duty outside the army. Development of "Socialist staff relations" refers to the outright bad staff relations in the Polish Army. There is a great deal of evidence that political officers see themselves as mediators between groups with conflicting interests, for example, regular cadre versus conscript personnel, officers versus other ranks, older soldiers versus new recruits, and so on. The above-quoted source contains the following statement:

> On many occasions when bad staff relations had been exposed either in the form of churlishness and callous disregard of human dignity or as Prussian-type discipline thinly disguised as service regulation requirements, it was found that the situation, so unworthy of the Socialist character of the Polish Army, happened and, what is more, persisted because the appropriate political officer had ignored information that was reaching him.[5]

Party Organization in the Army

The party organization has its party committees at various command levels: regiment, division, military district or arm of service, ministry. Their scope and duties are defined in instructions and orders of the Chief Political Directorate. The main tasks are to implement party resolutions, supervise the content and methods of work of lower party units, to promote ideological work, and to increase party membership. The party committee secretary, a full-time paid party functionary, is the key man in every committee.

As in the civilian party the basic element in the organization structure is the so-called Party Primary Unit (POP). The POP may be subdivided into smaller party units (OOP) or still smaller party groups (GP). This depends on such factors as size of membership, dispersed location, or separate functional entity. The average number of party members and candidate members of a POP is about 80. The

POP committee usually has seven members. A GP must have at least three members. The current business of a POP is run by its elected committee or, more exactly, by an elected secretary of the POP. The latter must not be confused with the committee and secretary of a party committee of higher command levels. For example, the party committee of a regiment controls the work of several POPs at the battalion level, including the one for regiment headquarter (HQ) staff party level. The secretary is responsible to the POP of the next higher level for the implementation of decisions. He organizes the work of the party committee and acts as its representative outside. He maintains contact with the commander of the army unit concerned and his deputy for political matters. He participates in briefings and meetings organized by the military commander, where he has the right to submit views and proposals on behalf of his committee. He is consulted before the commander takes decisions concerning personnel and on other important issues.

The party organization in the army has the right to go into all aspects of the life of military units in order to prevent shortcomings in the education and training of troops. By using criticism and self-criticism party members help the commander to eliminate deficiencies that may affect combat readiness. The party organization works closely with commanders and the political apparatus in matters concerning military and political training and strengthening discipline.

The party organization demands from its members active attitudes in their jobs and in unpaid social work. Infringements of the code of ethics and party discipline and moral offenses in private or service life are subject to criticism at party meetings. Only orders issued by commanders are exempt from criticism in order to safeguard the "sole commander" principle.[6]

POPs, which comprise personnel of command headquarters and central institutions of the Ministry of Defense, are said to be shouldering important and responsible duties:

> They comprise the army regular cadre known for its high
> ideological, political, and moral values, its honest gen-
> eral, military, and specialist education. The most telling
> proof of its high ideological and political standard is party
> membership, which in the case of medium- and higher-
> level headquarter staff reaches 100 percent. These POPs
> exercise very great influence on education, training, and
> on the command processes. They are to an increasing de-
> gree becoming a model for other POPs in the Army. . . .
> In addition to their contribution to an all-round improve-
> ment of staffwork they participate in ideological education
> work in army units and in the civilian environment.[7]

The scope and methods of work of a POP that comprises the personnel of a regiment headquarters is described in Appendix C. This gives a good idea of the waste of time and effort that results from party membership. If the whole Polish Army were to be a fighting army this would not be acceptable.

The level of party membership in the army is important to the political military because party members are subject to party discipline in addition to the normal military discipline. A senior officer of the GZP stated that the high level of party membership and political-professional skills of the regular cadre together with the well-thought-out deployment of party members in all the important parts of the army structure gave party members a decisive influence on training and work. [8]

The deployment factor is clearly visible, even from the limited amount of information on party membership in the army, which has been published in percentages only:

- In 1963 party membership at higher command levels was 100 percent; among officers generally, 72.7 percent; among regular NCOs, 36.8 percent. [9] In 1980 the 100 percent membership applied to higher and medium command levels.
- In 1972 average membership among officers was 85 percent and for the regular cadre as a whole 60 percent. [10]
- In 1979, in an artillery and rocket troops unit, membership among officers reached 92 percent. [11]
- In 1978, in the navy, membership among officers was almost 90 percent and for the regular cadre, including officers, nearly 70 percent. [12]
- In 1978, in an air force unit, membership among officers was over 80 percent, among warrant officers almost 50 percent, and among NCOs over 42 percent. [13]

According to a Soviet source, membership among officers was 40 percent in 1950, over 56 percent in 1955 and over 85 percent in the early 1980s. [14] A martial law purge in 1982-83 reduced party membership among officers to 64.3 percent. For warrant officers and NCOs it remained about 60 percent. [15] The implications are described in Chapter 12.

Party Youth Organization

The postwar Polish Army always had its party youth organization. (The term "youth" covers the age group from 15 to about 30, which is in line with the usage in other Soviet bloc countries.) It

formed part of the national Union of Polish Youth (ZMP). The ZMP
in the army was a mass organization because in the mid-1950s about
70-90 percent of officers and other ranks belonged to it. A senior
political officer wrote that the ZMP was from the beginning an ideological helper to the party organization and to commanders in the
training and education of soldiers and that its activities widened the
front of ideological and political work with the troops.[16]

The army ZMP was dissolved in 1957 together with the civilian
ZMP, which Gomulka considered a relic of the Stalinist era. The first
regulations that set out the aim of the organization said that it would
emulate the work of the Soviet Young Communist League (Komsomol).[17]

In 1958 the head of the Chief Political Directorate ordered the
forming of a new party youth organization known as Army Youth Circles (KMW), which again comprised the majority of the young in the
army. The KMW was not connected with civilian party youth organizations. For almost 15 years the KMW followed the program of work
that emanated from party resolutions, directives, and orders of the
ministry and from instructions and guidelines of the Chief Political
Directorate.[18]

This apparently was not good enough. A lead article in Wojsko
Ludowe (December 1973) stated that "the great drive to build Socialism
would get a boost from the new army youth organization SZMW, which
must become a militant organization with a distinct ideological and
political profile and solidly based on socialist ideology, socialist
patriotism, and internationalism."[19]

The SZMW (Socialist Union of Army Youth) was a new name for
the KMW. The adjective "Socialist" indicated the intensified political
indoctrination drive that began in the early 1970s. This was reflected
in two basic documents: Declaration of SZMW Ideology and Program
and Principles of SZMW Work, both issued in 1973.

Yet another change of name and objectives came in 1976 when
the SZMW became a cofounder of a national party youth organization
known as Union of Socialist Polish Youth (ZSMP). This is now the
name of the party youth organization in the army. Thus, after almost
20 years the army youth organization again became a part of the national party youth organization. Representatives of the army organization entered the central and regional offices of the national organization, which meant that it intended to play a major role outside the
army. The move must be seen as an element of the political army's
penetration of the civilian sector.

About 60 percent of serving conscripts and 9 percent of the regular cadre are members of the youth organization in the army. This
makes a massive total of about 125,000 people. The basic organization
and work unit is a group (officially called a circle), usually at company
level. Business is managed by committees at company, battalion, and

regiment levels. At division and higher levels are Youth Councils as advisory bodies, the composition of which is decided by the party-political organs of the same level. At the very top is the GZP.

The obvious function of the youth organization is to provide candidates for the adult party. It was stated that every year 80-90 percent of new party entrants in the army come from the ranks of the ZSMP. The performance of a ZSMP circle is often judged by the number of party members it has produced.

The youth organization has had for a long time four distinct lines of work: promotion and participation in the "lead and Compete Movement"; forming proper staff relations, especially among serving conscripts; special care of military equipment; and lecturing to small groups of soldiers. [20]

In general it provides widely based support for political officers and commanders in their ideological, political, and military training tasks. A good example is the development of brotherhood-of-arms with the Soviet Army. It was stated that the proximity of units of the Silesian Military District and of the Northern Group of Forces of the Soviet Army facilitated lively cooperation of the ZSMP organization of the military district with the Soviet Young Communist League. In 1978 and the first half of 1979 both sides organized 387 friendship meetings, 211 joint patrols, 2 seminars on cooperation, 170 exhibitions showing Polish-Soviet brotherhood-of-arms, 64 military-historical excursions, and a series of lectures. [21]

ZSMP work is centered on companies and company commanders are directly involved. They are responsible for the functioning of the group to their superiors and to the party organization. They take the job seriously when they realize that the ZSMP also works for them and their position in the army and that the success of the group is their success. [22]

One way for a commander to achieve success is to have his group win in the annual competition for the title "Best ZSMP Group" in the military district or arm of service. About 80 percent of all groups take part in an annual competition, which takes almost ten months of a year. Competing groups take part in stage one at regiment level, where the best three are chosen to go forward to stage two at division level and from there to the finals at military district and arm of service level. At regiment level the best three are chosen by a special commission, appointed by the regiment commander, consisting of one political officer, one member of the regiment party committee, one officer from the regimental HQ staff, and two representatives of the ZSMP committee of the regiment. Selection is based on a group total of points earned by individual members when they carry out special tasks in seven separate areas of activity: ideological education and culture, discipline and training, care of equipment, suggestion schemes, good deeds for the community, cooperation with civilian youth organizations, and work for the group itself at the very end. The declared aims of the competition are ideological and political in nature. [23]

The interesting point of the competitions is that selection is based on data supplied by the company commander and the group itself, in other words, by people who have the most to gain from the result of the competition. Even when all is aboveboard, and often it is not, the inevitable effect of these competitions is that company commanders are forced to waste time on useless paperwork to the detriment of their proper military duties.

CHANNELS OF CONTROL AND MAIN ACTIVITIES

The military Communist Party is a component of the Polish United Workers Party (PZPR) and is guided in its activities by the rules of the party statute and resolutions of the Central Committee. More detailed orders and instructions come from the minister of national defense and from the Chief Political Directorate of the army. [24]

The main object of its activities is to ensure that the army has the capacity to fulfill its internal role: the defense of the system. The threat to the system appears to be permanent and demands constant "combat readiness," which is to be achieved through continuous political indoctrination of all army personnel. Longer-term actions geared to the same objective are known as "educating a socialist citizen soldier" through various activities before, during, and after conscript military service.

Channels of Control

Decisions on key defense and army issues are taken at the highest levels of the party, that is, at party congresses normally held every five years and between congresses at plenary sessions (plenums) of the Central Committee. They are implemented by the Secretariat of the Central Committee and the Political Bureau. The political military were represented in all these bodies. General Jaruzelski has been a member of the Central Committee since 1964 and of the Political Bureau since 1971.

Intensification of ideological and political work in the army was decided at the 6th Party Congress held in December 1971. Its resolution outlined the tasks of the army in three main spheres: defense of the country, education of the nation, and developments in the scientific, technical, and economic fields. [25]

In June 1973 the 1st Ideological Conference of the Polish People's Army "debated the achievements on the ideological front in implementing the program evolved by the party at the 6th Party Congress and at the 7th Plenary Session of the Central Committee." The conference was attended by top-level party members in the army, namely members of the army leadership, commanders, representatives of military scientific establishments, army journalists, and party functionaries. The then head of the Chief Political Directorate, General Sawczuk, spoke about the need to widen and intensify the front of ideological education. General Jaruzelski spoke about the army's loyalty to the party and faithfulness to Socialist ideas, about strengthening the links within the Warsaw Pact and especially with the Soviet Army. He formulated the tasks facing the army in the ideological education field.[26]

There have been four such army ideological conferences (1973, 1976, 1978, and 1982). Each had to deal with problems arising out of a new political situation, define new lines of ideological education work, and improve its methods.[27]

The Secretariat of the Central Committee was the high-level party body that often dealt with political aspects of the army; and it issued a number of guidelines on party-army relations. The guidelines on party-army cooperation in the civilian sector issued in January 1978 (see Chapter 6) were in effect inviting the army to start political activities outside the army.

One of the secretaries, Stanislaw Kania, who replaced Edward Gierek as first secretary of the party after the emergence of Solidarity (September 1980), has been since 1972 the representative of the Central Committee for the army. The political military liked him. General Baryla paid him a tribute at the 7th Plenary Session of the Central Committee (December 1980):

We had in the army our own system of guarantees that protected us from aberrations and helped to maintain a good Marxist-Leninist condition. Comrade Stanislaw Kania played an essential role in strengthening these guarantees when over many years he supervised party-political work in the army on behalf of the party leadership. As a result the basic values that decide the strength of the army had not been affected in these exceptionally difficult times.[28]

This is not surprising. Kania, who at one time graduated from the School for Political Officers at Lodz, helped the political military to build up the political army. His appointment to the position of first secretary of the party was almost certainly arranged by General

Jaruzelski, who wanted a stooge in this post until he himself was ready for it (October 1981).

The Army's Internal Role

"We shall defend Socialism as we defend independence" was the slogan used by the political army throughout 1981 to draw attention to the internal role of the army. The average Pole was apparently not aware of this fact. A military publicist had this to say:

> In the press, radio, and TV we did not explain the essence of the army's function and tasks, its obligations to the nations and also toward the state. If people ever thought about Article 10 of the Constitution and its meaning they thought about the external role of the armed forces, defense of sovereignty, and independence of the country against aggression from outside. <u>Much too little was said about the internal function of the army in a Socialist country.</u> So little that up to December 13, 1981, the internal role was limited in the minds of the people to helping with grain and root crop harvests, rescue work during natural disasters, building factories and communications and other contributions. [29]

The inference was that the imposition of martial law represented fulfilling the internal role. He added that fulfilling that role did not always mean use of military force. Before that, the army exercised that role when it assumed "patronage" over schools, youth organizations, factories, and institutions and participated in the work of local councils, political organizations, higher utility bodies, and so on.

The concept of the internal role may vary depending on the internal situation in a given Soviet bloc country. General A. A. Yepishev, head of the Chief Political Directorate of the Soviet Army and Navy, wrote in 1972 that with the maturing of a Socialist society the internal role of the Soviet Army was dying away, that as regards the internal situation the Soviet Union did not need the army and that it existed only as an instrument of protection of Socialism against the growing threat of war from the imperialists. [30]

The Polish view, while to some extent reflecting the Soviet trend, gave the army some kind of internal role:

> As the rule of the working masses gets stronger the internal role of the army undergoes appropriate changes. The removal of class antagonisms, the consolidation of the basis

of the Socialist system leads to a gradual extinction of that part of the internal role of the Army that has military characteristics and to the development of army activities in the economic, cultural, and educational spheres.[31]

Jaruzelski expounded the same idea in slightly different terms:

> The concept of the internal role of a democratic, a people's, army is being continuously enriched by a modern approach to it. A true unity of the army and nation is the very essence and nature of our new type of army, a Socialist army. The Polish Army is deeply enmeshed in the life of society, takes active part in the development processes of the country, stands first in the front line of education and schooling, economy and science, technology and culture.[32]

It seems to have been Jaruzelski's dream to attain domination over Polish life by a slow penetration of society. The process was interrupted by the events of 1980/81, which led to the intervention with military means.

Combat Readiness: A Pretext for Political Indoctrination

In the Soviet bloc military doctrine, combat readiness is one of the basic factors that determines any army's value. A comparison is made that as in factories the main objective is the production of certain goods so in army units it is to achieve combat readiness. The defense of Socialism against the constant threat of imperialist aggression demands that the armed forces are in constant combat readiness.

According to the Small Military Encyclopedia, "combat readiness" is the capacity to undertake combat at a definite time. The general level of combat readiness depends on the moral and political worthiness of troops, their level of training and equipment, material and technical supplies.[33]

Combat readiness of the army, it is said in another source, depends on the following factors:

- moral and political worthiness of troops and units,
- ideological, political, and psychological resistance capacity of troops and their readiness to act in conditions of danger,
- effective functioning of the command system and dependable work of troops and HQ staffs,

- quantity and quality of arms and technical equipment,
- fire power and training of troops,
- efficient material and technical provisioning.[34]

According to General Yepishev of the Soviet Army the main task of army commanders, political apparatus, Communist Party, and party youth organizations in the army and of all soldiers is to achieve high combat readiness in every unit.[35] His counterpart in the Polish Army, General Sawczuk, agreed with him fully: "Our chief aim must be the further development of moral and political worthiness, which is the basic component of combat readiness and to this aim all our party and ideological work, military training, and organizational measures must be subordinated."[36]

General Siwicki, asked in an interview about current priorities (1975), said that ideological work, forming attitudes of commitment on the part of the professional cadre, and constant perfection of qualifications and skills would continue to be at the center of attention of commanders of all levels.[37]

Thus at all times and on all occasions the nonmaterial factors of combat readiness are given priority over material factors. This is certainly one of the main differences in approach to combat readiness between Warsaw Pact and NATO armies. The latter have no political apparatus, no political party activities, and no corresponding programs of ideological and political work, yet they apparently manage to achieve combat readiness and, on the Soviet bloc's own admission, become credible adversaries.

One Polish Army source contains a list of not less than 46 specific requirements concerning individual soldiers and whole units that, taken together, make up combat readiness in the Polish Army. Very few of them would be given any attention in a Western army. For individual soldiers they include virtues like:

- ideological commitment to the cause of socialism,
- deep faith in the noble ideas of Socialism and a desire to defend the fatherland,
- sentiments of internationalism and of brotherhood-of-arms with soldiers of allied Socialist armies,
- up-to-date knowledge about the aggressive plans of imperialists and their psychological warfare methods,
- approval of the military doctrine of People's Poland and of the Warsaw Pact countries,
- resistance to subversive propaganda and imperialist ideology,
- vigilance to activities of forces hostile to Socialism aimed at weakening the army.

For whole units the requirements are very similar except that a concerted response is expected. [38]

It is not difficult to see that this interpretation of combat readiness is a great asset to the political military. <u>It provides an excuse for unlimited political indoctrination and justification for maintaining in the army a huge political machine for eventual use outside the army.</u>

Educating the Socialist Citizen-Soldier

The Polish military never miss an opportunity to say that as they prepare the country for defense they are also educating a new type of Pole and that educating the nation is a long-term mission of the Polish Army, one with a very long tradition. The basic premise is that the army is part of the nation's education system in which it plays its part alongside other elements: family, school, youth organizations, employers.

The objective, they maintain, is to produce a citizen-soldier. Military service teaches strict execution of orders and self-discipline, and develops responsibility and care for public property without which modern society cannot function. For young conscripts military service is a phase during which characters are formed and full maturity is reached. On leaving the army they take with them the result of the ideological education as well as of the professional work of commanders and instructors. The result is not only a competent defender of the country but very often also a well-qualified worker. Every year almost half of those who completed conscript service acquired a trade that is useful to the national economy. The army has become part of the national system of training for trades and professions. [39] During the years 1947-77 the army handed over to the national economy about 150,000 qualified workers who had obtained or improved their qualifications during military service. Among them were 78,000 drivers, 40,000 signalmen, radio-operators, electromechanics, and many other specialists. [40]

Not so well publicized is the fact that "educating the nation" is only a vehicle for political indoctrination and thus is the domain of the political apparatus, party, and party youth organizations in the army. According to <u>Wojsko Ludowe</u> (1981) an officer not only prepares a citizen for defense by teaching the art of war but also transmits knowledge of social matters and makes him a politically conscious active member of a Socialist society. The scope of his work is very wide because it concerns the whole life of the nation and the state. [41]

"Educating the nation" also takes place outside the army in all sections of the population where defense training is carried out. The field of civilian education is one example. Jerzy Kuberski, minister of of education, said in 1978 that his ministry and the Ministry of Defense worked closely together concentrating their efforts on undertakings that served to shape ideological and patriotic attitudes of the young. Preparatory military training, a subject in the secondary school curriculum, contained educational values of a general social nature. It influenced the shaping of a citizen's consciousness, patriotism and internationalism, discipline, and respect for order in public life. By taking part in the teaching process and social life of schools the army cadre makes a contribution to the patriotic and defense education of the school-age population. The extent of the army's involvement with the young of school age is illustrated by the fact that each year about 1.5 million young take part in meetings with regular officers and 800,000 children and youngsters visit army units. Army units assume patronage over schools and in many of them with army help "national tradition rooms" have been organized. In recent years intensive cooperation developed between army officers and teachers in the matter of exchanging experiences in the field of patriotic and defense education. At least 40,000 teachers took part in such conferences and consultations.[42] General Baryla, head of the Chief Political Directorate, said more recently that every year the army was handing over to society a large number of patriotic Poles. It is repaying the nation with enlightened citizens who brought with them from the army characteristics that are today most valuable: respect for work, high discipline, and deeply engrained patriotic concern for the welfare of Socialist Poland.[43]

This citizen-soldier must of course meet one basic requirement:

The Polish armed forces have a duty to secure the building of Socialism. They educate the citizen and are an instrument of national integration. They must therefore still more effectively shape a citizen-soldier who is politically committed, hard working, and disciplined—one who understands that today patriotism is irrevocably linked with internationalism, and in particular with the ideological and arms brotherhood with the Soviet Union, the guarantor of Polish security and of peace in Europe.[44]

4
Indoctrination Methods and
Monitoring Political Reliability

"Party-political work" is the standard Polish name for
all types and forms of political indoctrination and group
pressure practiced on serving conscripts and the regular
cadre. The obvious aim is to ensure the political reliability of troops. An elaborate system of gathering and
recording of political information on individuals and of
assessing and reporting the views and attitudes of whole
social groups has been developed for this purpose. However, the staggering extent and great diversification of
these activities suggested that they were also meant to
give employment and practical experience to large numbers of political officers and party activists who were
groomed for a future political role outside the army.
Much later it was admitted that the system of ideological
and political training paid dividends during the preparation and operation of martial law. There is also no doubt
that these methods would be used by the political military
against the continuing political opposition in Poland.

DESCRIPTION OF PARTY-POLITICAL WORK

The various forms of party-political work are listed in the
Small Military Encyclopedia. A much-favored method is group pressure (literally "group influence"). Joint action by the group is said
to produce socially useful behavior, help to transform individual
thinking, and minimize negative influences. The occasions where
this happens are:

- meetings of the POP for members and candidate members of the party,
- general meetings for troops, usually at company level, concerned with current political developments, with training and discipline matters,
- conferences of party and party youth activists devoted to current policies of the party and government, new training tasks, discipline, service living conditions,
- Courts of censure for career NCOs, warrant officers, and officers, and similar courts for conscript soldiers and NCOs.

In addition to collective influencing there is an institutionalized form of individual pressure known as "personal party talks" (which will be discussed in more detail below).

Another form is participation of army personnel and sometimes of whole units in social and political activities in and outside the army. They help the development of the individual and forge solid links between the army and the people.

A third form consists of instruction and self-tuition:

- political instruction of all army personnel arranged as one- or two-year programs of instruction in groups under specially trained group leaders (more detail below),
- party instruction, in addition to the above, for party members and candidate members (more detail below).

Propaganda consists of:

- political information at company and battalion level meetings given by higher ranks,
- visits by VIPs (party and war veterans, distinguished commanders, government figures, and so on),
- lecture series, talks, meetings, quizzes, and so on.

The foregoing take place in connection with special events of international, national, or military nature, important anniversaries, competitions in general, and military knowledge. Quite separate are various forms of visual propaganda (posters, leaflets, notice-board information, news sheets), and central, regional, and military press and publications. Polish civilian mass media too have a substantial military content. To complete the list there are cultural-educational and artistic activities based on officer's clubs, reading rooms, and libraries.[1]

All these forms of indoctrination and pressure have been used by the political army when it was being built up, then during prepara-

tions for the martial law intervention, and finally under the rule of
the political military. They were used at first mainly against army
personnel and now against the Polish people as well. Some methods
are described in more detail in the sections that follow.

Political Instruction

Political instruction is described as one of the main forms of
ideological education. The objective is to instill Socialist patriotism,
the will to defend the country, the feeling of ideological and class
links, and brotherhood-of-arms with Soviet bloc armies. Political
instruction programs contain Marxist-Leninist ideology, progressive
and revolutionary traditions of the nation, building of Socialism in
Poland, development of the world Socialist system, current political
and military situation, and principles of Socialist morality.

The political apparatus organizes and directs political instruction in army units, headquarters, and establishments in accordance
with guidelines of the Chief Political Directorate, which define time
scales, methods, and principles of conducting political instruction
periods. The GZP also provides all training material.

All serving army personnel undergo political instruction, which
varies according to the level: higher-level commanders and party
members attend ideological-theoretical conferences; officers, warrant
officers, and NCOs attend ideological instruction; and serving conscripts get standard instruction with the use of modern didactic aids.
Members of the party-political apparatus get instruction on theory
and methods of political instruction. Instruction periods for the regular cadre are in the main conducted by a political officer, for serving
conscripts by commanders of army units. [2]

Personal Party Talks

This is an effective form of pressure and deserves attention.
The practice was first brought in after the 6th Party Congress (1970)
and became a permanent feature of the system. According to the party
statute, every year one-third of the members and candidate members
of party organizations attend a special interview. A member appears
before a special team appointed by a higher party authority for this
purpose. The team consists of the committee secretary and at least
two members of the member's POP.

Ostensibly personal talks are concerned with improving the contribution of a party member. According to one political officer the
talks activate members and help reveal personal problems and doubts

that arise from various happenings and events. They provide an opportunity to hear proposals on training and party and service life. The interview teams must find the right kind of approach to the comrade to be able to start a frank dialogue about interesting problems and matters of every-day life. They are able to do this because they acquaint themselves beforehand with the good and bad points of the comrade's character and consult his immediate superiors. The teams aim to ensure that criticism does not provoke an unfriendly, insincere, or defensive attitude but helps to evoke honest self-criticism plus a desire to correct one's behavior and to carry out party and service duties better. [3]

It is possible that many personal party talks fulfill a prophylactic role as described above. Many, however, serve a different purpose and are arranged as and when required and not at three-year intervals. It is well known that every political crisis in Poland has been followed by the expulsion of undesirables from the party. During the 1980/81 crisis many party members chose to expel themselves.

Here are two examples of how the practice was exploited in the army. In December 1971, at a meeting of party activists in the army, General Sawczuk, then deputy head of the GZP, said:

> Personal party talks helped many comrades to become
> aware of the demands of party membership and strength-
> ened the feeling of party responsibility. . . . As a result
> of these talks a number of party members and candidate
> members left the party. . . . The party does not need
> passive people, people who do not like party or service
> discipline, do not meet ideological standards or the
> requirement of additional unpaid work. . . . All agreed
> that the talks were also a source of information and re-
> sulted in proposals for improving the work of party
> authorities, of commanders and army units. [4]

The last sentence can mean only that some comrades, while defending their own record, were furnishing information about superiors that was later used against the latter. After all, former supporters of Gomulka had to be replaced by the new people of Gierek.

Another deputy head of the GZP, General H. Koczara, interviewed in connection with the 1974/75 exchange of party cards, had this to say about personal party talks:

> Party talks conducted as part of the party card exchange
> operation differed somewhat from the generally accepted
> type of personal talks in that they had to end with an as-

sessment of the party member concerned. This was because the Political Bureau decided that a party member
can obtain a new card on the condition that he had obtained
a positive assessment in respect to his party and professional activities, his ideological and moral attitude. The
assessments are just now and for the near future the most
important task for party committees, POPs, and the special interview teams. . . . The penetrating talks that have
already taken place achieved their objective. Comrades
who found themselves in the party by accident, who broke
the provisions of the statute, and who as a result got a
negative assessment already carry the consequences.[5]

Personal party talks also take place when a comrade commits
a major or a series of smaller service offenses. It is customary that
a commander would inform the secretary of the POP committee before
punishment is decided so that the latter can step in first. The offender
is then subjected to a nonscheduled personal talk with the interview
team. The matter may end there with a party admonition. The positive
and negative sides of this practice were often debated among political
officers. The view prevailed that the social pressure exercised by the
party organization is more effective than punishment by a superior.

Evening Universities of Marxism-Leninism (WUML)

This is a misnomer for a system of party instruction facilities
that has nothing in common with university or extramural studies.
WUML have existed in the Polish Army since 1950 as correspondence
courses for improving the ideological and political knowledge of career
officers. In 1958 they were turned into Centers for Sociological and
Military Sciences (ONSiW), which adopted a different program and
were based on military districts.[6] This was evidently one of the concessions made during the early Gomulka era when Marxism-Leninism
suffered a temporary setback in Poland.
      In the 1970s WUML became one of the more important institutions
in the political sector of the Polish Army. Following the recommendations of the 1st Ideological Conference of the Polish armed forces in
June 1973 the GZP prepared a long-term program of ideological-
education work in which a significant role was assigned to WUML.[7]
      Of the many reasons that one could find to explain why WUML
were instituted at that particular time, one seems more compelling
than the rest. In 1974 the first graduates of the political stream of
Higher Officer Schools were joining Army units. These graduates were
far superior in the areas of general education and political knowledge

to the average officer already in the service. Development courses under the high-sounding name "university" were intended to minimize the difference and raise the overall standard.

WUML activities are based on Centers for Sociological-Military Sciences that exist at military district and arm of service level. Most of the party instruction takes place at branches of WUML established in larger garrison towns or other places that offer suitable teaching staff or physical facilities—within Higher Officer Schools, the Military Historical Institute, but also with army units (the 12th Mechanized Division [General Jaruzelski's pet division]).

Party committees of all levels, from military district downward, are responsible for organizing the courses, selecting suitable programs, finding teaching staff and students, and so on. The main thing that distinguishes WUML activities from other forms of party and political instruction is that they depend on the initiative of local party organizations and the "zeal" of individual party members rather than on the full-time (established) training machinery in the army. Students are selected by their local party committees, which also monitor their attendance and progress. This is because a party member has a statutory duty to undergo party training. The student is obliged to keep a record of activities in an official log. In the main officers are chosen for these courses, although at one time 25 percent were regular NCOs. The aim is to put all the regular cadre through WUML courses. It has been stated that some units are close to achieving that target. This does not mean that the courses will one day be discontinued. They are described as being "continuous," which means that having finished one faculty one can continue at a second or even third faculty.

WUML have a large number of faculties from which branches can choose those that suit local needs most—for example, philosophy-sociology, economics, religion and ethics, foundations of Marxism, scientific Communism, esthetics and culture, pedagogy-psychology, legal problems, and crime prevention. WUML courses are attended by party members who are earmarked or are already working as group leaders of political instruction groups (for conscripts) or leaders of party instruction groups (for party members) and also as lecturers on party matters to young soldiers. Most of these posts are on the establishment of the army and this is probably an adequate incentive.

The two-year courses end with examinations and a diploma, which is considered an additional qualification. But the diploma is not obligatory and the examinations, according to some sources, are not taken very seriously.

There is evidence that some WUML courses were oriented toward the civilian sector, especially in the Baltic Coast region. Here are two examples:

The Faculty of Legal Problems and [crime] Prevention of the Szczecin Branch of WUML is attended not only by comrades from the military organs of prosecution and judiciary but also by commanders and educators who found that it helped them to learn more about penal law, the role and rights of superiors, international military law, military administration law, and legal aspects of discipline and prevention. Well-known specialists and people of great practical experience covered these subjects. In addition there were meetings with representatives of organs of prosecution, judiciary, legal help, legal defense, and prison service. There also were excursions to these places.

and

The Economics Faculty had the largest number of students. The studies that were far from abstract were complemented by meetings with political and economic leaders of the West Pomerania region. Economists of Szczecin enterprises and representatives of foreign trade organizations gave talks on current problems. Some practical exercises were carried out in factories and service establishments.[8]

It is interesting that the academic year of WUML begins and ends with ceremony and pomp and that WUML courses were organized also for the leading cadre of the central institutions of the Ministry of Defense and of military academies.[9] Quite clearly, those among the top brass who until the early 1970s did not have to worry about orthodox Marxism-Leninism were made to correct the deficiency.

Party-Political Work at the General Staff Academy

The General Staff Academy (ASG) is the highest training establishment of the fighting army. It is surprising that party-political work should be given much prominence in the work of the ASG. It has been described very fully in connection with its 30th anniversary (1977) by General Jura, its political deputy commandant.

Party-political work is organized and directed by the party-political organ of the ASG, which combines its political department and the party committee. The objectives in the ideological field were: raising the level of sociopolitical knowledge with special emphasis on the theory and practice of Marxism-Leninism; and educating the mili-

tary and civilian staff to become idealists, politically committed
patriots, and internationalists who fully approve and implement the
party line.

It is an accepted axiom at the ASG that ideological education,
the didactic processes, and scientific research all hang together.
The teaching of sociopolitical subjects and organization of practical
ideological education are geared to producing a modern commander
and staff officer who has been trained for organizing and directing
party-political work in army units. Political and party instruction are
the two main forms of ideological education of staff and students. They
are carried out in more than 100 groups that are run by officers of
the party-political organ and of the chair of sociopolitical sciences.
For the teaching and research staff the highest forms of political instruction are ideological conferences that take place two to four times
a year. Studies at WUML courses are the important form of party
instruction for party members and candidates. In addition there is
political information as the most direct form of transmitting topical
information about the situation in and outside the country and in the
army. Many high-level politicians and well-known scientists and
journalists visit the ASG for this purpose.

Cultural-education activities also have an important place in
party-political work at the ASG. The 1976-80 Program of Culture
Development in the army implies that an ASG graduate must show that
in addition to his wide professional military knowledge he is an effective party-political and social organizer, an educator with a striking
personality and a developed aesthetic sense, which should make him
a "patron of culture" in his place of service. Various cultural activities at the ASG are geared to this end.

The "Lead and Compete Movement," another form of party-
political work, was brought back to the ASG (its birthplace) in 1973
after a break of many years. It now is an integral part of the education and training of officers. It helps to motivate the teaching staff,
conscript personnel, and civilian employees of the ASG. In a wide
range of competitions, individual winners are given appropriate titles:
"For Service to the ASG," "Exemplary Student of ASG," "Distinguished
Graduate of ASG," "Exemplary Teacher of ASG," "Exemplary Worker
of ASG," "Exemplary Commander," "Exemplary Soldier," "Exemplary
Driver." The winners in group competitions are given collective titles:
"Leading Chair of ASG," "Leading Unit," "Leading Subunit," "Section
Excelling in Socialist Service," "Brigade Excelling in Socialist Work,"
"Leading Group under Instruction."

The influence of party-political work on scientific-research work
at the ASG makes itself felt on three planes:

- the direction of scientific-research work is party-politically
  inspired,

- the party committee and the political department of ASG are directly involved in the organization and execution of research,
- they carry out periodic assessments and surveys of the work done and formulate tasks for party members and party units in the area of research.

One result of the above was that from 1974 onward, students chose sociopolitical subjects for their diploma thesis more often than before. Among the problems taken up in this way were role and tasks of party-political work in combat operations on land and in the air, role of the party organization in strengthening the "sole commander" principle, importance of the morale and political factors on the battlefield of the future, and so on. Methodological problems of party political work in battle conditions were made the subject of a symposium (May 1977) that was attended by political officers of division level and above and those serving with institutions of the Ministry of Defense, military academies, and higher officer schools.[10]

Cramming the ASG program with political exercises of doubtful military value cannot be the true function of the party-political organ and of the political department inside it. Both institutions rank very high in the party hierarchy and exist normally at division level and above. Numerically the ASG could be compared not with a division but a regiment. What then makes the party-political work at ASG so important? The most likely explanation is that these high party authorities are there to ensure that future top-level commanders of the Polish Army are fully aware of the internal political role of the army and that they understand the implications. The heavy presence of the political army in the life of the ASG is proof of the high politicization of the whole army.

The "Lead and Compete Movement"

Various competition schemes have been practiced in the Polish Army since the late 1940s. An integrated system was brought in with the "Instruction on Lead and Compete Activities" issued by the Ministry of Defense in December 1972. It established new principles and forms of competition, raised the standards, and expanded the range of rights and privileges for winners. This and the sessions of the Military Council of the Ministry of Defense in 1975 and 1977 devoted to this subject gave the movement a very high standing and created favorable conditions for its development and a close correlation with training and education processes.[11]

The main elements of the system are individual competitions for the title "Model Soldier" and "Model Commander" and group

competitions for the title "Section Excelling in Socialist Service."
The "Model Soldier" applies to three levels of accomplishment denoted by bronze, silver, and gold badges. The awards correspond to
fixed points on the one to five scale of performance, which is in general use in the Army: 5 = very good, 4 = good, 3 = adequate, 2 = inadequate, 1 = bad. The minimum for a bronze badge is a 4.25 average
result during a six-month period in military training and combat readiness and moral and political condition and discipline; for the silver
badge, 4.35; for the gold, 4.51.[12] Different requirements apply to
the distinctions of "Model Commander" and "Section Excelling in
Socialist Service," but they too depend on the performance of individual
soldiers in the units concerned. The linking of awards with training
and service performance makes the system of competition a valuable
instrument in the hands of commanders. It has been stated that all
commanders had a duty to direct competition activities and that they
were helped in this by the party-political apparatus, the party, and
the party youth organizations in the army. The political apparatus
supervised the organization and promoted the ideas of the movement
and its various forms. This was to ensure that individuals and groups
taking part were fairly and objectively assessed.[13]

Stick and carrot are used to achieve large-scale participation.
Participation is, at any rate, a statutory duty of party members and
candidates and of members of the youth organization. Others volunteer
at meetings organized for the purpose. Some privileges are material
(additional leave passes, preference in promotion and appointments,
gifts, and even money payments), others exploit vanity (photographs
with citations on official display boards, entries in commemoration
books, photographs with unfurled regimental colors in the background,
place of honor at official functions, congratulation letters to families
and civilian employers, write-ups in the press, meetings with high-
ranking superiors, and so on).

The above "incentives" as well as continuous pressure seem to
work. It was stated that for every ten members and candidates of the
party, seven obtained the title of "Model Soldier." Among members
of the youth organization 50 percent and among conscript soldiers in
general 33 percent were holders of the "Model Soldier" title. In the
group competition 25 percent of sections in the ground forces and 33
percent of flights in the air force have obtained the "Excelling in the
Socialist Service" title. Average results obtained by individual soldiers and by units taking part in competitions were 0.5-1.0 grade
higher than in those not competing.[14]

In elite troops participation was even higher, in one instance
reaching 60 percent of all units. One source claimed that thanks to
the competition movement at the Higher Officer School of Mechanised
Troops at Wroclaw in 1975 over 55 percent of graduates obtained the
very good (5.00) result.[15]

Yet the competition movement was not an unqualified success. Many venerated army institutions and procedures were debunked by army personnel themselves during the 1980/81 crisis. The competition movement came under fire right from the start. The principle as well as the procedures and practices were systematically criticized.

MONITORING AND MAINTAINING POLITICAL RELIABILITY

In 1978 General Sawczuk, head of the GZP, said at a meeting of the Military Council of the Ministry of Defense:

> There is at present no issue of greater importance in the party-political and command and education areas of work than forming a high moral and political worthiness and a proper mood (atmosphere, climate) among the troops. Results obtained in this work should be one of the basic criteria for assessing the suitability of commanders and political officers for their posts. [16]

The meaning of the terms "high moral and political worthiness and a proper mood" was explained:

1. They are not the equivalent of the term "morale" used in the West. They have a wider meaning because in a Socialist army they represent a whole range of ideological, political, and social values together with combat and discipline qualities. Their outward signs (indicators) are the attitudes and behavior of troops. The elements of moral and political worthiness are described more fully in an article, "Moral and Political Condition and Military Discipline" in Scientific Papers of the Military Political Academy, No. 86, 1976.

2. Polish views on the subject fully agree with Soviet Army thinking, which links the moral and political worthiness with a psychological readiness of troops or mood. Mood is a reaction to various events that take place at home and abroad, in the army as a whole, and in own units, in the area of living conditions, human relations, and personal life. It is expressed in opinions, verbal declarations, gossip, and other behavior. The form in which it manifests itself depends on personality, life experience of a person, and level of ideological, political, and social awareness.

3. Mood is affected by outside influences and can be shaped. It is what American psychologists call "attitudes not quite formed." While attitudes result from intellectual processes and convictions based on knowledge and therefore have a lasting character, mood is

changeable, even spontaneous, because the rational element is dominated by emotions. Even so the relationship between established attitudes and mood is sufficiently close to be able to draw correct conclusions about the real moral and political state of a given army milieu from an analysis of the prevailing mood.[17]

Assessing and Shaping the Mood of Troops

It is a basic duty of commanders and political officers to assess the current mood of the troops and shape it as required. In 1977 the Minister of Defense issued recommendations on the use of scientific methods in the assessing and subsequent shaping of mood. In 1978 the head of the GZP issued an instruction about assessing and analyzing the mood of troops and informing about them. A practical guide on the subject was published in 1979.[18]

There exists an integrated two-way, up-and-down-the-hierarchy-ladder system of gathering information about the mood in the various groups and environments of the army and of reacting with instructions on ways and means of shaping a desired atmosphere. Reporting about opinions and views of subordinate soldiers, civilian employees, and families of professional soldiers is an important element of the process, but the aim is to form proper attitudes to given events and situations. Commanders and political officers must therefore ensure feedback of information to subordinate commanders and their political deputies that provides guidance on shaping the mood. The reaction is of particular importance when reports contain questions or proposals. Needless to say, superior officers should study and analyze the situation on the ground and find out what is or has already been done. Other general requirements are that information should be objective, come from as many sources as possible, and be timely.

Gathering Information on Mood

For gathering information on mood the following sources are used:

- Personal contacts of commanders and political officers with soldiers, civilian employees, and families of the professional cadre as well as contacts with officers who are superiors of the above
- Party and youth organization meetings, conferences, and so on, where the mood normally manifests itself
- Reports from officers who inspect units, attend meetings and briefings, from secretaries of Party committees, and through other activists.

- Civilian party organizations, local administration bodies, and military personnel on detached duties to the above organizations
- Periodic reports from subordinate commanders and political officers.
- Complaints registered by soldiers, civilian employees, and families of the professional cadre.

Appraisal of the Mood Situation

Appraisal is the next stage of the process. It amounts to a summing-up of the information and drawing conclusions. It consists of a number of separate operations: preliminary sifting of information from the point of view of reliability, organizing the material for analysis, analysis itself (this takes place once a week at regiment level and once a fortnight above that level), drawing conclusions in respect to desirable behavior, and preparing an outline of the report for a superior.

The most important of the above is analysis. It aims to describe:

- the mood that predominates in the various environments; it is shown against the background of sociopolitical and economic developments in the country, in the life of the army (with special reference to staff relations and living conditions), and developments abroad,
- the way in which mood manifests itself in the various groups,
- causes, extent, and intensity of the mood in each milieu,
- dynamism of development, tendencies to grow or wane,
- effect of means used hitherto to form the desirable mood.

Drawing conclusions amounts to determining ways and means for shaping the mood. These are incorporated in the plans of work of commanders, political officers, the party, and youth organizations. Shaping the mood consists of applying suitable "pressure" on individuals and groups with the aim to create positive behavior patterns in aid of combat readiness. Methods of achieving this belong to the area of military pedagogy, theory of command, propaganda, and so on. The mood-forming process must be integrated with the system of army education and training. [19]

A political officer of the rank of colonel criticized the above system. He was well qualified to do so, because in his own words, "at one time among his official duties were: analyzing, appraising, and inspiring the activities of the command and party-political apparatus of the Pomeranian Military District in respect to shaping the mood in units of the district." The main point of criticism was that

due to limited data processing capacity the time for information to
make the route from the political section of a regiment to its destina-
tion in the Chief Political Directorate was excessive and the information became stale. In his view information traffic should be speeded
up by 50-80 percent. A step in the right direction was taken when in
the Pomeranian Military District they began to use the general communication network of the army and the operational network for transmission of information on mood. This reduced the number and size of
written reports. The aim was to cut out the latter altogether in favor
of the teleconference method of communication. Written reporting is
susceptible to embellishment and pruning of information "unwelcome"
to superiors, whereby it ceases to be "live." Another weakness was
that the whole commitment of reporting and shaping the mood was
considered to be a responsibility of political officers alone, and of
lower-rank officers at that. The colonel suggests that many more
command and political officers of all levels should be involved, and
in particular the so-called first teams, that is, commanders of units
and their political deputies.

In general, according to the colonel, the system has been working very well. In the Pomeranian Military District it was possible to
organize this work so that in the majority of units political officers
and party and youth activists were in continual and direct contact with
their men. [20]

Territorial Centers of Political Information (TOIP)

These centers are described by the same source although they
are only indirectly linked with the subject. In 1977 they were a new
institution, but having proved a success they were likely to be adopted
elsewhere. The facilities of the 12th Mechanized Division at Szczecin
were used to form a TOIP for the Pomeranian Military District area.
It serves the need of fast transmission of reliable political information
from the Political Directorate of the military district to all outlying
units, military establishments, and institutions that are all linked to
the TOIP center. TOIP goes into action once a month, or more often
if necessary. There are three modes of communication:

- Representatives from outlying places meet at TOIP with a representative of the Political Directorate who hands out the necessary
  information and uses the opportunity to brief himself.
- A representative from TOIP calls at the Political Directorate to
  collect information for area representatives assembled at TOIP.
- A runner brings tape-recorded information from the Political
  Directorate to TOIP for reproduction and distribution to representatives from the area.

It is pointed out in the article that the TOIP facilities are additional to the existing channels of communication and do not interfere with them in any way.[21] It is worth noting that the above TOIP is located at Szczecin and not at Bydgoszcz, the location of the Pomeranian Military District HQ and of the Political Directorate of the district. Szczecin has been for a long time a politically sensitive area.

Closeness to the Troops

One of the party's rules is that activists of all levels maintain close and continual personal contact with the rank and file of the party. The principle has been embraced by the army not only because a good knowledge of subordinates is considered to be the secret of success of a good commander but also because the political army needs to know absolutely everything about individuals even before it starts working on them.

Getting to know the men is a continuous process that covers the whole period of military service of a conscript and the whole life of a professional soldier. A superior's basic duty is to find out all he can about the personality, character, abilities, and interests of subordinates so as to be able to develop their potential. He must above all establish which elements may play a decisive role in forming his personality and a high moral and political condition.

Personal Talks

Personal talks are considered the most effective method of getting to know the men. They are carried out in all units with all personnel by successive commanders. Several such talks arranged in intervals help the superior to learn about the background, personality, views, personal problems, and progress in the service. They also reduce the psychological distance between the superior and his subordinates.[22] According to another source, regiment commanders and officers designated by them, and commanders of all levels, carry out personal talks with newly inducted conscripts. Party and youth organization members have separate and additional talks with the secretaries of committees in the army. The talks take place in the first few days after joining the units and later, but during the early stage of training.

Prior to the meeting the superior studies the personal documents that have been prepared by the Army Recruiting Commission (WKU) and contain a registration card, biographic data, and a psychological pen picture. The documents give origin, education, address, marital state, work qualifications, employment details, membership of organizations, and health record. These documents are held in a separate folder. Information provided by schools, employers, the Citizens' Militia and other institutions, health records, and other information on the individual concerned or his family are examined but "should not prejudice the superior against the soldier." A well-prepared and properly conducted interview (both stages are described in minute detail in the article) should enable the superior to form a fairly accurate view regarding:

- influence of the environment and family on the soldier's make-up (13 aspects are covered),
- moral principles, world outlook, ideological commitments, motivation, attitude to military service and to life in general,
- personal circumstances (family obligations, employment of members of the family, girl friend) and problems, fears and anxieties,
- character and temperament (25 aspects covered),
- intelligence and abilities (10 aspects covered).

Because one interview does not provide all the answers, they should take place systematically, not necessarily as formal and prearranged meetings. Intervals during working or leisure time offer ample opportunities for "informal chats," which can be just as fruitful.

These interviews are separate from normal career interviews and personal party talks described earlier. The main difference is that apart from the superior and the person interviewed, no other people are present.[23]

A superior has a number of other means to find out all he wants about his subordinates:

Observation: Conduct and attitude to training, ideological and political instruction, involvement in social, cultural, and sport activities tell him a great deal about the individual, his conscientiousness, stamina, resilience, and readiness to help others. He can spot the activists and the informal leaders in a group.

Environment and family: Background information is obtained through personal visits to parents and the family of the soldier, by talking to soldiers who come from the same locality, and so on.

Written references, testimonials, commendations: These are provided by the authorities or by political and social organizations in which a soldier has been or is still active. Special notice is taken of the views and opinions of the cadre and duty personnel of neighboring units.

Storage and Exploitation of Personal Information

A superior has the duty to collect and store the information on individuals and to keep on verifying and updating it. It depends on the level of command how elaborate the system and how well protected it is against unauthorized access. Even the lowest records contain a photograph. The superior uses the information first of all for assessing the moral and political condition and the mood of his unit. It helps him to organize training and party-political work, to achieve a high moral and political condition and the required mood in the unit. Finally, it affects the choosing of personnel for appointments, distinctions, and difficult or responsible duties. [24]

Special Communication Facilities

In the 1970s two rather unusual procedures have become established institutions in the Polish Army. Known as "rooms and telephones of trust" and "hours of frankness" they were intended to facilitate communication between the troops and their superiors.

Room and Telephone of Trust. In the mid-1970s in some military units and schools the idea arose of introducing a facility that would enable soldiers and civilian employees to ventilate more freely (in an open or anonymous way) their grievances, bring to the notice of superiors conflict situations that make normal relations with colleagues and superiors difficult, ask for advice and help in matters they were not prepared to raise officially.

Such a room and telephone came into operation in May 1974 at the Center for Training Navy Specialists (CSSMW) and since then in several garrisons. They were manned on certain hours of the day by selected officers. The duty roster was on the unit's notice board, which gave the soldier a chance to choose the officer. It was found that the facility was used first for matters connected with transfer and change of speciality, leave, and passes; second for personal and family matters; third for matters connected with training, staff relations, discipline, and so on. A modified version of the system spread to units of the Pomeranian and Warsaw Military Districts. Here the troops had the right to phone the regiment commander or his deputies on certain days and hours and present their problems. The aim was to give the troops the feeling of security and of being looked after. For a superior "the telephone of trust" was a means of learning about the mood among troops and a chance to defuse a potentially explosive situation and to "eliminate negative factors" in discipline, staff relations, and training. It also helped him explain the matter and create a positive attitude to military service duties.

<u>Hours of Frankness</u>. This practice was introduced in the Warsaw
Military District and spread to other districts and arms of service.
The aim and function are the same as for the telephones of trust.
The "hours" are organized by commanders and deputy commanders
from company upward and are attended by members of one of the
groupings in the army—for example, conscript soldiers, regular
NCOs, wives of the regular cadre, and so on. At these informal
meetings army and even personal matters can be freely discussed.
The meetings take place once every two to three months within duty
hours. Immediate superiors of the assembled do not attend the meetings. The practice of "hours of frankness" has proved to be an effective means of learning about the mood in a given military milieu and
an instrument for forming desired attitudes and behavior. One of the
advantages of the practice is that relatively large groups of people
are involved at any one time. [25]

Reading the above, one is seriously tempted to dismiss it all
as irrelevant and childish nonsense. It certainly is that, but only from
a strictly military point of view and in relation to the needs of a fighting army. To the political military <u>these activities represented
exercises that were relevant to their political operations as normal
field exercises are to military operations.</u>

5
Army Social Sciences and Cultural Facilities Serve the Political Military

A huge organizational and financial effort was put into the development of social sciences in the army. This was an indication that the political army's ambitions extended far beyond the army. Among thousands of army social scientists there were many who worked in civilian centers and universities or cooperated with them. This was presented as the army's contribution to the development of Polish science as a whole but was in reality part of a slow penetration of the civilian sector. The same can be said about the army's big publishing empire, the army's say in the mass media, and its role as the "greatest patron of the arts" in Poland. Both the social scientists and the publicity men now represent important factors in the confrontation between the political military and the Polish people.

SCOPE OF SOCIAL SCIENCES EXCEEDS ARMY NEEDS

General Polanski, commandant of the WAP, justifies the extensive development of social sciences in the army in the following comment:

Among the many fields of science, social sciences occupy a special place because they concern human beings and human beings play the decisive role in the modern armed forces. The best equipment offers nothing more than an enormous potential, which needs soldiers with higher than ever before intellectual, moral, and political qualities to

73

become effective. Because of that, knowledge about man
and his motivation and about soldier groups and their
psychology has grown so much in importance. . . . Military social sciences provide the theoretical backup for
practical ideological education.[1]

The term "military social sciences" is apparently ambiguous.
According to Colonel Professor Dr. Habilitatus Mieczyslaw Michalik,
a well-known military sociologist and philosopher, it may refer to
social sciences that concern social processes in the army, help to
understand war as a social phenomenon, and facilitate functioning of
the army; or are practiced in military establishments irrespective of
whether they concern the army or social processes in general; or are
practiced by scientists who are members of the regular officer cadre.
Since many civilian scientists work in military establishments and
some consider this their first and main job, he suggests a compromise
definition: Military social sciences are practiced in military establishments by scientific personnel who work in them.

Professor Michalik says that as a result of a long process of
development in the area of military social sciences the following scientific disciplines eventually emerged: Marxist philosophy, including
history of philosophy, ethics, religions; general political economy
with special economics, for example, economics of defense; scientific
Communism with elements of political sciences; sociology of the army;
pedagogy, general and military, together with didactics; psychology,
general and military; theory of party-political work with theory of
propaganda; theory of culture; methodology of social sciences; military
law with elements of civil and international law; history of Poland;
history of international relations and of the international workers'
movement; and military history. All of these are currently practiced
in a significant number of army institutions, of which the most important are the Military Political Academy and, under its umbrella,
the Institute of Social Research, the Institute of Economics, and the
Institute of Military History.[2]

According to another source, sociology of the army (one of many
in the above list) studies the armed forces as a social institution,
their role in society, their influence on other social environments,
as well as the feedback influence of the latter on the army's functioning and development. It also studies the internal relations in the army
as a specific human environment. It has four distinct areas of interest:
(1) development of the army as a product and factor of society, (2)
role of the army in the life of modern societies, (3) attitudes of the
population to the army, and (4) internal relations in the army. Area 1
includes comparative studies of modern foreign armies, especially
those of the capitalist countries; area 3 involves studies on various
groups of the civilian population.

Among specific subjects covered by army sociological studies were: silhouette of a conscript soldier (attitude during military service, change in world outlook due to service, adaptation to condition of service, and so on), means of strengthening patriotic and international feelings among the troops, role of army youth organization in army life, current political climate and moral and political condition among various categories of soldiers, prestige of the army professional cadre in society, attraction of professional military service to youth of school age, attitude of various groups of the civilian population to matters of defense and to military traditions of the nation. [3]

General Polanski wrote earlier that social sciences in the army must not be limited to studies that help the teaching and education processes or are otherwise useful to the army. WAP has always increased its participation in the political and ideological life of the country. WAP scientists have a duty to contribute to the development of civilian social sciences. This would be a true measure of the scientific and party qualifications. "The Party had a right to expect that the WAP would effectively react against philosophical and social conceptions and manifestations of revisionism that came from abroad or originated in some opposition circles in Poland. "[4]

A few years later Professor Michalik explained that

although the social sciences research program was geared to the needs and objectives of ideological-education work in the army it also fitted the requirements of ideological-education of society as a whole. Studies by military sociologists carried out among soldiers and among the civilian population provided data for military as well as civilian sociologists and were therefore used in and outside the army. At any rate many army problems could be studied in detail only against a wider and more general background. [5]

Apart from that WAP scientists were engaged in work that concerned the whole of society directly. Such studies formed part of the WAP research program but at the same time also part of the national research program. Around the mid-1970s WAP scientists participated in the work on eight out of eleven national problems in the field of social sciences that had been formulated at the 2nd Congress of Polish Science (1973). In the program for the years 1976-80 the WAP was to coordinate research work on a number of subjects that were of interest to the army and to society at large—for example, "Role of the army in establishing the people's democracy system of government and after," "Contemporary bourgeois and antisocialist sociopolitical doctrines, including Maoism and Trotskyism. "[6]

Organizational Link with the Political Apparatus

The importance of social sciences to the army is reflected in the substantial resources that have been put at their disposal. It began with the formation of the chair of sociology at the WAP (1957) and of a Center for Sociological Studies of the Chief Political Directorate of the Army (1960). In 1963 a Scientific Council of the Ministry of Defense for Pedagogy, Psychology, and Sociology of the army was created. When the range of social sciences practiced in the army expanded, the council changed its name to Council for Social Sciences of the Ministry of Defense (1968). Its role was to initiate, coordinate, and assess the work done in the field of social sciences in the army. It was an advisory body to the minister of defense on all aspects concerning social sciences. The council consisted of military and civilian scientists and representatives of the army leadership. The head of the GZP was its chairman. [7] This was a visible sign that social sciences in the army were the domain of the party-political apparatus.

The WAP not only is the main center for training high-level political cadres but also is the home of most social sciences practiced in the army. General sociology and sociology of the army were subjects studied at all military academies and higher officer schools but a full sociological specialization was obtained through studies for master's and doctoral degrees in sociology at the Sociology Department of the chair of philosophy and sociology of the WAP or at comparable civilian establishments. By 1974 many WAP students obtained these high-level qualifications and that rate of specialization continued. There was also a two-year postgraduate course in general sociology and sociology of the army at WAP.

The majority of army personnel with high qualifications in sociology were political officers employed at various levels of the party-political apparatus or in command HQs. Some were given teaching or scientific research posts. It was planned to establish teams of qualified sociologists at military district or arm of service level where they would be working in the Political Directorates of that level.

Alongside the training effort of the Department of Sociology there was at WAP a large scientific research capacity centered in the Institute of Social Studies (IBS). IBS was formed in 1971 through the merger of the Center for Social Studies of the WAP, the Center for Sociological Studies of the Chief Political Directorate, and the Law Institute of the WAP. Its role is the conduct of interdisciplinary studies on the organization and functioning of the army from the human angle. [8]

IBS belongs to the WAP but is functionally subordinated to the Chief Political Directorate of the army. This and a flexible internal structure, according to its former commandant, Colonel Eugeniusz

Olczyk, makes it possible to maintain a close tie between the activities of IBS and the current needs of the army. One example of this is that IBS would carry out opinion polls among soldiers to establish their views on topical subjects. [9]

The organization and direction of scientific research at the WAP was further improved when a Scientific Department was formed to administer all types of research and when planning and direction of work were computerized.

The 1976-80 plan of research studies at the WAP identified four large areas of research: pedagogical, historical, economic sciences, and studies on behalf of the IBS. For all these areas together, 29 main lines or directions of research were established. These are further subdivided into 120 subdirections, 233 topics, and 552 subtopics forming a kind of subject pyramid. The content of the main directions is illustrated by examples in the pedagogical sciences area: "the army in the sociopolitical system of a socialist country," "direction and management of party-political work in the army," "improvement of the teaching and education processes in army units and military schools," and so on. [10]

Long- and short-term reports and analyses prepared by military sociologists find many users in the army. The findings of the Institute of Social Studies of the WAP were from the beginning used by the Chief Political Directorate and the Ministry of Defense for policy and other decisionmaking. [11] Although the ministry attached greater importance to comprehensive reports, operational needs often dictated the use of polls to get quick answers to specific problems. The growing demand for sociological information shows that military sociologists play an increasing role in the decisionmaking concerning the army as a whole. What is more, they help those who made the decisions to supervise implementation and monitor the effect. [12]

The scientific output of the WAP appeared in many publications in Poland and abroad. According to Professor Michalik, by 1976—that is, during 25 years of its existence—scientific workers of the WAP have published more than 300 books and about 5,000 articles and teaching texts. In the years 1971-75 they published 53 monographs, 329 scientific articles, 79 reports, and 429 other items. [13] Two publications, the Scientific Notes of the Institute of Social Studies and the Social Studies Bulletin of the Council for Social Studies of the Ministry of Defense, are the main channels through which sociological information is reaching the professional cadre of the army. [14]

Pursuit of Qualifications in
Social Sciences by Army Personnel

According to General Polanski, in 1973 there were about 1,000 officers with a scientific degree of doctor and one-third of them were doctors of social sciences. Not all of the latter were working in training and research establishments of the army.[15] The politicization of the army in the 1970s probably doubled or even tripled their number. One can assume that most if not all those specialists in social sciences are political officers, that is, members of the Political Officer Corps. They represent an intellectual elite among political officers and by extension an elite of the political army.

On another occasion General Polanski stated that during 30 years of existence the WAP produced 33 doctors habilitatus, 347 doctors, and 3,500 masters of social sciences. He added that in 1981 the teaching and scientific research staff of the WAP consisted of 11 professors, 22 assistant professors (readers), and 74 doctors. All had obtained their qualifications at the WAP. The WAP also regularly employs a dozen or so civilian professors and assistant professors.[16] A non-military source (1981) gives the names of 37 professors and assistant professors who are employed at the WAP, obviously including civilian personnel, and states that in addition there are 72 doctors of social sciences.[17]

Many more highly qualified specialists in social sciences are employed at other military academies and higher officer schools. At each of them, especially at the WSO with a political stream, social sciences represent a major part of the curriculum. This would be reflected in the number of social science specialists in relation to the total number of permanent staff. In this connection it might be useful to quote the total number of professors, assistant professors, and doctors at these military training establishments:[18]

	Professors, Assistants	Doctors
General Staff Academy (ASG)	40	81
Military Technical Academy (WAT)	74	282
Military Medical Academy (WAM)	54	160
Higher Naval School (WSMW)	26	83
11 higher officer schools	11	104
Total	205	710

It is estimated that about one-third of the above total of 915 professors, assistant professors, and doctors are specialists in social sciences. They and the staff of the WAP together represent a substantial intellectual capacity that is at the disposal of the political army.

It has been stated that unlike in the West, Polish military sociology from the very beginning based itself on military establishments
and on work by military personnel.[19] The reason, no doubt, was self-
protection against undesirable influences. However, once it established
its Marxist-Leninist basis and its position in the army it began to infiltrate the civilian social sciences. The WAP began to organize conferences and meetings that were also attended by civilian specialists.
In 1975 alone, WAP scientific workers took an active part in 60 conferences and symposia in and outside Poland. They organized joint
conferences with the Higher School of Social Sciences (WSNS) of the
Central Committee of the Party, with the Academy of Internal Affairs
(ASW), and various institutes of the Polish Academy of Sciences (PAN).

There were many ways in which WAP workers participated in
the development of social sciences in the country:

- contribution to the military and civilian press of popular-
  scientific articles of economic, political, ideological, and
  historical content (about 550 articles a year),
- lecturing on courses, especially within the framework of party
  instruction in and outside the army; among lecturers working
  for the Central Committee of the party were 19 WAP workers,
- working in many learned societies, on editors' boards of scientific periodicals, and in the Central Qualifying Commission
  for Scientists,
- propagation of WAP teaching methods and of planning and organizing scientific research.[20]

According to Wojsko Ludowe, by 1974 most military sociologists
were members of the civilian Polish Sociological Society and took
active part in its work. They also cooperated with the Institute of
Philosophy and Sociology of the Academy of Sciences, the Sociology
Institute of Warsaw University, the Institute of Science Policy and
Higher Schools, and the Center of Public Opinion and Program Studies
of Polish Radio and Television.

Polish military sociologists enjoy a high reputation among the
armies of the Warsaw Pact countries. They hosted many meetings and
visited their opposite numbers in the Soviet bloc countries.[21] It was
said about WAP that it maintained close and regular contacts with 62
scientific research centers in Poland as well as with military academies
of the Warsaw Pact countries and in particular with the "Lenin" Military Political Academy in Moscow.

Role of the Army's Social Sciences in the Post-1980 Crisis

Social sciences in the army were developed as an instrument of the political army. This is confirmed by an article in <u>Wojsko Ludowe</u> published shortly before the introduction of martial law. It said that social sciences, including those practiced in the army, have an important role to play in the process of renewal of the social and political life of the country and in overcoming the economic and political crisis. A great deal of research was needed in all those areas that concern the internal role of the army. The army faced the responsible and very difficult task of improving the content of ideological education, especially in respect to the patriotic and internationalistic attitudes of conscripts and of the young professional cadre as well. This was difficult because there had been mistakes, distortions, and even abuse of power by people who by reason of their high positions should have served as models of patriotism and citizenship. In this situation it was necessary to expose the sources of anomalies that were alien to Socialism and to restore the belief that all that was harmful to the nation could be overcome.

To counter the intensified activities of anti-Socialist centers, military representatives of social sciences wrote and published scientific articles in which they expounded the program of economic reform, attacked anti-Socialist views, and exposed anti-Socialist opposition groups in the country. Providing sound arguments in favor of Socialism and the defense of the country, showing the dialectic unity between the practice of administration and management and socialist theory were all among the most important tasks of the military social sciences.

Those who wrote carried responsibility as party members and as citizens for the content of their scientific and published popular-scientific material. Furthermore, they had the duty to combat anti-Marxist and anti-Socialist views in the works of other people in and outside Poland. The intensified propagation of an idealistic world outlook called for more studies on the forming of a scientific world outlook, on secularization processes in Polish society, and on changes in Catholic thought in Poland and abroad. Special attention and rebuff were to be directed to manifestations of attitudes and tendencies, be they nihilist, pacifist, or cosmopolitan, which negated the need for defense efforts.

In the context of socialist renewal the Council for Social Sciences of the Ministry of Defense proposed a number of themes that deserved some priority. One of these was that following an analysis of the post-1980 crisis it became necessary to define the role of social sciences in forming socialist convictions in society and in restoring the high rank of socialist ideological values. A second subject was the army's participation in the patriotic and defense education of Polish youth. This would involve a survey of the army's past work in this field and propositions for work in changed conditions. Finally, in view of the intensified imperialist subversion, directed against Poland in particular, there was need for a scientific analysis of the basic theory of bourgeois political and ideological conceptions concerning coexistence and international conflicts, together with an analysis of relations between the main capitalist countries and the Socialist countries.[22]

At the 4th Ideological Conference of the Armed Forces (November 1982) General Baryla, head of the GZP, spoke about the need for scientific backup on the ideological front in shaping the people's "awareness." Here was a role for Marxist philosophy, political economy, scientific Communism, and other political sciences as well as history, sociology, and pedagogy. The WAP was already doing that effectively and so was the Army Historical Institute in its field. But it appears that the capacities of other military scientific centers and of chairs of social sciences in military academies and officer schools were not yet fully utilized.[23]

In a speech at a session of the Council for Social Sciences of the Ministry of Defense made in November 1981 a prominent civilian sociologist said that the central aim should be to boost the national role of army scientific centers so that they reach out far beyond the army, radiating on to the civilian scientific field their intellectual, moral, and political potential. In practical terms this meant creating suitable forms of cooperation between army centers of social sciences and the scientific research centers of the party. The latter had suffered considerable losses, and had suffered more than other civilian social sciences. They needed help in a major reconstruction and transformation, especially because on the (civilian) academic front an offensive was developing that limited the initiatives of Marxists.

The above comment is significant. Professor J. J. Wiatr is director of the Institute of Basic Problems of Marxism-Leninism of the Central Committee of the party and author of a number of books that are considered classics of post-war Polish sociology. His statement must be seen as a surrender of sociologists of the civilian Party to their opposite numbers in the political army. The Party has in this way acknowledged that in one of its most vital areas of activity the "leading role" has passed from the civilian to the military party. It is not surprising that Wojsko Ludowe published this speech while in the past he was totally ignored.[24]

PUBLISHING AND PUBLICITY FACILITIES

The Army's Publishing Empire

Even in the early stage of its political development program the army had at its disposal a huge publishing machine in the shape of the Ministry of Defense Publishing House, some daily papers, and scores of journals and magazines. All of these are directly subordinated to the Chief Political Directorate of the army and have become a powerful instrument of influencing public opinion.

In the beginning (1952) the Ministry of Defense Publishing House published mainly books, training and propaganda material for the Chief Political Directorate, and regulations, instructions, and visual aids for the General Staff if and when required. After some changes in the 1960s a more permanent structure was established with three main divisions (military-political, military-technical, literary and documentary works) and ten editorial offices.

The editorial office of sociological and political publications produced, in addition to training and propaganda material for the GZP, military-political books for the open market. The majority were on the German problem and on the "true face of imperialism." Some of the books were published in conjunction with the Polish Institute of International Affairs. The scope of that editorial office widened when it began the series of "Ideology-Politics-Defense" (IPO) brochures in 1969.

In the first 25 years of existence the Ministry of Defense Publishing House has produced 5,000 titles with a total issue of 120 million books destined for the open book market. [25]

The army daily newspaper Zolnierz Wolnosci (Soldier of Freedom) is the mouthpiece of the political army. It has demonstrated this by incessant attacks on Solidarity throughout 1981 and after. It claims to be the direct descendant of the daily paper published first for the new Polish Army in the USSR on June 12, 1943. In addition to material on current developments in Poland and abroad it devotes its space to general problems of defense and the Army, to military thought, technology, army life and tradition. In 1980 circulation was 120,000. [26] For a short period at the beginning of martial law it jumped to 500,000. When in 1975 the head of the GZP established an editorial council for the paper the list included four generals and ten colonels, all serving officers at the time. [27] One of them was General Uzycki, who later became a member of the Military Council of National Salvation and is now the chief of general staff of the Polish Army.

Next in importance comes the weekly illustrated magazine Zolnierz Polski (Soldier of Poland), published jointly by the Chief Political Directorate and the country's Defense League. Its scope is similar to that of the daily <u>Zolnierz Wolnosci</u>. Its circulation in 1980 was 155,000 copies.[28]

There are also daily papers issued for each of the military districts: Warsaw, <u>Glos Zolnierza</u> (Soldier's Voice); Silesia, <u>Zolnierz Ludu</u> (Soldier of the People); Pomerania, <u>Solnierz Polski Ludowej</u> (Soldier of People's Poland). The monthly magazines of the arms of service known as <u>Przeglad Morski</u> (Maritime Survey), <u>Przeglad Wojsk Lotniczych i Przeciwlotniczych</u> (Air Force and Air Defense Survey), and <u>Przeglad Wojsk Ladowych</u> (Ground Forces Survey) have a limited political content.

All political aspects of the Polish Army are covered fully in <u>Wojsko Ludowe</u>, (People's Army), a monthly published by the GZP since 1950 for regular officers and, since 1972 in a more elegant form, for the whole regular cadre. In practice it still deals only with matters concerning officers, because, as was said earlier, regular NCOs have a limited political role.

The following subjects are covered regularly: party-political work in the army, social and political problems in the country and abroad, progressive traditions of the Polish Army and its predecessors, army sociology, psychology and pedagogy, social and cultural life of the army, and life in brotherly socialist armies. With its 112 pages <u>Wojsko Ludowe</u> is large compared with other military magazines. There are no pictures, only photographs of prominent political officers. For more than a decade there has been hardly any change in the contents and treatment of subjects except during the winter of 1980/81 when many of the army's sacred institutions came under fire in the magazine itself. It somehow came to life then and became almost readable. The editor in chief (since 1977), Colonel Zdzislaw Czerwinski, is the only one of nine members of the inner editing board, the so-called <u>kolegium</u>, who has been there since 1973. Many of the regular contributors are of lieutenant-colonel or colonel rank coupled with a doctor's or master's degree. Quite a number of civilian scientists also make contributions. There is a time lag of 3-4 months between event and its treatment in <u>Wojsko Ludowe</u>.

Military Component of the Civilian Mass Media

In order to reach the civilian population more effectively the army established inside the civilian Polish press, radio, and TV its own editing offices staffed with journalists working for the army if not also serving with the army. In the beginning the aim was merely to create a favorable image of the army in the minds of the Polish people. Later came the determined portraying of the army as a major factor in Polish life; later still, during the post-1980 crisis, as a savior of the nation.

Penetration of the civilian mass media at the central level is shown in the following events:

- In 1972 Zolnierz Wolnosci published a list of 35 authors of best contributions to military publications and to radio and TV programs. They received awards of the head of the GZP and heads of other departments in the Ministry of Defense.
- In 1973 General Sawczuk, head of the GZP, handed out annual awards (named after Z. Jarosz) to journalists who publicized army and defense matters.
- In 1973, in connection with the 30th anniversary of the Polish People's Army, scores of journalists were awarded the "Meritorious Service for Defense of the Country" medal for publicizing army defense matters in the central press, radio, and TV.
- In 1974 at the GZP a meeting of chief editors of the mass media and of military journalists working with them was held to discuss the results of 1974 and the tasks that faced the military editing offices of the press, radio, and TV in 1975. General Baryla, deputy-head of the GZP, described the main directions of ideological and political work.
- In 1976 the Press and Information Department of the GZP organized a meeting of journalists with the staff of the Ministry of Defense responsible for recruiting candidates for officer schools. [29]

Involving the mass media in propaganda for the political army also takes place at military district and even division level. The 12th Mechanized Division based in Szczecin cooperates with representatives of Szczecin papers, radio, and TV who are telling their audience "what happens behind the gates of the barracks." Thanks to the initiative of the military, 15 or more publicists operate as a group in the Szczecin Branch of the National Union of Polish Journalists, where they have formed a Club of Military Publicists and Reporters. The leader of the group was given an award by the minister of defense for his defense publicity work. He was full of praise for the divisional command, who provided all the necessary facilities, like press conferences, visits to units and training camps, trips to battlefields, meetings with war veterans, and so on. [30]

Civilian and military publicists who are members of the National Union of Polish Journalists are grouped in specialization clubs (sport, aviation, press photography, transport and communications, and so on). One of them is the Club for Army and Defense Publicity. Among the 150 members of the club there are some well-known army journalists, some from Wojsko Ludowe. The club's activities ensure that army and defense matters are taken up by the press more often. Ventures organized jointly with the army consist of seminars, conferences, and work trips. Good examples of these were: a demonstration of battle efficiency by an air defense unit and a meeting with the air defense command; a meeting at the Swinoujscie base about the cooperation of the Soviet, Polish, and East German navies; several symposia at the Journalist Center of Warsaw University devoted to publicity about defense matters.

Since 1969 members of similar clubs in the countries of the Warsaw Pact have met every year in a different country to discuss common problems. The Union of Polish Journalists hosted the 1975 venue at which the main subject discussed was precisely "The role of press, radio, and TV in the patriotic and defense education of society." The club discussed with the main board of the Union of Polish Journalists ways and means of improving its army and defense publicity work. It was decided to widen cooperation with other clubs of the Union and to extend the work to coverage of defense matters to civilian paramilitary organizations. One of the plenary meetings of the directing board of the Union was preoccupied entirely with publicity for the army and defense. At the 1978 congress of delegates from the 7,000-strong Union three prominent army journalists were elected to its directing board. [31] All this shows that the political military had established a bridgehead in the mass media field long before martial law.

Polish Television (TVP) shows regular programs devoted to army and defense matters. The programs, which are the responsibility of the Military Editing Office of TVP, are shown on fixed days of the week in a month. In 1979 there were four programs of 25 minutes each and one of 30 minutes per month on Channel 1, and three programs of 30 minutes each and one of 30–50 minutes per month on Channel 2. In addition there was one program a month for schools and nonscheduled programs on TVP.

DEVELOPMENT OF THE ARMY'S CULTURAL FACILITIES

The Polish Army has from the beginning paid great attention to the development of its own cultural facilities. Culture in this case means activities that make literature and arts generally accessible and popular and that at the same time provide entertainment and relaxation. It is necessary to make this proviso because in the second half of the 1970s the term "culture" has been given a wider and totally political meaning.

Traditional culture in the army is made by full-time professional army personnel and amateurs operating through a well-developed network of cultural and education facilities (KO), which consist in the main

of army clubs and leisure centers. These activities are described by
General A. Zyto, head of the Culture and Education Directorate of the
GZP.[32]

For light and music-hall type entertainment there are the central ensemble of the army and six regional ensembles with military
districts and arms of service. They produce over 2,000 shows per
year, of which about 35-40 percent are for the civilian population.
According to another source the central ensemble alone gives 150
performances a year for about 200,000 people, of whom half are
civilians.[33] The six regional ensembles and one of the Frontier
Troops together produce over 1,200 shows for the troops, with a total
audience of 1.5 million, and 600 shows for the civilian population,
with a total audience of 0.5 million. The army light entertainment
represents a substantial part of that type of entertainment in the
country. About 1,250 amateur groups with about 12,000 members are
also active in this field. They get a boost in the form of centrally
organized annual festivals.

In the theater and film area the army has no professional capacity of its own. In the theater field the efforts of the GZP are directed
to providing access to plays through cooperation with the civilian Society of Theater Culture and with the Ministry of Culture and Arts.
The latter ensures that army units benefit from all repertory theater
tours, but theater-going in the army remains unsatisfactory.

By contrast, viewing of films of all kinds is extremely popular
and is considered to be a great help in training, ideological education,
and the cultural development of troops. The main problem for the GZP
is the elimination of harmful and the selection of the right kind of films
for the troops. This is done in cooperation with the civilian Chief
Directorate of Cinematography and the Central Film Distribution
Agency.[34]

The army did have its own film production organization until
1965, when it was handed over to the Ministry of Culture and Arts.
According to an interview published in 1979 it still works mainly for
the army and most of its top personnel are serving officers. Each
year it produces some 120 short, medium, and longer films, of which
two-thirds were made for the army and one-third was commissioned
by the Ministry of Education and Polish TV. Historical, political, and
documentary films have an anti-German and anti-American bias. Current military matters are the subject of the military journal Radar
of which 267 issues had been filmed by 1979.[35]

In the army attention was directed to amateur film productions.
According to a report in Zolnierz Polski, a rapid growth in the number of amateur film-making clubs followed the first all-army showing
of amateur films in 1977. They now take place every second year.
This was in sharp contrast with the situation some years earlier when

"somebody thinking too far ahead supplied the whole army with cine-cameras that were never used." The same lavishness with funds of the political apparatus is hinted at in the report when it says that clubs offered better chances because "a club cannot be ignored and has easier access to the breasts which so generously feed many other Muses that are dressed in uniform."[36] It is perhaps also relevant that the Training Center for Political Officers at Lodz organized a 30-day course for amateur cinecamera operators. Seminars in the art of filming were held at the house of the Polish Army Methods Center. That organization is apparently providing the know-how to all kinds of amateur groups in the Army.

The army has a large number of military orchestras: the Central Representation Orchestra, six regional, and several all-garrison orchestras. Each year they take part in thousands of ceremonial events and concerts. The Central Orchestra alone gives annually about 150 concerts for about 280,000 people, of which on the average 60 percent are civilians. Several scores of other orchestras give over 3,000 concerts a year in addition to their ceremonial jobs.[37]

PENETRATION OF POLISH ART AND CULTURE

Where the army was unable to develop an adequate cultural potential of its own it brought into its orbit suitable civilian capacities. This process started in the early 1970s. In 1972 the GZP signed a cooperation agreement with the Union of Polish Painters and Sculptors (ZPAP). Subsequent exhibitions in connection with the 30th Anniversary of Victory over Fascism and the 30th and 35th Anniversaries of the Polish People's Army benefited greatly from that agreement. General Sawczuk said that every year the army spends huge sums on the purchase of the best works.[38]

General Zyto wrote about agreements between the GZP and the Union of Polish Writers, the Union of Polish Composers, the Union of Authors and Composers of Light Music, and the Ministry of Culture and Arts. These agreements were followed by intensive promotion activities among authors and artists, by competitions, exhibitions, and excursions to army units and training camps. Medals, awards, distinctions, and promotions to the next rank in the army reserve were given to authors and artists who had rendered meritorious service to the army. Most progress was made with painters and sculptors. Several hundreds of them produced work on defense themes and participated in competitions and exhibitions.

Many authors and artists were awarded scholarships from the Ministry of Culture and Arts enabling them to take up army subjects. In return many valuable works of art, literature, and music were produced. It was necessary to form close links between army commands of military districts and divisions, military schools, and other army institutions and the civilian cultural centers, institutions, associations, and unions in order to continue this cooperation.

The army would hire cultural workers of all categories to help to improve work in army clubs, ensembles, orchestras, and museums. Within the framework of the agreements, five-year plans of cooperation were to be worked out to give to these arrangements a more permanent character. Contacts with higher art schools would encourage students to make army themes the subject of diploma works and later maintain links with army cultural establishments. [39] The 1973 agreement between the GZP and the Ministry of Culture and Arts defines the duties of both sides in the fields of theater, films, music, light entertainment, plastic arts, and protection of cultural wealth. It provides for participation of both sides in the committees, councils, programs, and planning groups to ensure that army and defense themes get wide response in the civilian art environment. [40] To this end the Ministry of Culture and Arts called a meeting of higher art school presidents to discuss the matter of army themes in artistic studies. This gave General Zyto another opportunity to talk about cooperation between the army and civilian cultural centers. [41]

Items taken from a chronicle of events show that General Jaruzelski played his part in promoting culture:

- On November 21, 1975, in accordance with tradition, General Jaruzelski presented the annual awards of the Ministry of Defense for outstanding achievements in the field of defense to representatives of science, technology, literature, arts, and journalism. [42]
- On June 23, 1975, in connection with Navy Day, representatives of Polish science and culture were invited to meet top men in the Ministry of Defense. General Jaruzelski thanked them for their contribution to the ideological and patriotic education of Polish Youth. [43]

Patron of the Arts

The political army has been busy creating a myth that the army was a true "patron of the arts." In May 1978 the GZP, together with the Union of Polish Writers and Warsaw University, organized a scientific conference under the heading "Army-Literature-Arts." Like previous conferences of this type, this one was concerned with regular contacts between the army and the creators of culture, which amounted to patronage of the army over the arts. [44]

At the presentation of a commemoration medal from the Union of Polish Painters and Sculptors to GZP the chairman of the Union said that after the Ministry of Culture and Arts the army was the greatest patron of painters and sculptors. [45]

The Awards Commission of the "patron of the arts" medal at Cracow made a unanimous decision to award the medal to the Chief Political Directorate of the army. [46]

Professor S. Poznanski, a painter, whose work had been shown at army-sponsored exhibitions for over 30 years, said that the regular patronage of the army led to the formation of a group of painters on army subjects. He himself does it, he said, because of Polish conditions and the role the army plays in the life of society. He had been given the award of the minister of defense for 1979. [47]

Jan Bohdan Chmielewski, a sculptor of monuments that adorn many places, said in an interview:

> The patronage of the army over Polish art is a tremendous thing and has no equal in the world. The fact that the GZP has over many years been faithful to the principle of noninterference in the search for new forms of artistic expression created for many most favorable conditions of work. All they ask for is a clear expression of the idea. [48]

A declaration by W. Zukrowski, a novelist with strong army connections, may serve as a summing up:

> The Army is today a great patron of the arts. It helps sculptors to create monuments for the fields of glory. It buys works of art, has its own picture galleries. It helps to produce films that show the triumph of Polish arms. It has its own publishing house where our writings came out in large editions. It organizes competitions to find new talent and gives them a start. This army is worthy of our writing, painting, and music because it is our army. [49]

It is well to bear in mind that while the overwhelming majority of Polish writers, journalists, artists, film-makers, actors, and so on, oppose the rule by the political military, the latter can rely on the support of those whose livelihood they control.

A New Concept of Culture

In October 1977 a "Program for the Development of Culture in the Polish Armed Forces in 1976-1990" was introduced. It must be emphasized that the program covers a much wider area than that already described in this chapter. The content of the term "culture" has been changed and redefined. A lead article in Wojsko Ludowe contains this statement:

> Culture is one of the most sensitive sectors of the class
> and ideology struggle between Socialism and Capitalism.
> . . . Culture in its wider sense is a man's deep bond with
> general humanist ideas that are present today in Socialism
> and its system of values. . . . The aim of cultural activi-
> ties in the army is to produce a 100 percent citizen-soldier
> by instilling Socialist ideas, ethical and moral values, and
> by immunizing against consumerism, which is being
> smuggled in from the West.[50]

Another source says that the authors of the program included in the collective term "culture" a number of cultures: professional, intellectual, of community and family life, physical and health culture, of environment, aesthetics and hygiene, of leisure time, and participation in artistic activities. The stated conclusion is that in the wide panorama of cultures everyone should be able to find a creative role.[51] Many of the above we would regard to be elements of civilization rather than culture. It appears that in addition to "freedom," "democracy," "legality," "détente," and other terms that had been doctored to suit the Communist system there is "Socialist culture."

The functions and aims of Socialist culture have been formulated in the Resolution of the 7th Party Congress, which says that the main aim of creative and other cultural activities is to form in the most effective way proper ideological and civic attitudes with an honest approach to work and to create national, social, and ideological bonds. The program of cultural development defines what is to be done in the field of culture in the army. The following tasks are listed: civic and ideological education, creating Socialist human relations, shaping professional culture, intellectual development, increasing the participation of troops in artistic activities, rational use of leisure time, personal culture, and a Socialist life style.[52] The program was launched with the slogan, "Higher culture means better results in service, work, and training." General Sawczuk, interviewed in this connection, gave three reasons for its introduction:

1. Building the Socialist "developed" society demands that Socialist principles of human relations, of thinking, and attitudes become uni-

versal. Satisfaction of material needs must be accompanied by great care for spiritual and moral needs.

2. The ideological confrontation between Capitalism and Socialism manifests itself increasingly in the sphere of culture. Culture has become the main front in the battle of ideologies.

3. The Army has reached a stage of development that created new needs as well as new possibilities for the development of culture (author's emphasis).

Commanders of military districts and arms of service and their political deputies were made responsible for the implementation of the program. The actual work would be done in military units and garrisons.

Asked how this program relates to the "Principles of Ethics of Regular Soldiers" and other documents that cover similar ground as the program of cultural development, Sawczuk said that whereas these other documents described the objectives, the present program was showing the way to their achievement. In this way they complement each other. General Zyto, one of Sawczuk's deputies, when making the same point listed the other documents as: "Habitudes of Regular Soldiers," "Military Ceremonial," "Principles of Cadre Management," and "Program of Discipline Improvement."

General Sawczuk again referred to staff relations in the army. He said that the set of instructions, postulates, and recommendations contained in the program would ennoble human relations in the army and would eliminate all that is alien to the new type of army, namely lying, double-dealing, insincerity, selfishness, sycophancy, disregard of human dignity, vulgarity, brutality, and so on. He also linked General Jaruzelski personally with the project when he said that the authors of the program had broad access to General Jaruzelski for his comment, advice, and help.[53] According to General Zyto all the directives and program declarations of the minister of defense define a new and wider scope for cultural work in the army. Jaruzelski once said that more than anything else culture concerned the key issue of a Socialist army, namely human relations, and that a new quality of these relations would express itself in mutual respect, friendship and consideration, comradeship and solidarity, in the care of superiors for subordinates.[54]

The political military was right to attach so much importance to the problem of culture. During martial law and since then it found that in this area the opposition is toughest. This is not surprising. It is trying to counter a thousand years of Poland's Western cultural heritage with barely 40 years of a Soviet cultural experience.

6
Acting through Civilian Party
and
Paramilitary Organizations

In addition to social sciences and culture spheres the
political military used the machinery of the civilian
Communist Party and various paramilitary organizations for gaining positions of influence in society at
large. While involvement of the military in paramilitary organizations was justified and had a long tradition,
free access to decisionmaking in the civilian party was
given only when in the late 1970s the party needed the
help of the comrades in uniform to bolster its position
in the country.

PARTY-ARMY COOPERATION AT REGION LEVEL

In January 1978 the Secretariat of the Party Central Committee
issued "Guidelines on closer ties between party authorities (on one
side) and army commanders and army political organization (on the
other)." The guidelines were in effect an invitation from the civilian
party to the political army to increase its activities on regional and
local levels. The political military were quick to seize the opportunity
and soon became the major partner. The development may be seen as
the beginning of a long process in which the political military gained
full control over the civilian party. The document containing the guidelines was not given the usual publicity and their purpose was not clear
until 1980, when in three consecutive issues of Wojsko Ludowe nine
first secretaries of regional party committees presented accounts of
what had been done in their respective regions to implement the guidelines.

In his speech at the 8th Party Congress in 1980 General Jaruzelski had this to say about party-army cooperation:

> The guidelines of the Secretariat of the Central Commit-
> tee defined the content and forms of perfecting the links
> between the army and the nation. Party authorities and
> government representatives worked actively in the same
> direction. This is our common cause. We shall cultivate
> it, extend and perfect it. The army maintains particularly
> live and extensive contacts with the people. It has become
> a tradition that workers, scientists, artists, journalists,
> teachers, combatants, and the young visit our barracks
> and training camps, airfields and naval bases, the work-
> shop of the army and its frontline. [1]

By using the term "perfecting" General Jaruzelski wants it to appear that the guidelines meant nothing new. Indeed, Chapter 5 has already described numerous links between the army and the civilian sector. Why then the special guidelines in January 1978?

One possible answer is that the civilian regional and local party bosses saw army activities as unauthorized incursions into their area of responsibility. The guidelines were to regularize the position. At the same time they probably felt that the party could very well use some of the enthusiastic help from the army at the time when the political opposition in the country was increasing. Both reasons are confirmed in statements made by some first secretaries of regional party committees. One said that the guidelines have undoubtedly put the house in order as regards cooperation between his committee and the army and that it was now possible to tackle important ideological education and organizational issues. [2] Another said the guidelines have substantially improved existing cooperation, but whereas in the past the initiative came from the army, there was now a tremendous in-crease in party activity. [3] The statement implies that where before the army was poaching, it was now given a license to hunt.

The guidelines confirm once more that the Trojan horse of the political army is called "defense requirements." One of the secretaries said that the guidelines make the work for security and defense of the country and for unity of army and the people a principal duty of party authorities and organizations of all levels. [4] Yet another secretary made it quite clear that the guidelines meant cooperation of all party authorities with the party-political cadre of military authorities in the region. [5]

Implementation of the Guidelines

The substantial inroads made by the political army into the
civilian sphere as a result of the guidelines can best be shown by
relating briefly the information given by some of the nine first
secretaries.

The first secretary of Olsztyn Region wrote in an article entitled "In the Common Interest" that the guidelines were discussed
at a conference with representatives of the Regional Defense Committee (WKO), the Regional Military Staff (WSzW), and the Regional Inspectorate of Civil Defense (WIOC), and at the local level with commanders of military units and their political deputies, with commanders of Recruiting Offices (WKU), with local inspectors of Civil Defense,
and with representatives of paramilitary organizations (ZBoWiD, LOK,
KOR) and the party youth organization (ZSMP).

Next, the Regional Party Committee together with the Regional
Military Staff worked out a detailed "harmonogram of actions directed
toward creating in society the habit of thinking of the needs of the
Socialist state, its security and defense capacity, and of actions aiming at closer ties with the army." They included lecture tours on defense and meetings with army officers. The army officers, combatants, and reserve officers took part in propaganda and information
work aimed at young conscripts. Local radio and TV broadcast information about the life and work of units of the Pomeranian Military
District through their scheduled military programs. Education and
school authorities propagated military patronage over individual
schools, naming the latter after army heroes or army institutions
and units. Cooperation of army units with their adopted schools took
the form of army "open days," meetings of officers with pupils, organizing joint celebrations, equipping "national commemoration halls,"
and so on.

The party organized a conference of the Federation of Youth
Organizations (FZSMP) in the region, which adopted a program of
work in the area of defense. The conference was hosted by an army
unit. Party regional authorities maintain regular contacts with commanders and the party-political organization of army units stationed
in the region. Once every quarter members of the Secretariat of the
Party Regional Committee attend meetings where the state of discipline in units is analyzed.

Representatives of the army serve on party committees and local
national councils, especially in places that have military garrisons.
The same applies to reserve officers, of whom 69 serve on party committees, 123 on national councils, and 88 in civilian associations.
Army personnel take part in lower-level party committee meetings
and briefings. Local party organizations helped the army to establish

contact and cooperation with the work force and party and youth organizations in factories. As a result many large factories and institutions of the region cooperate with the army. The main elements of this cooperation are exchange of information on economic, political, and defense matters, exhibitions of military equipment, and visits to factories by military personnel.

The results of the two-year cooperation between the army and society were examined in October 1979 at a joint conference of the Regional Party Committee and other party organizations in the region with the command and party-political cadres of the Pomeranian Military District. The army comrades gave very high marks for this cooperation. Cooperation in the cultural field was greatly helped by an agreement between army and civilian cultural establishments.[6]

The first secretary of the Kalisz Region, in an article entitled "Defense—Our Common Cause," wrote that his party committee made sure that party cadres of the army were involved in political, defense, economic, and environmental problems of the region and that regional party authorities would provide the army with current information on everything that affects the social and economic life of the region and its defense capacity. When areas of possible cooperation were identified it was found that more effective army help was needed in the political and defense education of the population.

The Regional Party Committee adopted a program whereby: POPs were obliged to intergrate the troops stationed in their area into the social, economic, and cultural life of the locality; party authorities were to use army officers in their system of political education and provide them with access to civilian party training facilities, and party authorities were to bring Reserve Officer Clubs (KOR) into the system of defense training in schools and elsewhere.

Some tangible results of two years' work were 300 applications a year to officer schools with a 60 percent success rate. The number of KOR clubs in factories rose to 40 and army officers are well represented in offices in the party and state administration.[7]

In his report on the implementation of the guidelines the first secretary of Radom Region said that the Regional Party Committee and the Regional Military Staff together determined the lines of cooperation between local and factory party organizations and army institutions of the region. A regional coordinating body comprising representatives of the Regional Party Committee, regional state administration authorities, youth organizations, and the Regional Military Staff was set up to make the cooperation as fruitful as possible. When defense problems were discussed in the Regional Committee it was possible to take constructive decisions, thanks to the large presence of the military. Cooperation with the Political Directorate of the Warsaw Military District was very important. There was a plan to use army lecturers for training civilian party cadres because they were experts on the international military-political situation. [8]

The first secretary of Walbrzych Region spoke in his report about lecture tours organized jointly by the civilian and army political authorities for factories and youth centers. Regular army officers and NCOs have become a source of supply of organizers, lecturers, and instructors for the civilian party. [9]

The first secretary of Pila Region wrote that at least twice a year, in May and October, army officers attended meetings that were very popular in numerous factories, institutions, and schools. It has become a practice to involve the officer cadre in solving really important problems of the region's development. Officers receive regular monthly, quarterly, and annual reports of the region's Statistical Office on the economic situation. In recognition of their services many regular soldiers were awarded the medal "For special services to the Region" in 1978-79. [10]

The report by the first secretary of the Wloclawek Region contained a statement that the close links of the Regional Party Committee and of town and village party committees with the command and political authorities of the Pomeranian Military District made for a deeper unity between the army and the people, and the working class in particular. Party cadres of the military district take part in organization and execution of major sociopolitical campaigns. [11]

In each of the accounts by the first secretaries, considerable space is devoted to the role of paramilitary organizations in the party-army cooperation outlined in the guidelines. It appears that paramilitary organizations were meant to be an important element of the phantom unity of army and people.

A Net Gain for the Political Army

The successful implementation of the guidelines was ostensibly the result of a genuine party-army partnership. The "mutual interest" aspect was conveyed in the titles of their accounts. But it was an unequal partnership from the start. When the party accepted "unity of the army with the people" as one of the objectives of the cooperation, it admitted indirectly that the party itself had abandoned the idea of being "one with the people."

The political army was the partner who made most on the deal, having obtained from the cooperation very tangible gains:

1. The party, having recognized its own weakness and the considerable political potential of the army, became ready to "share" political control of society, at any rate at regional level and below.

2. The increased and official presence of the army regular cadre in the party machine, without reciprocal facilities for the party, gave the army access to internal party affairs and with that a positional advantage in any future contest for political supremacy.

3. The direct access of army personnel to party committees in factories and other establishments, again without reciprocal facilities, broke the monopoly party and working class link and must be seen as a major concession to the army.

4. On the grounds of cooperation the Regional Party Committee found itself "reporting" to the Political Directorate of the nearest military district as well as to its proper superiors, the Political Bureau and Secretariat of the Central Committee of the party. What is more, it was reporting as one of 15 or so regions (49 regions to three military districts). This was not a proper partnership.

5. In the process of implementing the guidelines the Regional Military Staff slowly emerged as an element of the political army operating in the region. The WSzW was consulted before the Regional Party Committee took decisions on matters covered by the cooperation.

6. Most important of all, the regional party organizations began to feed Army Intelligence and Security Services with information on the political and economic situation in their areas. This particular development must have played a vital role in the army intervention in the post–1980 crisis.

All these concessions were made with the blessing of the former party leader, E. Gierek. General Jaruzelski thanked him for that in his speech at the 8th Party Congress (1980) when he said that the army greatly appreciates his care and benevolence and always remembers them heartily. [12]

The party could hardly do otherwise. In this and many other situations the political military gained ascendancy through a clever use of semantics. It was agreed that party-army cooperation was in the interest of defense. Here one must remember that according to the "Code of ethics of a regular soldier of the Polish People's Republic" the term "Poland" means "Socialist Poland" and "defense" means "defense of Socialist Poland" or, more precisely, "defense of the system." The civilian party could not object to that any more than it could deny that defense was principally an army matter.

Earlier Political Army Activities on the Baltic Coast

Before 1978, army political activities in the civilian sector were not systematic and not general. The Baltic Coast was an area where they developed early in the 1970s. This was connected with the so-called December incidents on the Coast in 1970 when 56 people were killed and the Gomulka government was brought down. Since then the area has been considered politically insecure.

The 12th Mechanized Division at Szczecin was one of the places where "extramural" schemes began quite early. They were described in Wojsko Ludowe. Cooperation of the division with the work force of local factories is highly valued. Almost daily contacts take place on several planes: party, youth organization, cultural establishments, clubs, hobby groups, and also between army commands and factory managements. Altogether 25 enterprises are involved but with the six largest enterprises contacts are particularly live. In some cases they are regulated by special agreements that define mutual obligations. Before leaving conscript service, soldiers are informed about job prospects. As a result, some 400–500 reservists find employment in local enterprises.

The next biggest area of cooperation is schools. Here, too, there are agreements with individual schools, the regional education authority, and the Union of Teachers. Within the civic education part of the school curriculum, many officers give talks once a quarter. Units of the division assumed patronage over 51 schools, including one that is named after the division. The division, the regional education authority, and youth organization jointly organize an annual competition in defense knowledge and physical fitness. Every year some 40,000 school children visit units of the division. They learn about modern equipment and gain more lasting impressions in "halls of tradition" of units. Propaganda vehicles of the division show films with a military-defense content using walls of buildings as screens.[13]

An intentional reference to the 5th Kolobrzeski Mechanized Regiment of the division helped to notice the link between the political pioneering zeal of the 12th Mechanized Division and General Jaruzelski. He served in the regiment during the war and was commander of the Division in 1957–60, that is, just before he became head of the GZP.

PARAMILITARY ORGANIZATIONS
AS A CHANNEL OF PENETRATION

The importance of paramilitary organizations is that they provide the political military with wide access to large sections of society under the guise of training for defense. Premilitary service organizations comprising millions of people are the recipients of defense training that has a substantial ideological and political content. Ex-service organizations consisting of ex-combatants, postconscript service reservists, and retired regular army personnel together with serving personnel provide defense instruction interlaced with political indoctrination.

An entry in the <u>Small Military Encyclopedia</u> says that paramilitary organizations play a very important role within the OTK framework. Their wide-ranging activities among the population increase patriotism and the sense of responsibility for the defense of the country. By popularizing the role of the army, its traditions and close links with society paramilitary organizations play an important role in political life and education. Paramilitary organizations prepare the population for internal defense (the term used is "self-defense"). This is achieved by training and taking part in the work of appropriate internal defense formations and units that the paramilitary organization helps to form. The military effort of paramilitary organizations is directed toward: premilitary training of conscripts for special service in the army (drivers, signals personnel, pilots, skin-divers, and so on); military development of army reservists; organizing and training of self-defense units; and general training of the population for defense against weapons of mass destruction.

The law on universal defense obligations (1967) gave a great boost to paramilitary organizations in that its provisions created a proper legal basis for their functioning.[14] The 1979 amendment to the above law regulates how paramilitary organizations discharge their defense duties in close cooperation with the army. These provisions made it necessary to amend the then existing charters of paramilitary organizations. In the Official Gazette of 1979 new charters were published for the Union of Fighters for Freedom and Democracy, the Defense League of the Country, the Polish Red Cross, the Polish-Soviet Friendship Society, and others. All the paramilitary organizations enjoy the special status of "public service societies," which means that they fulfill certain duties delegated by the state in return for certain facilities in the field of organization and finance. The public service status and the charter are conveyed by a decree of the Council of Ministers.

The presence of high-ranking serving officers as full-time officials in the national (central) governing bodies is a common feature to all paramilitary organizations. This gives the political military great influence over organizations whose membership runs into millions.

Paramilitary organizations are now mainly referred to as "social defense-type organizations." The term "social" means that members carry out duties on a voluntary unpaid basis. This does not apply to instructors, lecturers, and organization managers, who receive remuneration for full-time or part-time duties. The economic factor was one of the reasons why the political military could count on the allegiance of these people, which was needed particularly during the early phase of martial law.

Union of Fighters for Freedom and Democracy (ZBoWiD)

ZBoWiD was formed in 1949 through a merger of 11 veteran and combatant organizations. In 1970 it had 360,000 members organized in 4,338 local groups; in 1979, 640,000 and in 1983, 660,000. The large and growing numbers are possible only because inmates of Nazi concentration camps and prisons also qualify. In addition ZBoWiD is practically the only place where an individual can establish his statutory right to compensation for his contribution in fighting the Germans. At one time only those who fought the Germans on the Soviet side were admitted, but after 1964 membership was extended to those who fought as members of the Polish forces in the West. Those who fought the anti-Communist resistance in 1944-48 are the cream of the organization and staunch supporters of the political military. ZBoWiD has always been fully committed to Socialism and cooperated with the army in the political indoctrination of Polish youth. At the 6th Congress of the organization in May 1979 General Jaruzelski said that ZBoWiD represented for the army a great moral hinterland. ZBoWiD was the power base for a political group known as the "Partisans" led by General Moczar. They had roots in the state security apparatus but probably did not support the political army's line.

ZBoWiD has a well-developed organization network that follows the state administration structure with branches at locality, region, and central levels run by direction/management boards. At the central and regional levels there are commissions of which the verification, welfare, propaganda, and youth commissions are the busiest. There is a foreign commission for contacts with similar foreign associations and a commission for cooperation with Poles living abroad. 15

Reserve Officer Clubs (KOR LOK)

The organization was formed in 1956/57, after a major reduction in numbers of the Polish Army, to assist a large number of regular army personnel to adjust to civilian life. It assumed a wider role in the early 1960s when it became an integral part of the Defense League of the Country. This gave the clubs an opportunity to use their military skills in work with the young organized in LOK. They became the official source of supply of organizers and instructors for LOK. Another boost came when the OTK system was brought in and began to develop. Locality and factory defense units set up within the OTK system were keen to get members of the KOR to work with them because of their military knowledge. Almost 5,000 KOR members function as commanders of Civil Defense units and services and 3,000 as instructors. The number of clubs grew from 869 in 1967 to 1,400 with about 60,000 members in 1972 and to 2,220 in 1979.[16]

It appears, however, that the political military was not happy about the composition of the clubs. In 1974 in the country as a whole reserve officers proper—that is, those who came into that category through conscript service in a reserve officer school—represented the majority of reserve officers but their share in the clubs was only 20 percent. The remaining 80 percent were older, retired, regular officers.[17] It was obvious that the domination of the clubs by retired regular officers deterred the conscript service officers from joining the clubs. The two groups had very little in common.

Nevertheless, strenuous efforts were made in the second half of the 1970s to attract as many young reserve officers to the clubs as possible. It was openly admitted that

> these young people would soon have a considerable say in matters that affect the whole country because they held directing positions in the national economy, education, and culture. Defense issues should not be outside their field of vision and it would be a good thing if most of them were to join the Reserve Officer Clubs.[18]

The aim was to establish KOR in all main enterprises. Since they consisted mainly of conscript-type reserve officers, further military training was given more attention than before. A training program especially designed for clubs allotted 16 hours out of a total of 64 to political and semipolitical subjects. The army made available its own training facilities, instructors, and lecturers. Many regular officers were working with the clubs on a voluntary unpaid basis.[19]

KOR gained still more importance when the number of young reserve officers grew as a result of the 1979 amendment of the law on defense obligations, which made graduates of civilian universities undergo one year of conscript service.

There is little doubt that for the political military the new type of KOR was a means of extending its influence to large factories and establishments. The clubs also provided access that was not controlled by the local civilian party organization. KOR and another organization of exservicemen, the Union of ex-Regular Army Soldiers (ZBZZ) formed early in 1981, played a major role in the imposition of martial law and provide solid support for the military rulers (see Chapters 10 and 11).

Defense League of the Country (LOK)

Known until 1964 as League of Friends of the Soldier, this organization has 2.5 million members, mostly of school age, organized in groups operating mainly in schools. LOK runs training groups and training centers to teach the young skills useful to defense, like motoring, water sports, signal communications, shooting, model-making, seamanship, and so on. The general role is to instruct the population in local defense and protection from the effects of weapons of mass destruction and in the nonmaterial sphere to propagate the concept of universal and total defense, to educate in patriotism, and to form closer links between the civilian population and the army.[20]

As can be expected for an organization of that size, LOK has a big organizational superstructure: a central Chief Directorate, regional HQs, and local offices in towns and villages. The head of LOK is a serving army general. Regular army personnel and reserve officers are well represented at all levels of the organization and thousands work as instructors and lecturers. KOR forms an integral part of LOK. There are commissions for KOR matters at medium and higher levels of LOK. According to one source, over 6,000 reserve officers are active in the organization side of LOK, many more as instructors on the training side.[21] The standing of LOK and its links with the political military are shown in the following events:

In 1973 Generals Jaruzelski, Tuczapski, Baryla, and representatives of the central institutions met members of the Presidium of the Chief Directorate of LOK and of regional directorates for discussions.[22] All three were later members of the Military Council of National Salvation.

In 1976 the GZP organized a conference of representatives of Regional Directorates of LOK and of Regional Military Staffs to discuss forms of cooperation between LOK and the army in patriotic and defense education of the young and in preparing them for conscript or regular service in the army. Representatives of central institutions of the Ministry of Defense and of military districts and arms of service also attended the conference.[23]

The massive character of LOK is reflected in large-scale competitions. For example, in 1976 as many as 21,000 local branches, 1,100 clubs, 200 training centers, and 40 regional LOK organizations took part in choosing a local branch, training center, club, and regional organization of LOK that achieved the best results in popularizing defense sports.[24]

Polish Red Cross (PCK)

The Polish Red Cross differs greatly from Red Cross organizations in the West in its aims, organization, and functions, which are geared to defense requirements. This fact is generally not appreciated. A study of the new PCK charter (1979) shows that within its sphere of humanitarian and normal Red Cross work (care for hygiene, medical-sanitary emergency help, free blood donation, and so on) the PCK fulfills certain tasks of the state administration in the field of civilian health service, army health service, and civilian defense. This is borne out by the fact that the main sources of PCK funds are allocations from the state budget by various sectors of the state administration and national economy "in connection with tasks delegated to the organization." That is perhaps why in addition to 83 elected members of the PCK Main Management Board and its Presidium there are eight members appointed by eight key ministries.[25] PCK membership in 1979 was about 5 million, of which 2 million were the active young element of the organization.[26] PCK is therefore a mass organization in the true sense of the word. Work is done in tens of thousands of groups ("circles") in villages, towns, districts, institutions, factories, and schools under the direction of local and regional PCK offices that are subordinated to the Main Management Board in Warsaw. This organization structure follows exactly the system of OTK and is the best proof of the military character of PCK.

There is a considerable army presence in the PCK. Personnel of the Army Medical Service help with the sanitary defense training. Army doctors represent 80 percent of lecturers at first aid training courses held for PCK teams in schools and places of work. It is stressed that the training has specialist and ideological education aspects.

In the central and regional offices there are 149 regular soldiers, mainly of the Army Medical Service. The Chief Quartermaster's Service and the Inspectorate of Civil Defense of the country also play an important role in the army's cooperation with PCK. In the years 1974-78 numerous commitments that were essential to defense were accomplished, thanks to the work of PCK. In recognition of the contribution made by the army, 2,381 regular and conscript personnel were in the years 1974-78 awarded the PCK Medal of Merit. Similar awards were made to some military units and institutions.[27]

In 1976 PCK and OCK heads signed an agreement of cooperation at all levels concerning medical-sanitary defense tasks. PCK subsequently prepared a program of work that, compared with the contribution of other social organizations to Civil Defense, is the most extensive and concrete.[28]

PCK is heavily involved in promoting free blood donation and organizing clubs of free-blood donors. It can claim some credit that there were in Poland in 1981 over 1 million blood donors and 3,793 clubs. In 1980, 449,774 liters of blood were collected, of which 391,376 liters were given free. [29]

Polish Scouts Association (ZHP)

The original ZHP was a youth organization with an excellent prewar record of service to Poland and a truly heroic wartime conduct in resisting German occupation. It was denied existence in People's Poland because it was not prepared to substitute true Polish patriotism with the Socialist brand. The ZHP organization that was put in its place retained the name and all the outside characteristics but, as stated in the Small Military Encyclopedia,

> is now under the ideological leadership of the party, co-operating with schools in the Socialist education of children and the young. In the area of defense its activities are closely linked with the army. ZHP members work in sections to achieve a given military specialization (air force, signals, medical help, parachuting, fire-fighting, civil defense, and so on) and as local defense sections in schools. [30]

The specialized sections are organized in schools for pupils between the ages of 15 and 18. They go under the collective term "ZHP Service to Socialist Poland" (HSPS). In the Civil Defense area ZHP concentrates on training Civil Defense youth instructors for civil defense work in the youth environment. [31]

At the end of 1981 ZHP had 1.8 million members, which makes it the largest youth organization in Poland. [32]

ZHP receives extensive help from the army in materials and equipment for its camping program and as instructors. Regular and conscript soldiers who have a ZHP background are given facilities to develop their qualifications as youth leaders. They are given special leave to attend camp. ZHP camps are run on military lines with army drill, procedures, and even ceremony. For this the army lends personnel who lack training as youth leaders. The army treats all this as a good investment, as valuable premilitary training. [33]

The skills learned in the specialized military sections are tested in the annual "central paramilitary exercises of ZHP" (CMTO). The 1980 maneuvers described in a civil defense monthly were held for the seventh year running. The aim is to create interest in developing defense skills and physical fitness that are useful during military service and for service in civil defense units. In the spring elimination trials were held at local and regional levels. These were followed by competitions at the military district level between the best teams of the regional ZHP organizations. From these came the finalists for the central maneuvers.

In all over 800,000 young of school age took part in the exercises, the majority ZHP members. The organizer of the exercises, the ZHP main HQ, was assisted by the army, the Ministry of Education, and other institutions. At the school level help came mainly from teachers of defense subjects; at local and regional levels, mainly from employees of the Civil Defense Inspectorates.

The exercises also commemorated the 35th anniversary of victory over fascism and the 25th anniversary of the Warsaw Pact. Competitors were given the opportunity to meet veterans and army and Civil Defense personalities. [34]

ZHP has a nationwide regular commitment to protect and look after "places of struggle and martyrdom of the 1939-45 war" and to do the same in respect to other national monuments. A place of honor is reserved for ZHP at all army celebrations or army-organized venues. In this and other ways the political military exploit the good name of the original ZHP for its own purposes.

Union of Voluntary Fire-Fighting Units (ZOSP)

Following a new law on fire protection passed in 1975, locality and factory voluntary fire-fighting units (OSP) were given a new charter and an umbrella organization: the Union of Voluntary Fire-fighting Units. The latter has a structure that corresponds to the OTK system.

The main roles are fire prevention, fire fighting, protection of water reservoirs, and dealing with effects of floods and heavy snowfalls. At the 6th ZOSP Congress the organization accepted additional commitments: support of civil defense measures and public order and forging closer links with the army and the militia.

In 1979 there were over 25,000 fire-fighting units based at localities and factories or large establishments. Among them were 6,000 units with 90,000 members consisting of young people, including women's teams. The congress recommended that every unit should form a youth team and that fire-fighting teams should also be formed in schools. Stressing the army, Civil Defense, and militia links indicates the political army's interest in ZOSP. The explanation could be that in remote villages OSP are often the only form of organized life and can provide a foothold for the army and militia. They had a good anti-German resistance record during World War II. In 1983 ZOSP had nearly 800,000 members.

DEFENSE AS A SCHOOL SUBJECT

The activities of LOK, PCK, and ZHP are linked with defense training in schools (PO). "Preparation for defense" is an integral part of the curriculum. It begins in the last year of the seven-year basic (primary) school and goes on for the two or three years of secondary school. At the latter the program provides for over 200 hours of lectures and exercises (which amounts to two hours per week in the school year). The aim is to form Socialist attitudes of patriotism, internationalism, love of freedom, and sense of responsibility for the fate of the fatherland. At the same time PO prepares for military service and Civil Defense duties. It encourages choosing a military career.

The subject is taught by teachers who are members of the school staff and have specialized in the subject. They are known as "teachers PO." In a class of 30-40 pupils they need help, especially during practical work, and this comes from auxiliary instructors. In the course of the first year, two to three promising pupils are selected to attend a four-week summer camp, where they are trained for the role of "instructor-helpers to the teacher PO." The summer camps are organized by the regional education authority but are run on military lines (organization in sections, platoons, and companies, uniforms, fixed timetables) with a military training program.

Army units help with organizing and running the camps by providing staff, transport, and camp equipment. Ideological and patriotic education takes the form of excursions to "places of struggle and martyrdom," of visits by veterans, political and military VIPs, and so on. Candidates to officer schools as a rule come from those who have been at the camps.[35]

General Zygmunt Huszcza, deputy-minister of education since 1972, said in an interview that PO was not new because premilitary training existed in prewar Poland but only People's Poland found the energy and the resources to implement it fully. In his view instruction in civil defense and preparation for military service were important, but more important was the establishment of patriotic attitudes and the emotional and rational binding of the young to Socialism and preparing them to work for the country. Preparing the young for the defense of Socialist Poland was for the schools as important a task as preparing them for a profession. General Huszcza stated that since 1946 over 3.5 million pupils in primary schools and over 4 million in secondary schools have had the benefit of defense training. It was therefore the most universal means of defense training and not an expensive one. He said that in the last few years, every year 16-17,000 pupils have attended instructor-helper training camps.[36]

With the imposition of martial law in December 1981 General Huszcza became military commissar for that ministry. One of his first declarations made in that capacity was that he was considering introducing a post of "school deputy director responsible for patriotic and defense education," which would be available to teachers of PO defense classes and selected regular or reserve officers.[37]

Colonel Tadeusz Bieniasz, head of the Defense Education Department in the Ministry of Education since 1972, described in Wojsko Ludowe a project of far-reaching reform of defense classes in schools. The reform was connected with the planned transition from seven-year primary and three-year secondary system schools to a "comprehensive" ten-year school that was to take place in 1985. Although the defense classes program could not be introduced before that date it was almost ready by 1978. Bieniasz said that the Defense Education Department attached great importance to improving the quality of teachers for defense classes. Until 1972 they had no special training and had been recruited casually from among former army officers and reserve officers. They did not have university-level education, normally required for teaching at a secondary school. In 1973 it was decided to train new teachers and give further training to existing teachers at the Cracow and Bydogoszcz Teacher Training Colleges, where special defense facilities had been established for this purpose. In 1978 the four-year master degree courses were attended by 400 full-time and 450 extramural students.[38]

It appears that the post-1980 crisis prevented the introduction of the reform, but the political military is most likely still considering it because under its terms all young people aged 15–18 would be exposed to indoctrination, whereas before it affected only pupils of the old-type secondary schools.

Colonel Bieniasz stated in an interview that he had been seconded to the Ministry of Education by General Jaruzelski himself.[39] It appears that General Huszcza and Colonel Bieniasz had been planted in the Ministry of Education as far back as 1972, that is, much earlier than was the case with other ministries.

EXTENT OF ARMY PENETRATION IN CIVILIAN SECTOR

The extent of penetration of the civilian sector by the army (see Figure 3) can to some extent be gauged from published figures. It was stated in 1981 that there were almost 33,000 military personnel working in the civilian sector, that is, outside the army. This figure is broken down further: civilian party authorities of all levels, 585; elected members of national councils (all levels), 634; culture, education, and health authorities, 159; Front of National Unity (FJN), 1,059; local and factory defense organizations, 1,100; scientific establishments, 4,000; custodianship service, 625; local self-govern-

FIGURE 3: Presence of Army Regular Personnel in the Civilian Sector (33,000 in all; prior to December 1981)

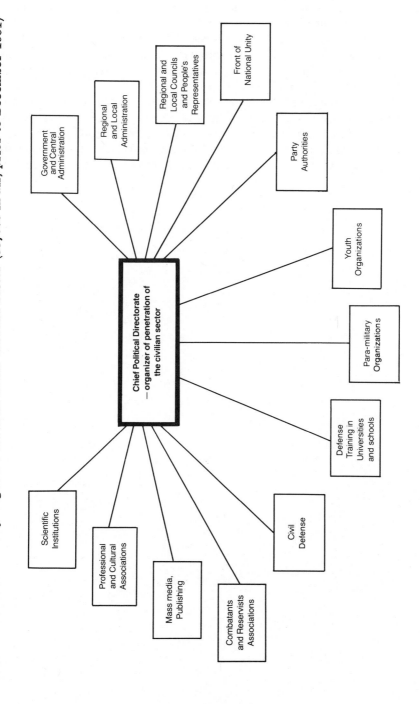

ment, 4,677; youth organizations, several thousands; other organizations, the remainder.[40]

It is not easy to reconcile the above figures with those published in 1973 and 1972. In 1973 the following figures were given: civilian party authorities, 483; state administration bodies, 814; various social and professional bodies, over 35,000.[41]

In a speech at the 6th Party Congress (December 1971) General Jaruzelski gave the following figures: regional and local party authorities, state administration, youth organizations, 5,000 (approx.); Front of National Unity, Union of Polish Teachers, Main Technical Organization, Polish-Soviet Friendship Society, 6,000 (approx.).[42]

7
Impact of Solidarity
on the Army

Taken at face value the information presented so far
radiates the political army's confidence that they
controlled a large and efficient political machine and,
through it, the whole army and large parts of the civilian sector. Thus the time when they would become
masters of the whole country was in sight. The declin-
ing influence of the civilian Communist Party made
this almost inevitable. But it appears that like the
party and the government, the political army also
suffered from illusions created by the propaganda of
pseudosuccess that permeated Poland's public life for
most of the 1970s.

The emergence, official recognition, and initial success of
Solidarity found a natural response in the army. Here it took the form
of a heated debate, if not confrontation, about party-political work
that took place within the party organization of the army. It had the
appearance of an attack by line officers on political officers as those
responsible for the politicization of the army. It was very likely a fight
between those who opposed the use of the army against Solidarity and
the political military who favored such a course of action. The extent
of the opposition to the political military manifested itself in a large
number of demands and proposals that had been formulated at party
meetings and conferences held in connection with the 6th (September
1980) and 7th (December 1980) Plenary Sessions of the Central Committee of the party. The sessions were called to decide the party line
toward Solidarity.

The great majority of the demands were concerned with the party-
political area of the army. As the opposition could not question the

111

raison d'être of the political apparatus and party-political work, it called for changes in the organizational structure, content, and forms of party-political work that would have effectively decreased the role and position of the political military. In this the opposition did not succeed.

NUMEROUS DEMANDS FOR REFORMS

From mid-September to mid-December 1980, during the early part of the Solidarity era, at party meetings and conferences held at all levels in the army, a large number of postulates and demands or proposals for change were formulated and submitted to various departments of the Ministry of Defense. If accepted by the latter they were sent to a specially constituted Coordination Commission of the ministry for study and decision on implementation. Altogether 1,685 postulates and proposals reached the Coordination Commission. The Chief Political Directorate of the army received the largest number of demands. It rejected 36 and forwarded 266 to the commission. Next came the General Staff, with 148 postulates and proposals.[1]

The 1,685 items would be a modest figure if they were the total number of demands and proposals. In fact, less than one in ten got through the weeding-out and combining stage, which took place at party conferences at military district and arm of service levels. The ratio is based on the example of the Party Committee of the Air Force where, according to the same source, out of 500 only "several tens" went up to the Ministry of Defense. If one were to apply that ratio to the army as a whole it would mean that about 17,000 postulates and proposals had been looked at at the command levels immediately below the Ministry of Defense. One could therefore say that the "creative unrest," a euphemistic term for the fault-finding process, was a widespread phenomenon. Furthermore, the demands for change had originated in the party organization of the army, which consists almost entirely of the regular army cadre. Conscript servicemen had practically no say in the matter.

Regarding the nature of demands, they concerned all areas of army life. According to the same source, the demands fell into three main categories, one of which was "longing for justice." This heading covered superior-subordinate relations, personnel matters (promotions, distinctions, money awards, and so on), preferential access to army facilities (transport, holidays, accommodation, and so on). The second category, called "against nonsense," included mindless bureaucracy, excessive amounts of political training and political activities, bad planning and organization of work. The third category concerned "necessary guarantees" on the organization and functioning of the party itself, which included "return to Leninist norms," creating barriers against aberrations, social and economic policies, accountability of party leaders, program of solving the current crisis, autonomy for lower party levels, and use of party funds.

For each of the above categories the author of the article provides some examples and either supports or argues against them. The latter is an indication that certain demands simply had no chance of success—for example, officers of the Technical Services submitted to the Party Committee of the Air Force a proposal to abolish political classes during the two periods when equipment is being prepared for work in different climatic conditions. The author argues that the officers concerned obviously thought that political classes were a waste of time that could be used more sensibly and for a worthwhile purpose. They seemed to forget that the aim of political classes was to make oneself and others aware of the values and objectives of their service and provide the necessary motivation for long periods of exhausting work. [2]

Call for Structural Changes in the Party-Political Apparatus

Some of the proposals made in 1980/81 concerned fundamental issues such as the organizational structure of the party-political apparatus in the army. According to the same source, some comrades proposed to form at the central level an elected party body that would allow a different subordination of lower-level party organizations and enhance the authority of the army party committees and of their secretaries. It was said that the existing system gave the decisive and final word to the appointed element of the party, with the result that a typically military style of work by orders and instructions were transplanted from the service sphere into party organizations. The result was centralism without democracy. [3]

On the same subject another source said that during the pre-congress campaign hundreds of proposals on organization structural matters had been addressed to the Chief Political Directorate. Many of these changes would be incorporated in the new instruction on party organizations in the army. The position of the Party Committee secretary has already been enhanced by making him a member of the respective command HQ. However a proposed splitting of the party-political apparatus into political apparatus and party organization and the creation of a Party Committee for the whole Polish Army did not get the approval of the "top." In conditions of the fierce political confrontation when the question of "to be or not to be" of Socialism in Poland was still not decided, the introduction of such major changes would be pointless. [4]

This is easy to understand. The demand for a Party Committee for the whole Polish Army would have meant the creation of a rival army central committee. This might have been an attempt to discontinue the subordination of the party organization in the army to the Central Committee of the civilian party and to its instrument, the Chief Political Directorate of the army. It might have been merely a wish to dissociate the party in the army from the discredited civilian party, although the general clamor for more democracy makes the first interpretation more probable.

The idea of a separate central committee for the army was rejected. General Jaruzelski's aim was to dominate the civilian party, not to dissociate himself from it. He proved this by becoming first secretary of the party in October 1981. As for dividing the party-political apparatus, which amounted to a separation of the party organization from the political apparatus, it was rejected on the grounds that the system was tried in the late 1950s during the so-called October thaw of Gomulka and did not work.

There was to be no more discussion on the subject because the draft of a new "instruction about the duties, competences, structure of party-political boards, of the political apparatus, party authorities, and primary party organizations" said clearly: "Party-political work and ideological education in the armed forces is controlled by the Central Committee of the party through the Chief Political Directorate of the army to whom party-political organs are subordinated."[5]

Although the above fundamental change in structure became a nonstarter, major changes were contemplated. Otherwise there would have been no need for a new instruction when the existing one was barely a year old, having been introduced in July 1980.

Excessive Central Control of Party-Political Work

Many of the complaints referred to excessive "steering" from above. The most convenient way to demonstrate what was meant by this is to give paraphrased examples of comments from political officers that have been published:

1. The exaggerated central control, which degenerated into directing and deciding on every detail, gives the impression that many regular officers, especially those who work in HQs and higher-level institutions, are paid salaries for punctual arrival at work, remaining there for a prescribed number of hours, and for waiting to receive some orders. One could not say for sure that they are paid for work in which they use independent thinking and initiative and in which they can usefully apply their capital of knowledge and experience. Hitherto

at all times and in the smallest matters one saw the imprint of higher authority. The latter defined the issues, formulated tasks, and described in detail the way of execution. In conditions of excess control people slowly turn into automatons that work according to the formula: task-superior's predilection-execution. As the social crisis grew, the tutelage disappeared because the superiors themselves were somewhat lost. What was one to do? There was no way of knowing how superiors would view any independent action. One waited for guidance and when it did not come, one pressed questions on what to do and what to say to the troops. It is in the nature of things that higher levels of authority try to impose their will whether it is necessary or not. On the other hand, submissive acceptance of detailed instruction from above suits many people, if only because it frees them from any responsibility. Intermediate levels were equally undecided and did not dare to issue their own instructions.[6]

2. Under the present system, Plenary Sessions of the Central Committee of the party are followed by meetings at military district, division, and lower levels. This is the traditional way of transmitting the contents of resolutions from the top to the masses and turning them into concrete actions. But supposing one were to reverse the direction of flow, beginning with POP meetings up to the top? Then on the basis of proposals and conclusions reached at lower levels it would be possible to evolve more realistic programs of work. Centralization should not mean simply transmitting orders from above. Yet, as somebody said, in 1980 seven out of twelve meetings of the POP were devoted to subjects that had come down from the very top. This did not give much time to discuss problems arising at lower levels.[7]

3. During several terms of office a secretary of a party organization became used to getting guidelines and recommendations from above at every opportunity. On the one hand he was urged to show initiative, on the other he was effectively hindered in doing so. One could quote scores of examples. In consequence, lower party levels had a small margin of freedom and either did not have a chance to discuss their own problems or handled them very superficially.[8]

The Commander-Party Interface Problems

The need to reconcile the "sole (one) commander" principle with the presence of a party organization in army units is a continual source of worry for the political army. This is not surprising in view of the official line:

Without the support of the party-political apparatus, of the party and party youth organizations, without their

enlightenment work that ensures conscious submission to
the orders and will of the commander, without their contribution in building up his authority, the commander alone,
though empowered with certain rights, would have great
difficulties in discharging his duties. Even if he were to
manage he would not be able to create the team atmosphere
of striving for best results and the climate of understanding,
confidence, and involvement. To be a good commander he
must base his actions on the rich experience of the collective, listen to their views, assessments, and conclusions
and be their leader.[9]

From what has been written on this subject over the years one can
say that the above formulation is not reality.

As could be expected, the issue figured prominently in the
criticism during 1980/81. Again a few published examples:

1. All the problems that arise in the commander-party relations
area can be traced back to Higher Officer Schools (WSOs), where too
little attention is paid to instruction on party-political work. What is
done is largely theory, with no attention to forms and methods of work.
There is no good textbook on party-political work. Not much is taught
about the sole commander principle and its nuances. Commanders are
not aware of the problem. Here and there one sees the inclination to
issue orders at party meetings. Of all the things young officers know
least about, ideological education work is one. They know nothing of
psychology, of the art of talking to people, and do not like it either.
Their line (nonpolitical) superiors believe that training in the field is
the only thing that matters and forget that they are responsible for
ideological education. There is nobody to tell them differently. Two
things need to be done: changing the program at the WSO and reorient-
ing quite a few of the (commander) comrades to those parts of their
duties that concern political and education matters.[10]

2. During the informal part of the report-election meeting a
member of the HQ staff said that every attempt to say where the service plane ends and the party plane begins presents serious difficulties.
They are so intertwined. Yet a distinction must be drawn because
otherwise party meetings will lose their function as a platform for
party members and turn into service briefings where everything goes
by rank, position, and terms of reference.[11]

3. All the time there is the problem of areas of responsibility.
Perhaps it is a good thing that the party is concerned with all aspects
of army life, but it means a dissipation of effort, not to mention the
incredible burden. One feels that there should be clearly defined planes
of work, one for the party organization and the other for the commander.

The Party Committee should be responsible mainly for ideological matters (shaping attitudes, changing political opinions, increasing party membership, and so on), whereas the commander should have a decisive say in training, work organization, methodology, and so on. At present, the Party Committee secretary is in practice responsible for training, orderly conduct during exercises, and for any messy or small business. Here is a source of bad feelings because it is impossible to satisfy all. [12]

4. Unfortunately there still exist commanders who go it alone: form the idea, issue orders, check execution. Others are there to carry out orders. These commanders have fallen for the temptations of absolute power. . . . Watching some commanders in action one can hardly avoid the conclusion that they are not aware that the team under their command was not handed to them for some flashy experiments, satisfaction of command, or personal ambitions, but for carrying out certain public duties. They try to subordinate the party organization to themselves because they see in it a force that could limit their appetite for power. Once that is achieved they have secured for themselves impunity, no matter what they do. In some cases commanders would query decisions taken by the Party Committee or party meeting and ask that they be reexamined. Among less blatant cases of ignoring the party organization of his unit are: neglecting tasks given by the party, sporadic attendance of meetings, and limiting their party obligations to the payment of dues. [13]

5. Some procedures have been transplanted from the service to the party plane of activity. This is wrong. The strengthening of intraparty equality and guaranteeing that all party members, irrespective of rank and position, have equal rights and duties just now call for special care. The language of commands is one for field training and the battlefield. At party meetings a language of comrades is needed. When commanders, with the help of the party, have learned not to order people about, a big step forward will have been made toward renewal in the army. [14]

6. One hopes that the practice of bringing rank and position into the party area will finally disappear. One sometimes has the impression that the higher the rank the greater the degree of infallibility. It came to the point that party members quoted from speeches of their superiors in the false belief that this was adding weight to the argument. [15]

AILING IDEOLOGICAL EDUCATION AND PROPAGANDA

In February 1981 the board of editors of <u>Wojsko Ludowe</u> held a discussion with regular correspondents on the effectiveness of ideo-

logical education in the past and on future propaganda needs. On that
occasion a prominent official of the GZP lauded the achievements of
the political army in that area. He said that the army was the only
"environment" in Poland that had regular ideological education in the
form of systematically implemented programs of patriotic and internationalist education of troops. The system had proved itself, although
effects were disproportionate to the outlay. One shortcoming was that
tasks were set and new tasks were tackled without analyzing results.
The other was that the "top" issued guidelines without consulting the
lower levels. In consequence, propaganda decisions did not always
take into account the existing climate of opinion. On the whole, however, the army avoided the mistakes the civilian party made with its
"propaganda of success" because the army had a great deal of autonomy
in party-political work.[16]

The positive, though guarded, appraisal was later attacked by
one of the army's chief propagandists, Colonel Dr. A. Gaszczolowski.
He did not accept the view that the army managed to avoid the deformations caused by the propaganda of success and that the ideological
education system in the army had proved itself. He and others like
him did not agree that it would be sufficient merely to improve the
system and to update the contents of programs. A fundamental reorganization was urgently needed, discarding all that had outlived its
usefulness and ceased to be effective.[17]

Other comments made in the discussion were:

1. One of the reasons for difficulties was that propaganda in the
army had no strategy and its tactics were nothing more than justifying
the party line, which in turn meant justifying the decisions of individual party leaders. Propaganda that functioned in this way was one of
the sources of future crises. It was a defensive propaganda and produced no results.[18]

2. What little was known about the state of knowledge and the
attitudes of troops did not reflect the true position. This and the over-
optimistic belief about the systematic rise in the level of education of
the people were probably some of the reasons for the gap between the
intellectual capacity of troops and the ever higher and more ambitious
targets in ideological education work. Special studies revealed that
many soldiers did not understand basic terms, had a limited ability
of expression, and made cardinal mistakes in writing. It was important to assess their readiness realistically and see that demands did
not exceed their capacity.[19]

3. Among the things that had a bad effect on ideological education results were first of all formalism and clinging to traditional
methods. There was the exaggerated belief that success and results
of education depended mainly on an orderly conduct of classes. Politi-

cal hours need a relaxed mood. They must be essentially different from military drill and instruction in army regulations. It is not easy to form political convictions when "standing to attention."[20]

In May 1981 a conference of propaganda activists of the army was held in Warsaw. Some more critical comments were made:

1. Colonel Dr. Z. Rozbicki said: "It is a sad situation that after 36 years once again the army has to make propaganda for the party, the people's rule, and the Socialist state." He added that the frontal attack on the system had been prepared over a period of years. Lack of action on the part of the former leadership of the party allowed the enemy to establish favorable starting positions for launching the attack.[21]

2. Hitherto the system of information and propaganda was based on hierarchy. The higher the level the fuller and more "honest" was the information that was made available and vice-versa. In this situation the official propagandist had an easy role. The fact that he obtained information from above gave him ascendancy over the troops and great authority. Now the troops and the propagandists are in the same boat, that is, both have access to information from various sources. What is more, this information is also diverse regarding reliability, truthfulness, and in other respects. This raises the question whether propagandists should inform or interpret information. Also, hitherto the approach was rather formalistic. Although propaganda was directed on to separate groups (first-year conscripts, second-year conscripts, regular personnel, and so on), the material was the same and was served in the same way. This made the work less effective because the material was differently absorbed, that is, in a positive, relatively positive, neutral, or negative way.[22]

3. Since August 1980 those who work in the ideological education area of the army have been sitting a kind of examination of maturity. Once more it has become clear that their role should be continual persuasion, continuous conversations, and permanent confrontation of views. Experience has shown that many fell down on the job. Many activists not only forgot how to talk with people but also have demonstrated through their work that they are not familiar with the theory of scientific Socialism and with the dialectic approach to the fast changes taking place in society. The present situation also brought out the difference between those who know how to lecture and those who also know how to talk with people. Only the latter have a chance to shape views and influence the personality of others. There is, of course, the problem of "access to information depending on level." The senseless division into low, medium, directing, and other levels of information access does not help communication between people.

No amount of "initiation into secrets" will replace access to honest and objective information. [23]

The weaknesses of ideological education in the army also came to light in the working of the Evening Universities of Marxism-Leninism, one of the more venerated institutions of the political army. According to a senior political officer, studies at WUML are surrounded by a mythology of their own about the "high quality" of teaching staff and students. There is an invincible fascination with their "mass" character, the result of the slogan "Every officer is an educated Marxist." The price for the latter and for the pretense to be of university-level standard were mediocrity and shallowness of the content of WUML courses. Unselective recruitment of students brought in less-than-average talent. In addition, the existence of far too many faculties and of narrowly specialized courses created teaching staff problems. The discrepancy between actual teaching capacity and the demand to teach ever-changing new subjects was the cause of frequent conflicts and simplicist solutions. The excessive range of subjects caused an acute shortage of lecture notes, textbooks, and teaching aids. Although the weaknesses and neglect have been known for a long time, they have now created an urgent need for a radical reorganization of the structure of programs, for changes in the recruitment of students and provision of qualified teachers. The author then describes a new three-stage system of party education. The new system should provide a chance to liberate the existing WUML system from such undesirable features as universalism, excessive theorizing, and pretentious scholarship.

In general, the author said, lecturers and propagandists had a great deal of catching up to do. The time of conflict-free teaching had passed. Students now have access to various sources of information and pluralist commentaries. They will accept and trust only those lecturers who are well prepared and able to answer their queries convincingly. The situation calls for a critical reappraisal, bold initiatives, and fundamental changes. These are the conditions that must be met before one can start an offensive on the ideological front. [24]

Other Relevant "Deformations"

The wave of criticism and self-criticism of 1980/81 did not spare other undesirable practices, including some sacred cows. One of them was the "Lead and Compete Movement" (see Chapter 4). One young political officer wrote that one hears and reads a great deal about the noble aspects and benefits that result from the competition movement. Yet when one looks closer at the obligations that were "voluntarily taken on" as part of one or another drive, one feels like committing oneself to getting up in the morning. There is no point in solemnly taking on obligations that are in the list of one's duties.[25]

The institution of competitions was mercilessly attacked by two other political officers. They said that treating the competitions solely as an instrument of achieving better "statistical" results in training and combat readiness deprived them of their original ideological and social motivation and gave rise to many negative features in their execution. Troops were pressured into participation and this in itself was bad. They were motivated by concrete rewards—for example, generous allocation of "reward leave" and other privileges—for winning this or that title, and not, as is maintained, by the noble desire to be first. Organizers of the competitions themselves complained about the commercialization of the movement, faults in organization, and unfair decisions. In order to gain popular support the competition movement must become morally clean.[26] A year earlier one of them wrote a four-page article describing the malpractices of competitions. He said that all that increased doubts as to the purity of intentions of those who take part and of those who have a say in the final shape of results.[27] (A new instruction on the "Lead and Compete Movement" was issued in 1982.)

Bureaucracy was another much-criticized aspect of the political army. "We have become a paper army" was the opening phrase of one comment on the subject. There was great satisfaction at lower levels when a decision of the chief of the General Staff drastically reduced the number of documents that are kept at company level. But bureaucracy was not only an excessive number of documents kept in units. People wanted fewer guidelines or telephone messages and more personal contacts.[28] Another source explained that the General Staff's decision cut out 60 documents at company level that concerned personnel and planning data and various returns. The same was done at regiment level, where in addition 40 different competitions (outside the "Lead and Compete" drive) were eliminated. They were found to be of little consequence but consumed much time and money and kept people from more important duties. The criticism directed against deep-rooted bureaucracy in the end did some good.[29]

A high-ranking political officer said that for many years in all their work they were taught to follow directives, instructions, and recommendations from above. Hundreds and thousands of telegrams, letters, and other documents contained ready schemes and instructions on what to do and how to proceed and even how many events to organize in a given area. This style of work did not help to develop independent thinking and initiative among propaganda workers.[30]

The propaganda of pseudosuccess that is blamed for many ills of pre-Solidarity Poland was, according to the criticism of 1980/81, due to the language of that propaganda known as "newspeak." Colonel L. Wojtasik, a top expert on information services, wrote that in the 1970s a kind of language for official speeches was developed known as newspeak, which reached society via the mass media. It is a poor, tendentious, and primitive language, operating with slogans, stereotype expressions, and overworked metaphors. The aim of newspeak was to hide the discrepancies between propaganda pronouncements and the true situation and to give the semblance of social unity. The reading of speeches was not only to ensure that the contents were prepared and approved in advance but also to separate the official and private views of the speaker. At the 9th Party Congress one could already see that some speakers loosened the corset of newspeak. [31]

A comment by another source was that in order to improve the effect of propaganda in the army it was necessary to bring in a new language. In the past in the army and, if it is any consolation, outside the army, there were two circuits of communication: one using newspeak, the conference jargon, and the other with a real living language that called things by their name. [32]

CONTROLLED CRITICISM OF THE POLITICAL APPARATUS

The information already given in this chapter amounts to a condemnation of the political apparatus of the army. It is curious that it should have been provided by Wojsko Ludowe, its main organ. One can think of several reasons:

- The criticism was part of the "Socialist renewal" drive in the Communist Party that was to be an answer to Solidarity and its demands; confessing past sins carries the suggestion of contrition and decent behavior in the future.
- If the debate was unavoidable it could at least be steered in a more desirable direction, away from key issues.
- A "frank and honest" debate encouraged the opposition to reveal itself as did Solidarity leaders outside the army.

In order to repair the damage done to the morale of political officers during the early Solidarity era, the same Wojsko Ludowe started after mid-1981 a lengthy discussion about the political apparatus itself under the heading "Need for a New Approach." In the course of it political officers, while admitting weaknesses, blamed the "machine," individual officers (scapegoats), but mainly the civilian party and the economic crisis.

In the September 1981 issue the board of editors invited a general discussion on three points: reasons for adverse feelings toward the political apparatus, factors that reduce or enhance the authority of political officers, and future role of the political apparatus. In introducing the subject the board stated that the spring 1981 elections to party offices and the elections of delegates to the 9th Party Congress were a sign of critical attitudes toward the political apparatus. Some political officers with distinguished party and service records were not elected (see Chapter 8).

The board stated that criticism of the political apparatus of the army was an extension of the "calling to account" actions undertaken in the civilian party. The full-time political apparatus in the army, like the civilian party leadership, was made guilty of the propaganda of pseudosuccess. It must be pointed out that the political apparatus of the army was bound by party and service discipline to carry out tasks set by the Party Central Committee.

Further, one cannot accept the view that the apparatus should be blamed for all that was wrong in the past. One must not forget its great merits in creating conditions in the army that to a considerable extent were limiting the sources of those mistakes and aberrations that were at the roots of the deep sociopolitical and economic crises in the country. Finally, the apparatus had organized a systematic ideological education, which though not free of weaknesses was generally implemented. It did not lose head during the first stage of the crisis, often taking on itself the main burden of defending the principles of Socialism. It moved with the times and switched itself into the process of renewal.

The board agreed with those who offered constructive criticism but thought that some of the criticism was unjustified and a negative attitude to the apparatus showed lack of understanding of its functions and duties.[33]

As a result of the invitation Wojsko Ludowe was able to publish in its No. 9-12 1981 issues 13 full articles on the subject that were contributions by prominent or less prominent political officers. The articles are the main sources of the information presented below. As the information cannot be easily presented under separate subject headings, it is arranged in two larger groups: one group of comments that admit the apparatus's own faults and mistakes, and another that shifts part of the blame from the apparatus on to others, mainly the civilian party. The information is paraphrased and represents only a small part of the content of all 13 articles.

Admission of Guilt

1. It was not Marxism-Leninism and Socialist ideas that diminished the authority of political officers but the fact that under pressure from above they were publicizing false slogans ("Second Poland," "Developed Socialist Society," "Moral and Political Unity of the Nation") that were backed by pseudo-Marxist quotations alone or the authority of the officer's position.

Much harm to their authority was done by pomp, airs, and graces that were bordering on the absurd. This refers to stage-managed visits (preceded by cleaning operations of several days' duration) and to conferences and meetings. At a party conference a high-ranking political officer instructed the assembled: During Gierek's speech they were to look at the officer and applaud more loudly or less, depending on what he, the officer, would be doing himself. This was a great pity because there was no doubt that in most cases these officers had an excellent party and service record and were convinced that they had done the right thing for their organization.

Much harm was done during the present troubles when political officers were using information that was incorrect and sometimes contradictory. When one has to retract what one had said the previous day one naturally loses face. The loss of esteem did not apply to the whole Political Officer Corps but to officers who were not up to the job.[34]

2. In recent years political officers distanced themselves from the rank and file in the army. When officers of the Political Directorate came visiting they saw the officers of the command HQ but could not find the time to meet the troops. In consequence they became removed from the realities of life. Many comrades thought that those who held high service and party positions spent too much time at the desk and there was not enough time for working with the people.

People are tried in adversity. For the political apparatus such a test came in August 1980 when the demand for more information simply exploded. Political officers were blamed that information about the social and political situation was both unreliable and stale. The criticism was in part justified. In the past, one is sorry to say, the apparatus did not always assess people's motives correctly. An officer was expelled from the party and cashiered for having criticized A. Karkoszka, member of the Political Bureau and first secretary of the Warsaw Regional Committee of the party. Steps had been taken against people who dared to criticize strongly or bring a matter to an open forum.[35]

3. We appreciated the help given by the Chief Political Directorate in the form of propaganda material or when in connection with anniversaries speakers came to give interesting talks. But why were

talks not given also during the most difficult period? I have a grudge against the comrades in the GZP and the Political Directorate of the military district that when things turned ugly they were not to be found. [36]

4. There is no doubt that the prestige of people who work professionally in the area of ideology, politics, education, and so on, has definitely declined. One even hears that they are disliked and that there is a crisis of confidence. I have doubts whether the accepted system of training political officers at Higher Officer Schools is conducive to the development of an independent, critical, and open mind and of a nondogmatic approach to the material they learned. My observation of graduates of the political stream of WSO confirms my belief that while WSO studies create certain specialist abilities they contribute to a decline in general culture, knowledge, and interests of the individual concerned. In those respects the WSO graduate who takes up a post in the political apparatus has only just reached the level of his subordinate soldiers.

Some years ago I asked among soldiers how they see a political officer. Most said that he is the officer who supervises the afternoon cultural-education activities, is sometimes interested to know whether a meal was good and sufficient, and has a say in the matter of leave and passes. Some said that he is an officer in whose presence one does not say too much. [37]

5. Whenever one asks about the results of party-political work in a unit the political deputy commander produces various documents as evidence of results achieved. The documents consist of all kinds of minutes of meetings, tables, work sheets, and so on. Laboriously completed columns remind one of the efforts of medieval monks. The purpose is to convince the inspecting superior officer that nothing had been neglected and that all that is expected has been and can be documented. Otherwise the lack of a register of personal party talks could be construed as neglect of the activity. [38]

6. The methods of certain officers were and are still criticized, but there is no attack on the political apparatus as a whole. They were criticized mainly for verbalism and hollow phrases, for lectures in which economic output curves went up and up when in reality things were getting worse all the time. Setbacks and difficulties were to be drowned in a flood of words. They now have to eat their words. And it did not end on lectures because people also remember the well-polished reports about the mood in units, the stage-managed meetings with precisely allotted roles when one or the other was to say something or applaud. Not all political officers condemned cases of sham and pretense and the depressing race for indexes, positions, and distinctions. [39]

7. We must bear in mind that political officers are accustomed

to certain methods of political work and will be inclined to continue to use them without realizing their inherent faults. It is a fact that existing methods of ideological education are not very good and sometimes outright wrong.[40]

Mitigating Circumstances Claimed

In addition to the large number of highly critical statements about the political apparatus there are many that while admitting the malfunctioning of the apparatus do not blame its personnel, the political officers themselves, for this state of affairs. Without going into the merits of this attitude the views expressed are worth relating.

1. If the authority of political officers in the regiment has fallen then this was mainly due to the social and economic situation in the country and the situation in the civilian party. Political officers are to some extent thought to belong to the latter and are identified with the mistakes and deformations that were at the roots of the August 1980 crisis. These were factors of an objective nature and had nothing to do with the political officers themselves.[41]

2. Political officers often with the best intentions in the world and with a tenacity worthy of a better cause were trying to convince people about the validity of the paper slogans dished out by the propaganda of pseudosuccess. For some time the situation in the country seemed to confirm the validity of these slogans, but . . . .[42]

3. Many opinions about the political apparatus are, to say the least, controversial. They are based on the belief that political officers do not overwork and often only go through the motions. Those who criticize operate with generalities. Small incidental failings that do occur in our work are made into major vices that discredit the role and importance of ideological education. On such occasions political officers are also held responsible that the process of Socialist renewal has stopped at the entry gates to the barracks.[43]

4. Because the political apparatus was implementing the policy of the party, setbacks suffered by the latter were interpreted as malfunctioning of the apparatus. Recent developments have shown up the discrepancy between propaganda and reality. The result of that was seen in the party elections. It is sad that in many cases this affected people who were truly dedicated to Socialism and practiced unity of words and deeds. They should not be saddled with the responsibility for the mistakes of the former leadership. To do otherwise is most unfair to these people. One cannot ignore the fact that although the apparatus carries the policy of the party into the army area, it has no real influence on its content. It appears that many have forgotten that.[44]

5. The political apparatus carries full responsibility for the state of discipline in units. This is the reason why in the minds of many party members the apparatus is regarded as a kind of "stocks" for those who violate army regulations. There were cases when political officers were punished because somebody in the unit used forbidden methods, whereas the commander was not in any way made responsible. What is worse, nobody stood up for the political officer concerned. [45]

6. The "universal" role of the political apparatus meant that all kinds of tasks that were far removed from ideological education were heaped on it. It landed the apparatus with excessive paperwork, continual planning, and rendering innumerable returns. This, together with long and ineffective conferences and briefings that political officers attended ex officio, did not leave much time for work with people. Furthermore, the nature of the job involves taking unpopular decisions in matters of discipline, staff relations, political and moral issues, or as members of commissions that supervise distribution and other procedures. [46]

7. The sociopolitical and economic crisis produced in a large number of party members in the army a certain complex of guilt, a kind of moral hangover. To get rid of it they want to pass the blame for their own lack of understanding of the situation at the time on to political officers. The army of a Socialist state is subordinated to the party whose ideas form the ideological makeup of the army. Political officers cannot be blamed for having defended the party program. This truth is not generally understood, nor are the basic functions of the army, the place and role of party organizations in the army, and the relationship between the political apparatus and the elected party authorities in the army. [47]

8. A political officer has a vast range of duties. It would be easier to say what does not come into his area than what does. He takes too much on himself that it is no wonder he cannot cope with his duties. One thing is taking interest—for example, in the food or sanitary conditions of troops—and another to be responsible for that sector. Inspecting officers have acquired the habit to ask right away what have the political officers, the party, and youth organizations, done about it. A political officer's performance is noted by his superiors but even more by the troops. It is not easy to gain the trust of the latter without falling foul of the "top." It is not easy to say definitely who is right and who is wrong. [48]

9. One political officer was asked by a military correspondent why they have lost their self-assurance and are avoiding the troops. He gave a disarming answer. Political officers were only human. They must be given time to recover. Anyway, there is not much to tell the troops. One does not know what line to take. Superiors maintain a

strange reserve and reticence. Most times they keep silent as if they, too, had no opinion and were waiting for instructions. Some information, at first very general and often contradictory, did get through. Lately there was more information but still mostly in the form of comment, whereas everybody wanted facts. To justify his lack of enthusiasm, he said: "In my life I have had to 'reorientate' four times already and four times I burnt my fingers. I worked hard to convince people about something that after a time turned out to be a misunderstanding."[49]

10. With disbelief and surprise I listened to denunciations made at a party meeting that was attended mainly by officers of the political apparatus. True and imaginary personal wrongs were pursued. Mistakes and deformations in training and ideological education were denounced. The attacks were directed against named people and the motivation was revenge. Victims are easy to find when one applies the rule that only those who criticize are not guilty of irregularities. Such behavior was bordering on nihilism.[50]

IS THE ARMY IMMUNE AGAINST THE SOLIDARITY VIRUS?

Protecting itself against ideological and political subversion has been very naturally a primary duty of the political army. It managed to do this effectively throughout its existence. Whether the emergence of Solidarity posed a real threat in this respect or not, the political army has decided to make the army's "steadfastness" into the first major victory over the enemies of Socialism.

At the end of January 1981 the Chief Political Directorate organized an ideological-theoretical conference for the top leadership of the army. It was to decide the line of action in the command and ideological education fields under the new conditions of Socialist renewal. The starting point for the discussion was a statement that

> thanks to the purposeful, well-organized, and effective
> ideological education the army was coming safely through
> the period of social tensions without major upheaval, calm
> and intact. Numerous structural features introduced in the
> course of the past decade in all the important sectors of
> the army saved it from deformations. For this reason
> Socialist renewal in the army will differ in character and
> scope from that in the civilian sector. There is no need
> to reject anything or to build from scratch. All that is
> necessary is to ensure that the efficient functioning of
> the existing schemes and of their optimal exploitation.[51]

The "numerous structural features introduced in the course of the past decade "of course represents all that makes the political army. General Baryla of the GZP calls them "a specific system of guarantees that protected the army from deformations and allowed it to maintain a good Marxist-Leninist condition."

Piotr Jaroszewicz, former prime minister now in disgrace, explained the background to the increased political activities of the army since the early 1970s. He wrote in 1973 that with the progress of détente and the resulting increase in trade and other contacts anti-Communist and anti-Polish centers would try to exploit the latter for the ideological and political disintegration of Polish society. Ideological subversion had to be countered with a cohesive ideological and moral front of the nation. Ideological education had to create psychological barriers that even the most insistent and sophisticated propaganda of the class enemy would not be able to cross. Party conferences in the army, especially the recent Ideological Conference of the Armed Forces, had shown that the well-developed system of ideological education coupled with a determined effort in this field were in fact building such barriers.[52]

The above is confirmed by other sources. One said that the Army's steadfastness was due to the fact that beginning with the 6th Party Congress (1971) everything possible was done to make ideology the daily bread in the life of the party organizations in the army. Thanks to that they did not suffer a shock and weathered the storm, always remaining in control of the situation.[53]

It was also stated that the army avoided the mistakes made by the civilian party, which allowed forms of ideological work like party instruction, political instruction, personal party talks, and so on, to die out and so left the entire field of shaping public opinion to the mass media. The army always attached greatest importance to ideological education and that was the reason why moral and political worthiness were high.[54]

One senior political officer stated with satisfaction that when during the workers' protest action in Gdansk he was among soldiers of the Gdansk garrison he became aware how very right was the ideological education conducted for years with obstinacy and consistency. In the new situation it bore the most essential fruits, namely calm, discipline, prudence, and everything else that represents the army's strength.[55]

Some, even well-known, political officers had reservations. According to one the statement that the army did not stray from the general line of the 6th Party Congress and that there were no deformations did not excuse everybody and everything. The truth was that to some extent all (the politicals) practiced propaganda of pseudosuccess, especially when trying to prove that what came from above always brought the expected results, and if it did not it was the fault of the lower levels who were unable to read the intentions of their superiors.[56]

8
Ideological
and
Political Mobilization
of the Military Party

There is no doubt that in winter 1980/81 and spring and summer 1981 the political reliability of the army was seriously impaired by dissension in the army and in particular by the attitude toward the political military. This was one of the reasons why the political military had to postpone its martial law intervention for almost a year. Combat readiness, the one thing on which the whole army led by the political military was supposed to have been working all the time, was simply not there. To be more precise the political machine that they have been building and perfecting over the years was still there but had broken down. A major organization and propaganda effort was needed to get it working again and this became the preoccupation of the political military in 1981. The imposition of martial law was proof that they succeeded but success was only partial, it seems. It is not clear whether it was by design or necessity that the full ideological and political mobilization was directed onto selected parts of the army. It is a fact that during martial law and since then General Jaruzelski has relied to a great extent on support that came from outside the army.

SOME INITIAL MOVES

The political military came onto the stage much earlier in the crisis than is generally accepted. The 6th Party Plenum held on September 5, 1980, replaced Edward Gierek with Stanislaw Kania as first secretary; endorsed the concessions made to Solidarity in the so-called Gdansk, Szczecin, and Jastrzebie agreements; and decided on the peaceful solution of the conflict. General Jaruzelski stated in his speech at that Plenum: "Together with the party and the Central

131

Committee the Polish Army has decided for a peaceful solution of
the conflict." He also made it clear that Stanislaw Kania was
his choice (see Chapter 3).

Addressing himself to the Polish people directly, General
Jaruzelski said that although the army had tha love and confidence
of the party and the people, there recently had been cases of misunderstanding, insinuations that the army had excessive privileges, and
even inexcusable affronts. But foul forces would not succeed in driv-
ing a wedge between the army and the people. The army regular
cadre was doing a difficult and responsible job, not for 8 hours a day
but often for 12-14, and even 24 hours, which never counted as over-
time. He said that stabilization of the situation in Poland was an
important element of stability in Europe and referred to the Soviet
Union as the guarantor of Poland's frontiers. The latter is a permanent feature in every one of his speeches. He took a conciliatory
line on Solidarity, saying that the agreements with Solidarity created
conditions whereby in pursuance of the workers' just interests the
Socialist reality may be perfected.[1]

A similar line was taken by the ideologists and sociologists
of the political army. The great authority among them, Professor
M. Michalik, wrote that the peaceful method of solving the conflict
was chosen although there had been other views and tendencies. But
it was a solution taken in line with the character of the socialist state
and its ability to solve its internal contradictions. It served the
interest of society and proved a political and moral maturity of
society and of its representatives in the State authorities, notwith-
standing the resistance, disagreements, and differences that existed
before the choice was made. He also said that one of the basic ways
of countering the opposition would be to deprive it of its arguments
by an effective, open, and visible elimination of mistakes,
deformations, and abuses.[2]

The pragmatists of the political army knew that the above
suggestion would have meant concessions to Solidarity that were
unacceptable to the system. At the 7th Party Plenum (December
1980) General Baryla produced an interim program of the political
army. The aim was to strengthen the party, rebuild its authority,
and help it to regain confidence of the people. To him this was the
basic condition for beating the crisis, continuing the socialist renewal
of the social and economic life, and for building a prosperous Socialist
Poland. Those party members who concentrated on calling to account
the guilty were unaware of the seriousness of the situation. The
time had come for battle with the enemies of the system, with irresponsible extremists. Already one noticed more intensive intelligence
activities on the part of NATO staffs, revisionist and revanchist forces,
and of the imperialist subversion center. The time between the 6th

and 7th Plenum was wasted in the army. Party-political and propaganda work was intensified. The party in the army gained new members. The links between the civilian and military party organizations were becoming closer. Cooperation with the Citizen's Militia and the Security Service would be improved. As always in the past, one could count on the cooperation of combatant, veteran, and army reservist organizations. Baryla concluded with an assurance that the army was fully dedicated to serving the party and the nation.[3]

Briefings at Military District and Arm of Service Levels

In December 1980 plenary sessions of party committees of the commands of the three military districts and three arms of service took place. This is the level immediately below the Chief Political Directorate, the General Staff of the political army, at which policy is translated into a concrete program of action. This means that by then the political military had decided on its response to the situation in the country created by the rapid expansion of Solidarity. The decisions taken at these conferences, or rather that part of them that had been published, are worth relating.

At the session of the Silesian Military District it was stated that in November 1980 in all administrative regions in the area covered by the district there had been meetings with the military cadre who worked in the civilian sector or on the borderline between the army and the civilian sector. These were mainly officers working in regional and local civilian party offices, members of councils, teaching cadre of defense courses at universities, officers working in paramilitary organizations, and so on. The aim was to arm them with arguments and prepare them for more aggressive confrontations with people holding other views. The meetings helped to gauge the political climate in various places and to prepare for action in them.

The program of work adopted at the session instructed all commands and party authorities and organizations of the district to:

- show the extent of the threat from counterrevolutionary forces and the roots, aims and methods of anti-Socialist forces; create ideological and organizational resistance to enemy propaganda, and develop close cooperation with the Army Security Service and the militia;

- highlight in all party work the Polish reason of state, especially the importance of the political economic and defense integration of the Warsaw Pact countries as well as the brotherhood-of-arms with the Soviet and other Socialist armies;

- build full confidence in the policy of the party, explain the essence of Socialist renewal of party life and of the political and economic life of the country, learn more about the reaction of troops to events in the country; and

- improve the situation in the Army in respect to military training, discipline, and human relations.[4]

One should note the role played by military personnel on detached duty outside the army since there were 33,000 of them at that time.

At the plenary session of the Party Committee of the Pomeranian Military District attention was drawn to penetration of alien ideas, of firebrand-type opinions and provocative rumors into army barracks. This happened in localities where anti-Socialist forces and political hooliganism had developed. New conscripts, including members of Schools for Reserve Officers, came still hot with passions of 1980 and with a load of slogans and opinions. It was not easy to calm down temperaments and to correct deformed views. They were not easy to counter with propaganda methods used hitherto. There was greater demand for daily fresh political information, objective comment, and for an official party assessment of developments. Political instruction hours had to be geared to current needs and interests of the troops.

One, Colonel W. Kawula, referring to the December 1970 events on the coast, said bluntly that there was no need to feel remorse on that score. The army did not tolerate anarchy; it had no choice. This fact should be brought to the knowledge of soldiers in a gentle but consistent manner. He added that the liberalism of the authorities who negotiated the agreement of Gdansk, Szczecin, and Jastrzebie had taken the army by surprise and caused dismay. He also suggested that as the civilian party authorities were now showing less haughtiness one should form closer links with them and "inspire" them to devote more attention to defense matters, in particular to living conditions of the Territorial Defense Troops and to Reserve Officer Clubs. It was worrying that some members of the latter were going over to the other side.

In addition to strengthening the party and fighting anti-Socialist forces the program of party-political work was to include observance of social justice, better human relations, improved living conditions for military personnel, and exposing irregularities in the distribution of goods. In all matters concerning personnel, the views of the party secretary should be taken into account because 20 percent of the demands for improvements concerned personnel matters. Strict measures would be taken against superiors who persecute or physically assault their subordinates. This applied also to second-year soldiers who usurped the right to order about the younger ones.

Those party members who in the current climate of accusations have been unjustly maligned should be protected. [5]

At the plenary session of the Warsaw Military District it was stated that there had been a marked improvement in the flow of information and in methods of work with the troops. Here once again direct work with individuals and informal contacts between the educators and their charges had proved very effective. In the Report of the Committee the expansion of political education work was to become a duty of every party member. Army personnel who work in the civilian sector have the same obligation in respect of their environment.

General J. Jarosz, a member of Jaruzelski's Military Council of National Salvation, made the interesting comment that the present political situation in Poland and in the world was so complex that many find it difficult to understand. If even very experienced and politically enlightened people have difficulties with a proper interpretation of events, one can easily understand the problem this presents to young soldiers. They need intellectual and ideological guidance. Unfortunately, among those who have not involved themselves in political education work with the troops are many who graduated from Evening Universities of Marxism-Leninism, experienced party members, and staff officers. The evident need to calm down emotions, to form views, and weight-up arguments demands greater use of their talents.

Many who spoke underlined the importance of true knowledge of Marxism-Leninism for the analysis of the very complex economic situation in the country and of the causes of the moral and political crisis. In the main report and in subsequent discussions much attention was given to internal party matters, to human relations, and to the climate of contacts between the troops and the working people in towns and villages. These relations had always been good and the soldier's uniform was always respected. This is still so but anti-Socialist forces were trying to sow seeds of discord. Separate addresses were given by Generals T. Tuczapski and W. Oliwa, who are members of Jaruzelski's Military Council of National Salvation. [6]

According to the main report made at the plenary session of the Party Committee of the Polish Navy Command, the strikes on the Baltic Coast changed the style of party work in the navy. Decisions had to be made without waiting for instructions from above. The big strike of August 1980 put party members in the navy to a most difficult test. The committee thought that they passed it very well; but "renewal" is treated by some in a one-sided way. It should ensure protection of statutory rights of a party member but also proper discharging of obligations.

The adopted resolution obliged all Party authorities of the command to establish closer links with the troops. A heavy price had been paid for ignoring this requirement in the past. One means to this end were the so-called days of meeting the soldiers. Their object was to give to higher-level officers the opportunity of obtaining reliable first-hand information on conditions of service and on current needs of troops. They should also serve to explain current problems, inform about future tasks, convince the troops that the advocated policies were right, and so win them to the cause. Officers who prefer "lecturing" to a discussion and who turn party meetings into service briefings did not like the innovation. [7]

ADJUSTING POLITICAL WORK TO THE NEW SITUATION

In the summer of 1981 a group of party-political workers discussed with representatives of the board of editors of Wojsko Ludowe the nature of "renewal" in the army. The following conclusions were reached:

- part of the regular army cadre did not see any need for or did not understand the problem of renewal;

- the younger, less experienced comrades, ignoring the specific function of the army would want to change almost everything;

- the obvious way forward was to continue what was good or modify or reject what had become obsolete. [8]

Propaganda Work

Propaganda work in the army was to assume new characteristics. This emerges from two articles by one of the chief army propagandists, Colonel Dr. Z. Rozbicki. In an article published early in 1981 he stated that the new political situation demanded that the content and form of propaganda assume the character of a political fight, which means being ahead and reacting immediately to steps taken by the enemy. This was now generally accepted but the ways of achieving it have not yet been properly worked out. The pressure of events force one to adopt ad hoc and partial solutions. There simply was no time to develop a propaganda strategy. Yet some elements of a new approach should now be formulated:

- A new style of propaganda, with changes in the mode of control from the Chief Political Directorate down to the political section in a regiment and with clearly stated priorities;

- widening the range of propagandists beyond those who are involved by reason of their job and position;

- separating positive propaganda for Socialist principles from criticism of wrong doings;

- exposing anti-Socialist forces in the country and their links with foreign centers;

- making political instruction hours the main element of the political struggle;

- giving to leaders of political instruction groups all possible assistance because they were in the forefront of the political battle. [9]

In an article written ten months later Colonel Rozbicki provided further detail about army propaganda but did not say that the key issues have been solved. He said that political instruction given twice a week and political information once a week presented the main opportunity to form political convictions and attitudes of the troops. They provided a chance to present in a systematic and programmed manner who is who in this confrontation and which side is right. All is done in the form of dialogue and informal discussion, which puts further demands on the abilities of group leaders.

The other form of propaganda work known as "political information" depended largely on the efficiency of the information transmission system. Information was often slow in coming because it was held up in the various tiers of the system. Distribution was as important as preparation of information. In urgent cases telex was now used more often. Banks of information kept at various levels of the political apparatus were a great asset. Every officer should know that the propaganda instructor was in possession of material that could be made available at short notice.

In the last few months there have been big changes in the structure of the propaganda sector but there was room for more stream-lining, for example, at the military district level there were a Propaganda Department, a Center for Ideological Training (OKI), and editorial boards of newspapers. All these would benefit from greater integration. The main object was to adjust the propaganda sector to the sharp political fight against anti-Communist groups that operate in the country. [10]

Mood of the Troops

In the new conditions the assessment and informing about the mood of the troops grew in importance. A leading army expert on this subject wrote that compared with other areas of society, for example, the civilian party, the army system of informing about the mood of the troops worked very well. However, in view of the situation facing the army in 1981 it was necessary to improve the reliability of information. In the past, returns and reports were subjected to "makeup" (beauty) treatment. Only the current situation was considered to be of interest and not much thought was given to the possibility of a new situation arising in a given place or time. As a rule, information went up and concerned a given part of the army structure; there was not much feedback in the form of guiding information from above. This needed to be corrected. There were factors in the existing system that produced distorted information. Among them were subjectivism of the originators of reports and sifting and summing-up processes as the information went up the rungs of the hierarchy ladder.

The information on mood reached the so-called central control of ideological education work in the army via two main channels. One was the system of reporting from the Political Directorate of military districts or arms of service and from Political Departments of divisions or equivalent. The other channel was research conducted on this subject by the Institute of Social Studies (IBS) of the Military Political Academy. Both these systems worked independently of each other. There is no doubt that with more cooperation and some organization changes, sufficiently reliable information could be produced. The results obtained by the Institute of Social Studies, or at least some of them, should be made available down to the Political Department level. The latter would then have the chance to compare the state of morale in the army as a whole with that in their own units and draw conclusions.

As regards the state of public opinion outside the army, it had been for many years the object of studies by the Polish Radio and TV Public Opinion and Programs Center. The result of this work should to a greater extent than hitherto be made available to the political apparatus of the army, at least to the Chief Political Directorate.

An important aspect of information on mood was the capacity to anticipate the arising of a certain mood in a given place at a given time. It made it possible to prevent the forming of a negative atmosphere or limit its extent and intensity. Moreover, anticipation was necessary because of the fast-changing political situation and the fact that some developments had a local character, affecting units stationed in a given area and not the army as a whole.[11]

Ineffective Propaganda Lines

The so-called Polish reason of state and Polish-Soviet friendship were two favored topics of the intensified ideological and political
work in the army. They were meant to counter the most catching
Solidarity call that for Poland to be Poland it was necessary to end
Poland's domination by the Soviet Union. It is somewhat surprising
that all the social science experts of the political army were unable
to produce any convincing arguments in favor of their proclaimed
policies that said that Poland's interests are identical with those of
the Warsaw Pact countries, that is, of the Soviet Union. Some of
the arguments used were so weak, sometimes even ridiculous, that
they must have been counterproductive. Even without that contribution
the insistence of the political military on a Polish-Soviet friendship
in the present political constellation represents its Achilles heel.

Special Meaning of the Polish "Reason of State"

The Polish reason of state (raison d'état) as a term came to be
more widely used only in the last few years, and its frequent use in
1981 was meant to be a warning to Solidarity. At first it looked as
if the official propaganda machine simply needed a highbrow term to
describe anti-Socialist activities as activities directed against the
state. There is more to it.

It is curious that a term that did not merit an entry in the
13-volume Polish Large General Encyclopedia (last volume published
in 1970) should appear in the Small Military Encyclopedia, Volume
3, 1971, as a carefully worded long definition, one that bears the
imprint of the mentality of Jaruzelski himself. It is given here in full:

Reason of state is a justified preeminent interest of the
state, mainly political but also economic, military, and
so on, which stands above all other interests of the
community or the individual; it is the highest obligation
of a certain behavior to which moral or even legal norms
are subordinated. The preeminent nature of reason of
state finds its expression in the entire foreign and internal
policy, in the system of alliances and the membership of
international systems, in what attitude the state authorities take toward social and political events in the world.
As regards internal policy, reason of state may justify
the introduction of certain limitations in the sphere of
rights and freedoms of citizens, use of organs of security
and law and order and even the use of troops for the purpose
of maintaining public order, correct functioning of state
organs, protection of public property, and of people''s safety. [12]

The <u>Small Military Encyclopedia</u> is an authoritative source of information for the army's regular cadre, but this totally amoral, totalitarian, and un-Polish precept was not practiced, even in the army, until the imposition of martial law. It is as if the disease needed a ten-year incubation period. When it broke out its scale and intensity were unexpected and its true nature was not known. Admittedly, in the year preceding martial law there had been numerous official and unofficial warnings that measures would be taken to protect the Polish reason of state but few, except the top political military, understood the full implication.

General Jaruzelski gave his interpretation of the "justified, preeminent interest of the state," which was to be protected. In the speech in which he broke the news of martial law, he said: "The Polish-Soviet alliance is and will remain the cornerstone of the Polish reason of state, the guarantee of integrity of Poland's territory."[13] In this way Jaruzelski's long but incomplete definition of 1971 was thus spelled out in full. The Polish people finally learned that Soviet interests, represented in Poland by the political military, stood above all other community or individual interests and that moral or even legal norms would be subordinated to them. Martial law provisions allowed the political military to follow the official definition of reason of state to the letter.

Drive against Anti-Soviet Propaganda

An undercurrent of anti-Soviet feeling has been present in Poland's political life throughout the postwar period, sometimes even in top party and government circles. It was to be expected that they would erupt during the Solidarity era. It was also certain that the political army leadership would try to halt what to them was a dangerous development. In a drive that grew in intensity during 1981 and with the approach of martial law, the political military appealed to the minds and to the hearts of the Polish people. The general line was that the anti-Soviet feelings were fueled by incidents artificially created by Solidarity extremists. An early example was a declaration by the Szczecin branch of Solidarity led by M. Jurczyk, which said that Stanislaw Kania, first secretary of the party, had no right to speak in the name of the Polish people when he addressed the 26th Congress of the Communist Party of the Soviet Union (CPSU) in March 1981. In that speech Kania assured the delegates that "counterrevolution in Poland would fail."[14]

Quoting a number of incidents <u>Wojsko Ludowe</u> provided the comment that under cover of fictitious organizations offensive anti-Soviet cartoons were distributed, walls of barracks of Soviet Army units painted with slogans, and war graves and "monuments of

gratitude" desecrated.[15] Another comment in Wojsko Ludowe said
that enemies of Socialism working under the protective wings of
Solidarity have for months been conducting a bitter anti-Soviet campaign. They were injecting the venom of hatred against Poland's
natural ally in thousands of leaflets and newssheets and at all kinds
of meetings.[16]

In September 1981 the Central Committee of the CPSU and the
Soviet government, in a note sent to the Polish authorities, drew
attention to the growing number and intensity of anti-Soviet incidents
that had reached dangerous proportions.[17] According to the army
daily, Solidarity carried the responsibility for all these incidents,
although Lech Walesa and the Solidarity leadership have officially
dissociated themselves from these activities.[18]

The need to counter anti-Soviet propaganda and to condemn
profanation of Soviet Army war graves brought back the myth of the
600,000 Red Army soldiers killed in the process of liberating Poland.
As far as it is known this extraordinary claim was made first in 1972
by the then chief editor of Wojsko Ludowe, Colonel Edward Skrzypkowski, who stated: "600,000 Soviet soldiers gave their lives for our
freedom as they fought on Polish soil."[19]

In October 1981 a protest mass meeting against anti-Soviet
activities organized by the Polish-Soviet Friendship Society (TPPR)
adopted an appeal addressed to the Polish people. In it young Poles
were asked to bear in mind that the 600,000 Soviet Army soldiers
who died for the freedom of Poland were as young as themselves.[20]
A further twist to the story was given later in the Army weekly:

> The five Soviet Army Fronts that were involved in the
> liberation of Poland had 2.5 million troops. Of these,
> 600,000 fell and rest on Polish soil. For the families
> of the dead the soil in which their fathers, brothers,
> and husbands rest is sacred soil.[21]

As an item of propaganda the above example is one of the
weakest ever made up. Apart from the fact that it is absurd to
maintain that the Soviet soldiers died for Poland merely because
their war route led through Poland, the figure itself is grossly
inflated. What the great majority of Poles think about "liberation by
the Red Army" is yet another matter.

Numerous articles in army publications presented political
and economic arguments for a close Polish-Soviet partnership. The
Chief Political Directorate published in October 1981 a booklet
entitled "Polish-Soviet Economic Relations—Facts against Myths."
A comment in Wojsko Ludowe said that it provides ammunition
against "enemies of Polish-Soviet cooperation who would do anything

to distort the true nature of these relations, who spread lying information, gossip, false statistics, and pure calumnies to create the impression that the terms of Polish-Soviet trade are unfavorable to Poland."22

Colonel J. Borgosz, professor at the Military Political Academy, came out with unusual reasons why Poland's place was at the side of the Soviet Union. He wrote that after World War I Poland gained independence after 123 years, thanks to the October Revolution that overthrew the Russian Tsars. But the prewar Polish governments rejected cooperation with the Soviet Union and Poland lost that independence after a mere 21 years. They had backed the wrong horse, namely the West. Had they backed the Soviet Union, Germany would not have dared to attack the combined Soviet, Polish, and Rumanian forces, and if it had done so the war would have been fought on German territory. Thus, he wrote, the campaign of 1939 finally proved that Poland's independence can be guaranteed only by the Soviet Union and the Socialist community.23

One can forgive Colonel Borgosz his historical ramblings and that he repeats the story of the 600,000 of Soviet dead, to whom he added several hundred thousands of wounded (a curious ratio). He is a Marxist philosopher, not a historian. It is not so easy to understand Colonel M. Leczyk, a prominent historian and professor at the Military Political Academy, who believes that after October 1938, when Germany presented its first territorial demands for Polish territories, there was still time, forgetting all other considerations, to form a Polish-Soviet alliance.24

Propagandists of the political army produced many other historical reasons for and evidence of a lasting Polish-Soviet friendship. One of them was that about 130,000 Poles sided with the Reds during struggles of the October Revolution and Civil War.25 This too was a feeble argument. Leaving aside those who did not side with the Reds one is entitled to question the motivation of the Poles who did. The fact that they fought the Tsarist system, the established enemy of Poland, does not mean that they fought for Communism.

As was to be expected, the drive against anti-Soviet actions was opened by Jaruzelski himself when at the 9th Party Congress he declared that Polish-Soviet friendship and brotherhood-of-arms were matters of the greatest importance.26

THREE MAIN DIFFICULTIES

The ideological and political mobilization of the military party ran into serious difficulties, which stemmed from three main causes: large-scale changes of personnel in directing party posts, dissatisfaction among the young regular cadre, and intakes of conscripts infected by Solidarity. One must assume that the political military was able to neutralize the undesirable effects before it embarked on its martial law operation, but there is evidence that it has not yet solved these internal problems.

Changes of Directing Party Personnel

In spring 1981 at all levels of the party, report cum election meetings and conferences were held to review past activities and to elect new party officeholders and delegates to the unscheduled 9th Party Congress (July 1981). The internal army opposition to the political military (see Chapter 7) seized the opportunity to launch another attack on the political apparatus and political officers. Their much-criticized performance during the accounting period and before gave the opposition sufficient grounds to oust them from office and elect their own people. This was against the long-established practice that all important party posts were held by political officers. Available evidence shows that this was a development of the greatest significance: It was a massive vote of no confidence in the political military. According to a leader in Wojsko Ludowe in the spring of 1981 elections, all first secretaries of party committees of military district and arms of service commands as well as 80 percent of secretaries of the division command level had been replaced by younger people who had not held office before. It added that this created a new situation as regards quality (of work). [27] It is perhaps significant that similar elections in the civilian party did not produce such drastic changes of directing personnel. [28]

Extracts from military publications throw more light on the result of the elections and the effect this had on current party-political work in the army:

1. In the Pomeranian Military District 90 percent of the newly elected committee secretaries had come from outside the political apparatus. They had to be put through courses in "organization and methods" and were helped in their daily work by political officers and more experienced party members. [29]

2. In the air command area over 70 percent of personnel in party committees and 66 percent of party committee secretaries held office for the first time. Thus the period from spring 1981 to the imposition of martial law could be called "baby crawling," although it was a period of great efforts to maintain morale and political reliability of troops, including party members and candidates. The absence in party authorities of experienced political

officers put party organizations in a difficult position, especially during the strained political situation.[30]

3. In the 1st Warsaw Mechanized Division, party work was affected by the fact that 80 percent of personnel in some committees consisted of young, energetic, and ambitious people who had no practical experience of party work. It took time before they began to work effectively, and this only after periods of intensive training. But the situation in the country forced them to learn quickly and to adopt an offensive style of work.[31]

4. Members of the Warsaw Military District Party Committee who had been reelected are in single figures. The majority of new members come from outside the political apparatus. One could safely say that they were carried to the top on the wave of criticism of the party's activities in the past decade and by "calling to account" members of the full-time party apparatus who in their view were guilty. This line probably brought them popularity.[32]

5. Political officers suffered setbacks in the precongress elections. That is taken as a sign that other officers disapproved of them. While it is true that more should have been elected because they are best qualified, one must not forget that they had little time for canvassing because the all-pervading bureaucracy limited live contact with people. It is a great pity that in their place blusterers were elected who had nothing better to offer than loud words.[33]

It is not surprising that in these conditions party activities in and outside the army were at a low ebb. One political officer complained that when after the 9th Congress the editorial board of Wojsko Ludowe addressed a letter to 53 comrades, mainly secretaries of party committees, asking for comment on proposals for improving party work that was based on the congress resolution, there was not a single reply. The officer was prepared to assume that this was the period of greatest attacks by Solidarity and that party organizations were totally absorbed by the political fight inside as well as outside the army.[34]

Dissatisfaction among the Young Cadre

In the Polish Army, as in any other social group, there is a generation gap, but one gets the impression that it has special characteristics that probably stem from the disparity of background of older and younger officers. One well-known political officer wrote that the older cadre resented the fact that young officers who joined their units were very self-assured and confident. They knew how to obey and carry out orders of their superiors but also how to demand what was due to them. They shouted when they needed assistance, refused quarters that were heated by stoves, questioned work organization, and loudly criticized wrong decisions. The old were annoyed that the young wanted more free time, hated working several days without a break, and immediately attacked inefficient use of working time. The young wanted to have at once everything that the old had to wait for for a long time, showed little respect for the life experience of the old, and judged people by results. It was therefore sometimes difficult to establish a lasting understanding between the old and young officers.[35]

One senior political officer seems to blame the older generation for the state of affairs. He wrote that achievements in ideological education work had for many years been marred by evident failure to eradicate in a substantial part of the cadre the wrong and socially so very harmful habits of peremptoriness, brutality, unfriendliness, haughtiness, and lack of understanding for human problems. Formalistic, autocratic, or bureaucratic behavior passing as efficient handling of affairs still make life difficult for many. This was in too many instances still a barrier to normal friendly relations between people.[36]

Another senior political officer was very critical of the young cadre. He wrote that they appeared to be susceptible to Social-Democratic and Christian-Democratic propaganda. They were fascinated by ideological pluralism and tried to bring into the party pseudodemocracy with compromise on different world outlooks. This no doubt was the result of the divergence between Socialist theory and the reality of daily life. Workers of the ideological front would need more political culture to deal with the young cadre, with its passions aroused by the present situation, its emotional approach to many political and economic issues affecting the country, its uncritical acceptance of opinion from outside, its lack of responsibility in the use of words, its rush utterances of various demands and postulates.

Other unwelcome characteristics of the young cadre, according to the same officer, were the increasingly critical attitude toward superiors of all levels. This manifested itself as excessive criticism of many aspects of military life and training and referred mainly to long working hours that, they maintained, prevented them from having an orderly family life and developing personal interests. Yet a great deal could be done to eliminate the artificial conflicts among the cadre if only by reducing the discrepancies between army regulations and everyday practice. Fair treatment of young people was another important matter.[37]

A member of the board of editors of Wojsko Ludowe reported grievances that had been aired at a meeting with a number of political

officers. One of them was that people hoped renewal would bring
some easement in daily life. The latest rules say that working hours
for the cadre are from 7:30 A.M. to 3:30 P.M. They do not say who
does the job before and after these hours. Those who work from
daybreak to late at night say they do not expect free Saturdays but
would like to have a free Sunday.

Another complaint was that since officers give up free Saturdays
of their own free will, they should not be made to do so under some
flimsy pretext of an inspection or competition, because that creates
bad blood. Officers often stay four to six weeks away from their
base and have no free Saturdays. It was suggested that they should
get financial or other recognition. One political officer said he was
asked to explain why, under the same field conditions, officers of
central institutions of the Ministry of Defense and military districts
were entitled to a food norm K, which in monetary terms is almost
double of norm D, the entitlement for division and regiment staffs.
People were extremely sensitive to injustice.[38]

A colonel of the Higher Officer School of the Air Force quoted
a Comrade Szewernicki as saying:

> Our superiors, beginning with the Ministry of Defense,
> force us to violate ethical and moral standards by
> continuously adding new tasks; our targets for 1981
> are greater than for 1980, although calculations made
> in the unit show that they are unrealistic and impossible
> to achieve; many of the theoretical subjects are entered
> in the logbook as fulfilled although they had not been
> done, so that this could be shown during an inspection.

And another comrade said that "those who plan the training schedules
for units in a deliberate and planned way also ruin people's strength
and health because we already work 12-14 hours a day including
Saturdays and Sundays; in this situation even the equipment cannot
be examined as prescribed by the regulation."

Changing the subject, the colonel condemned those who from
the pulpit fight against crime, nepotism, play-safe, bad behavior,
and mismanagement but act quite differently themselves. Then there
were those who once held high positions in the army and having
retired begin to malign the army.[39]

Adverse working conditions seem to affect the private lives
of the young cadre. From a research project on participation of
young officers in cultural life some interesting figures (for 1978)
have emerged:

Theater going	40.5 percent did not go even once a year and 42.7 percent went 1-3 times a year (even when they were stationed in large garrisons with at least two theaters)

Attendance at:

museums	61.5 percent not even once a year, 23.6 percent 1-2 times a year
fine arts exhibitions	83.2 percent not even once a year, 10.3 percent 1-2 times a year
opera and concerts	84.2 percent not even once a year, 9.3 percent 1-2 times a year
light entertainment	61.2 percent not even once a year, 22.3 percent 1-2 times a year
cultural events at army establishments	49.7 percent not even once a year, 37.0 percent 1-2 times a year
reading a daily paper	53.4 percent every day, 31.7 percent several times a week
the army daily Zolnierz Wolnosci	42.0 percent (obligatory subscription)
military periodicals	62.7 percent do not read regularly

The author comments that, generally speaking, participation of young officers was better in units where good organization of work allowed more free time and a chance to satisfy individual interests.[40]

A colonel stated that from many interviews during career reviews he reached the conclusion that reading of military books was alarmingly falling. It was difficult to believe, but some officers have in fact in their 15 years of service not read a single military book and have not bought one either. He had established that in a certain library the only publication on the Warsaw Pact exercises "Tarcza-76" (Shield-76) had not been touched and that the same applied to a description of the NATO "Wintex-77" exercises. For years the same applied to the reading of military periodicals. He knew that graduates of civilian universities who undergo the 12-month conscript training formed a very low opinion of the military knowledge of some officers.[41]

General Baryla admitted in his speech at the 9th Party Congress that the service of the regular cadre had become particularly difficult because of high work demands, unlimited working time, on-call duties, big responsibilities for people and equipment, frequent separation from families, and everyday problems with the supply of goods and services.[42]

Conscripts Infected by Solidarity

Conscripts with a Solidarity past were a major problem for the political army. This is reflected in a number of extracts.

1. It was important to realize that the conscripts who came in the autumn of 1980 had a somewhat different life experience from their colleagues who came six months earlier. Many of them had taken part in strike actions and had been exposed to propaganda calling for reforms directed against Polish interests. The duty of commanders, and army educators of party members in particular, will be to help these lads sort out their opinions and check out hastily formed sympathies and antipathies. Views formed under such conditions are not based on an objective appraisal of facts but on youthful emotions.[43]

2. One must remember that education aims take a long time to materialize. Effects appear some 15-20 years after a given system is introduced. Education problems that we now face have their sources far back in the 1960s. They now appear in a compounded form. Many still do not realize that the next intake of conscripts will have their own vision of what was acceptable in Socialism. This has been clearly demonstrated during the workers' protest where the 25-35 age groups played the main role. It appears that human relations will have to be radically changed.[44]

3. At the plenary session of the Party Committee of the Warsaw Military District (August 1981), most who were present were aware of the consequences of the new autumn intake of conscripts, with large numbers of members of Solidarity who had been affected by propaganda hostile to the party and the government and had taken part in all kinds of protest actions. This creates a completely new situation for which party members must be prepared. In the view of the committee executive the improvement of forms and methods of ideological and political work becomes one of the main tasks of party organizations.[45]

4. Since autumn 1980 propaganda work has not been easy. Soldiers have been more inquiring, more critical. Many are simply politically disorientated. Terms like Socialism, social justice, and democracy are treated with reserve and suspicion. They suffer from internal conflicts and frustration. For these reasons the cadre for work with first-year soldiers was carefully selected and leaders of political instruction groups were thoroughly trained.[46]

9
Propaganda Line
on Solidarity

Intensified propaganda against Solidarity was an important element of the ideological and political mobilization described in Chapter 8. The initial attitude
that showed sympathy and understanding for the workers'
cause soon gave way to attacks that contained more
venom as martial law was approaching. An article
about Solidarity by Major-General N. Michta, a leading light of the political military, published in Trybuna
Ludu of September 15, 1981, is an assessment that
reflects the middle view between the two extremes:
Solidartiy intended originally as a trade union movement absorbed millions of people. The bulk are workers
but there are also hundreds of thousands of technical
and nontechnical intelligentsia who are employed in
state administration, the economy, education, trade,
transport, and services and there are self-employed
persons and individual farmers. The organization was
soon penetrated by enemies of the existing political order
who became its advisers, experts, and consultants. It
gradually assumed the character of a political organization determined to take power.[1] An abridged version
of the article is given as Appendix E.

Because political power was already in the sights
of the political military, Solidarity had to be discredited
as an organization. Since then the line has been that dissident groups exploited the workers' grievances for their
own political ends and that the groups themselves had been
aided and abetted by Western imperialists who had
decided to use Poland's difficulties for an all-out attack

on Communism and the Soviet bloc. Attempts to prove
that known U.S. agencies were spearheading the attack
were a daily occurrence.

INITIAL ATTITUDES TOWARD SOLIDARITY

The initial view of some political military that Solidarity was
a genuine and justified workers' protest and that its aims and aspirations could be accommodated within the Socialist renewal sponsored
by the civilian and military Communist parties was short lived. It
was replaced by learned arguments that Solidarity was incompatible
with the system of government in People's Poland and this in turn
was followed by accusations that Solidarity was manipulated by
dissident groups—the Social Self-Defense Committee (KSS-KOR) and
the Conferederation of Independent Poland (KPN) in particular.

Ideologists of the political army were at first showing sympathy
to Solidarity's cause and even claiming Communist parentage. This
is reflected in extracts from military publications:

1. The development of People's Poland was creating forces
that opposed the building of Socialism from above. Without the
achievements of people's rule there would have been no Solidarity. [2]

2. The Socialist system developed aspirations and ideas that
created the workers' protest and gave it the form (of Solidarity) it
assumed. Socialism implanted in the masses a deep feeling of human
dignity and created aspirations to joint decision making, joint government, and joint responsibility. [3]

3. Solidarity sprang from the social protest against wrongdoings
and injustice. Renewal in the party had the same roots. In the cooperation of both these movements was the main chance for a Polish
revival. The weaknesses of the party were its diverse and contradictory interests and its social composition in which the center and
top of the social pyramid predominated. By contrast, Solidarity
gathered all groups that lived in poverty or were threatened by it.
It comprised a large number of people who had suffered during the
successive phases of mistakes and vitiations. [4]

4. The most important thing that happened in Poland in the last
few years was that society ceased to be passive (an object) and became
active (a subject). People began feverishly to organize themselves
and to negotiate with the authorities as equals to secure their rights
as subjects, not objects, of power. These ideas and sentiments
were propagated by Solidarity when in its program published after
its first congress it stated that "every human being has the right to
realize his individual goals and aspirations." To talented young
people who hitherto had no chance to prove their worth this was a

Most attractive program. This attraction stems also from the traditional forming of personality by the Catholic Church, which puts the individual above social values. Poles are brought up in a cult of full individual independence; it is their historical tradition. In this area the party has sinned most. The technocratic treatment of people as objects is today the most serious and weighty accusation. Discontent led to a violent confrontation with authority. The Socialist state and the workers' party found themselves in a position of confrontation with their own class. Irrespective of intentions it is in the nature of martial law that it leads to a drastic limitation of human rights and consequently to greater treatment of people as objects.[5]

These and similar declarations of sympathy and understanding had no practical meaning. By the end of 1980 the political army leadership stated that Solidarity was dominated by dissident anti-Socialist groups. These were described in a ten-page article in Wojsko Ludowe by Colonel Professor Dr. J. Muszynski of the Military Political Academy. Muszynski wrote that by 1980 Polish dissident groups that had been formed in 1976-79 decided that the growing economic and political crises had created a unique opportunity for seizing power or at least exercising so much pressure that the authorities and the party would be forced to make concessions allowing them legal and free operation. The groups aimed to transform themselves into a legal opposition to the party, thereby questioning its leading role. By doing this they ignored the truth that Socialism and political pluralism are incompatible. The dissident groups aimed to use the newly formed structures of the Free Trade Union's "Solidarity" as a platform for political activities, although the latter had officially declared their apolitical character and accepted the Socialist economic and political system when they signed the Gdansk agreement on August 31, 1980. In autumn 1980 members of various anti-Socialist groups became members of strike committees in which they acted as advisers, expert consultants, and informers of foreign media about the situation in Poland. Although anti-Socialist groups in Poland did not represent a major political force, they were not to be ignored but should be identified and fought as enemies of socialism.[6]

Colonel Z. Czerwinski, editor-in-chief of Wojsko Ludowe, made his belated attack on the anti-Socialist forces in July 1981. Czerwinski listed the sins of the opposition. They were saying that almost 40 years of effort were lost, that the principles of Socialism, not the deviations from them, led Poland into a blind alley, that under Socialist rule no good was or could ever be done, not a single problem had been solved. Of course, he argued, none of this was true. At any rate, the party had accepted the justified protest of the working class and decided on a program of total renewal of the social and economic life of the country. This sincere move was interpreted

by the opposition and its foreign masters as weakness of the party
and government that were to be exploited in the so-called second
phase. As soon as the popular demands were acknowledged the never-
ending protests began to resemble counterrevolution. How the opposition managed to spread discontent and channel all passions against
the party, the country's alliances, and the Socialist system is still
a mystery. However, it is easy to understand why the main NATO
countries and their military circles were so interested in the
developments in Poland. Their aim was to facilitate the process of
political disintegration in Poland and so weaken the defense capacity
of the Warsaw Pact and through this the global position of Socialism. [7]

SOLIDARITY MANIPULATED BY DISSIDENT GROUPS

Muszynski identified the groups that were allegedly manipulating
the workers organized in Solidarity as:

- Social Self-Defense Committee (KSS-KOR), formed in 1976,
  revisionist in character, led by Jacek Kuron. It was by far
  most effective of all groups.

- Human Rights Movement (ROPCiO), formed in 1977, representing neoliberal tendencies.

- Student Solidarity Committees (SKS) formed in several uinver-
  sity centers in 1977 and 1978, revisionist and reformist.

- Peasant Self-Defense Committees (KSCh), operating in some
  regions only, formed in 1978 and 1979, an agrarian movement.

- Poland's Youth Movement (RMP), formed in 1979 in Gdansk by
  members of the Student Solidarity Committees, right-wing
  nationalist.

- Confederation of Independent Poland (KPN), formed in 1979,
  right-wing nationalist, led by L. Moczulski.

- Association of Mobile Universities (TKN-LU), formed in 1978,
  by members of KSS-KOR.

He said that a common characteristic to all the groups was that they
had no real constructive alternative to Socialism. [8]

Four other contributors of Wojsko Ludowe clearly disagreed
with the above. In an article on ideology and program of the anti-
Socialist opposition they listed the following common aims of the

groups: political pluralism, parliamentary democracy, free elections
(universal, secret, equal, direct, proportional), human and citizen
rights, social self-government, and free trade unions. They added
that all the demands except the last were incmopatible with principles
of Socialism and their introduction would amount to the liquidation of
the Socialist system.[9]

Under a general heading "Geography of the Political Opposition
in Poland," Wojsko Ludowe started in 1982 a series of articles by
Dr. J. Kossecki. He is described as the founder of the Polish
"school of social cybernetics." He runs the Research Unit of Social
Cybernetics at the Higher Pedagogical School at Kielce where he is
assistant professor. He and his team study political confrontation
and information war problems.

In the introduction to his first article Dr. Kossecki said that
in the second half of the 1970s about 37 opposition organizations
came into being. Some had an openly anti-Communist line, some
were trying to hide it, and there were some that were not anti-
Communist. He said that he would be describing only organizations
that had not been registered and were publishing uncensored material.

The articles covered eight separate opposition movements (he
calls them currents): Liberal-Masonic, Neo-Pilsudski, Social-
Democratic, Trotskyist, Neo-Nationalist, Peasant, Christian-Democratic, Free Trade Unions.[10]

Another source says that there are only three main "currents":
nationalist, with roots in the prewar National Democratic Party, and
another line with traditions in the prewar Pilsudski camp—both are
decidedly anti-Soviet: Social-Democratic, oriented toward West
European social-democratic parties: and Christian-Democratic,
politically and ideologically not uniform, subject to influence of the
Catholic Church.[11] Two dissident groups—KSS-KOR and KPN—
received more attention from the military press than other groups.

KSS-KOR

Kossecki described KSS-KOR under the heading "Liberal-
Masonic stream" of the political opposition. He said that at the core
of this group were activists who in the late 1960s went under the
name "Commandos" and had organized the student unrests in 1968.
They were in the main the progeny of high party and government
officials of the Stalin era. At that time they were linked with the
Trotskyist 4th Internationale but in the 1970s the two main leaders,
J. Kuron and A. Michnik, became Social-Democrats. After the 1976
workers' unrests they formed the Workers' Defense Committee
(KOR) to give financial, legal, and medical help to victims of repression. In 1977 the committee changed its name to Social Self-Defense

Committee, (KSS) and later to KSS-KOR. the Association for Scientific
Courses (TKN) and the Independent Publishing Organisation NOWA
formed in 1977 were KSS-KOR subsidiaries and recipients of the
greater part of the material help coming from the West for opposition
activities in Poland.

KSS-KOR attracted people of various political orientations
who then organized action groups in their environments. These
groups and KSS-KOR itself used mafia techniques. Only about 30
people were named as leading members. When in the summer of 1980
the strikes on the Baltic Coast began, KSS-KOR and representatives
of other groups, for example, Clubs for Catholic Intellectuals (KIK)
and the Discussion Group "Experience and Future," offered their
services to the workers and soon became the effective bosses of
Solidarity. Of the 896 delegates to the 1st National Congress of
Solidartiy in September 1981, 150 were activists of KSS-KOR.

The main ideological precept of KSS-KOR was "the good of the
individual is a supreme value." Its political program aimed at self-
government, democracy, and pluralism. Kossecki admitted that the
aim was to improve the existing system of government, not to
change it.

KSS-KOR officially dissolved itself at the 1st National Congress
of Solidarity. This meant only that KSS-KOR activists found it easier
to penetrate other organizations under a different guise. At any rate,
in November 1981 a group of KSS-KOR leaders began to form a new
organization called Clubs of Self-Governed Poland—Freedom, Justice,
Independence. This organization was quite definitely aiming for a
change of the system.

Some KSS-KOR leaders managed to evade internment when
martial law was declared. Among them was Zbigniew Bujak who
became a member of the Underground Solidarity leadership.[12] J.
Kuron, A. Michnik, H. Wujec, Z. Romaszewski, and many others
are in prison awaiting trial.

Colonel Wojtasik, the chief propagandist of the political army,
explained that the influence of KSS-KOR in Solidarity was due to the
skilful use of mafia-type social engineering (socjotechnika), by which
he meant fomenting of all kinds of negative social emotions to gain
support for a demagogic program.

KPN

Much venom of the army media was directed against the KPN.
According to Colonel Wojtasik the influence of the KPN in Solidarity
greatly increased in the second half of 1981 when Solidarity was
heading for a confrontation with state authority. KPN was a chauvinist,
nationalist, and extremist group and this was reflected in its program

and actions. In the program that was evolved by Leszek Moczulski there were no constructive or rational elements, only a vision of total destruction, anarchy, and incredible risk-taking. Moczulski advocated breaking the law, attacks on state authorities, all types of actions directed against security of the state and defense and against Poland's true allies, namely the Soviet Union. He did not exclude the possibility of a general uprising to achieve his so-called Third Republic. Any compromise with the government was excluded.

KPN had the character of a military-type underground organization. Open or clandestine members were obliged to take an oath. They formed groups of three or five members. KPN also had two separate structures, open and clandestine. The latter would step forward should action be taken against the official leadership. (The leaders of KPN have already been given long prison sentences.)

KPN had the greatest following in the Silesia, which produced its most radical leaders. This resulted in the fatal casulties at the beginning of martial law. [13]

"MADE IN THE USA" LABEL

It suited the political military to maintain that Solidarity was manipulated by an unspecified number of extremists who in turn were exposed as mere tools in the hands of Western, mainly U.S., intelligence and subversion agencies. For propagada use this was a more acceptable formulation than an admission that it was a home-grown popular revolt against an alien system.

General Baryla said at the 4th Ideological Conference of the Armed Forces that at the end of the 1970s and the beginning of the 1980s Western strategists had reached the conclusion that the international situtation worked in their favor and they decided to exploit this. Poland became an object of particular interest. [14]

In his speech to the Seym on January 25, 1982 General Jaruzelski said:

> Speaking frankly and leaving diplomatic niceties aside, the dismantling of the postwar balance of power in Europe and in the world was to have started on Polish soil. In order to achieve destabilization and unilateral superiority, it was decided to destroy the foundations of peace in Europe, namely the Yalta and Potsdam agreements. The cost of this plan would have been paid by the Polish people. The imposition of martial law caused the plan to fail. The goal is still to be achieved by the use of threats, boycott, and so-called sanctions. [15]

Manufactured evidence that the U.S. government was behind all that was produced much later. In July 1983 <u>Wojsko Ludowe</u> published extracts from a secret report—"United States Policy toward Poland"—alleged to have been prepared by Zbigniew Brzezinski of the National Security Council and submitted on March 17, 1978 to President Carter and a narrow group of top personalities (Secretary of State Cyrus Vance, Secretary of Defense Harold Brown, and CIA Director Stansfield Turner).

One extract said:

> Having analyzed the situation in individual countries we
> came to the conclusion that Poland is the weakest link
> in the Soviet domination of Eastern Europe. Poland is
> also most vital because through Poland run the communi-
> cation lines between the USSR and its mighty armed forces
> in the GDR[East Germany]. It is proposed that the
> United States and its allies concentrate attention on
> Poland without neglecting other opportunities that may
> present themselves elsewhere.

Brzezinski allegedly saw four possible scenarios of future developments in Poland. Scenario No. 3, the one most desirable from the U.S. point of view, is described thus:

> Antigovernment demonstrations will reach such intensity
> and form that they will endanger the position of Gierek
> himself. In that case it will be possible to form a coa-
> lition government composed of "moderate communists,"
> independent economists, members of the opposition,
> and church leaders. If this evolution is steered with
> sufficient subtlety and intelligence it is possible that
> Moscow would accept that as a <u>fait accompli</u>, which
> could not be reversed without causing damage to the
> standing of the Soviet Union in the world.[16]

In an interview given to a representative of the London Polish emigré weekly <u>Tydzien Polski</u> Brzezinski said:

> I state categorically that the above memorandum is from
> beginning to end a forgery produced by the KGB. . . .
> Secondly there never have been any links between KSS-
> KOR and the U.S. government. The use in the indictment
> [against KSS-KOR] of a document forged by the Moscow
> masters is degrading for Poland and makes the authorities
> of the Polish People's Republic look ridiculous.[17]

An article by a senior political officer contained many more revelations. Large specialist staffs were continually analyzing the over-all situation and trying out new concepts and theories aimed at liquidation of Socialism. In the case of Poland the organizers of this war were greatly helped by the country's serious indebtedness, doors excessively open to the West, and the fact that anti-Socialist forces were allowed to grow under the cover of human rights. Credits were granted not out of sympathy but for the sole purpose of making Poland economically dependent so as to be able to dictate terms, in particular one: full freedom of action for anti-Socialist groups.

At the same time by other, clandestine, channels leaders and activists of the opposition were being trained for the overthrowing of the Socialist system. Far back in 1975 at a Geneva meeting organized by Western intelligence agencies, leaders of the opposition were given outline program and promises of support. At the end of September 1980 representatives from Poland attended a briefing conference at Garmisch Partenkirchen in the German Federal Republic. It took place within the framework of an international studium on the USSR and Eastern Europe. When one compares the recommendations made by the studium with subsequent Solidarity actions one sees that they were followed to the letter. Important decisions taken by Solidarity leaders were cleared in advance and then controlled by certain people and institutions in the West.

After August 1980 Solidarity functionaries frequently traveled abroad and always to the West. In the United States a special contact office was established. It was now more or less known whom they contacted and about what. Solidarity established close contacts with foreign trade union organizations, especially the international ICFTU in Brussels, the AFL-CIO (United States), and the DGB (West Germany).

Solid evidence of Western control over Solidarity was the "Message to the Workers of Eastern Europe" adopted at the 1st Solidarity Congress in September 1981. This declaration of a program for the liquidation of Socialism in the countries of Eastern Europe had been "sold" to Solidarity leaders by the 4th (Trotskyist) Internationale. Further evidence is the massive support by Western mass media and the decision to apply economic and other sanctions when the elaborate Western plans were thwarted through the imposition of martial law. [18]

Solidarity relations with Western countries were also described (1981) by a deputy minister of the interior, Militia General W. Pozoga, in an article about Poland's Security Services. He wrote that in the crisis situation the possibilities of penetration by enemy intelligence agencies were increasing as were the destructive activities of the internal enemy. In one of the program documents of NATO it said that never before was Poland as important as it now was. It has been

established that official NATO representatives have been developing
contacts between controlled Western trade unions and Solidarity,
developing their own contacts with Polish intellectual and cultural
groups, and forming close ties with suitable Polish journalists.
Western countries combined intelligence with subversion activities
in order to achieve a lasting destabilization in Poland. Material
help for opposition groups took the form of semiofficial gifts, illegal-
ly channeled funds, prepared propaganda materials, modern printing,
and radio and television equipment. [19]

Western organizations were accused of direct subversion in
Poland by Cezary Maski writing in Wojsko Ludowe. He repeats the
story that Western credits to Poland were meant to be an economic
trap to extract political concessions.

Among many organizations that work against Poland, he gives
the leading and coordinating role to the International Communication
Agency (ICA). He says that in ICA plans for 1981 Poland was
described as "the part of the Soviet system that is most susceptible
to Western influence." The program had been approved by the U.S.
government and was being implemented by the center as well as ICA
functionaries in Poland. When, thanks to the imposition of martial
law, the plan of taking Poland out of the Warsaw Pact came to nothing,
ICA was charged to start a propaganda war against Communism
modeled on the 1950s. Keeping Poland in a state of permanent unrest
is thought to be the best way of destabilizing the Communist system.

Second in the propaganda-league table, according to Maski,
was the Board for International Broadcasting (BIB), which controls
the broadcasting stations Radio Free Europe and Radio Liberty
(RFE/RL), as well as the Voice of America. The latter broadcasts
mainly to the USSR. The RFE/RL technical base was radically
improved in 1981 when 11 transmitters of 250 kilowatts (kw) were
installed. Both stations now had at their disposal 20 transmitters of
250 kw and 25 of 100 kw situated in Western Europe. Of the 553 hours
beamed on to Eastern Europe every week, Poland's share was 133
hours, or 19 hours a day. In 1982 broadcasting time was further
increased. The annual budget of RFE/RL was close to $100 million.
Maski highlights the fact that in March 1982 Zdzislaw Najder, who
lived in Poland until 1981, was appointed head of the Polish Section
of RFE. This was a break with the practice of appointing only emigré
Poles to this post. The move was intended to increase authenticity
of the broadcast material. Najder had very close links with Kultura,
a monthly political-literary publication in Paris that served Polish
communities the world over. Kultura was listed in the article as the
third most important center of anti-Communist subversion. Then
came French radio stations, especially "France Internationale,"
and finally the BBC. Both were described as mere tools of American
propaganda. [20]

It is strange, but information on the same subject given by Colonel Wojtasik of the GZP does not agree with the "foreign-made" label of Solidarity. He wrote that "in some instances Solidarity propaganda and information activity was clearly inspired by external forces," or "in the first months of Solidarity's existence its foreign contacts were of a passive character and were limited to receiving representatives of foreign organizations who were offering material assistance with the obvious intention of gaining influence on future activities of Solidarity," or "after 1980 one could see distinct tendencies on the part of foreign institutions to instruct and train Solidarty members who traveled abroad and to exert in this way some influence on the ideology and propaganda of Solidarity," or "with the passage of time we notice more frequent contacts with Western centers of ideological subversion and even NATO special services, using contacts made earlier by KSS-KOR."[21]

Colonel Muszynski of the WAP wrote about the early period of Solidarity in a similar vein.[22]

Colonel Wojtasik also said in his article:

- Before the imposition of martial law more than 50 official Solidarity delegations visited about 30 Western countries; about 300 Solidarity activists went on tourist trips.

- The U.S. labor organization AFL-CIO made a gift of $200,000 out of a total of $3 million collected for Solidarity.

- Radio Free Europe has always been the propaganda trumpet of illegal anti-Socialist groups in Poland; it was also used for instruction and inspiration of certain actions to make stabilization in Poland very difficult.

- The Polish-language monthly Kultura in Paris was supplying various Solidarity publishing facilities and the Independent Publishing Organization "Nowa" with suitably selected propaganda literature. Kultura propagated the development of anti-Soviet and anti-Socialist publishing activities of Solidarity.[23]

In spite of the wealth of information on Solidarity published by the military media it was not possible to get any on the numerical strength of the so-called anti-Socialist forces in Solidarity. One possible reason is that if figures had been given it might have been difficult to justify the huge scale of Jaruzelski's martial law intervention. However, two extracts throw some light on the subject:

1. "If one were to take into account KSS-KOR members employed full time in the Solidarity organization structure, in its illegal

publications sector, in the Independent Students' Union, in creative culture associations, and various enterprises one would get a figure of several thousand professional revolutionaries."[24]

2. "How did it happen and why that several hundreds or several thousands (if one goes by the number of those interned) were able to paralyze the minds of millions, gain their confidence and cooperation?"[25]

Several hundreds or several thousands? There probably is no other case in the annals of military history when so many had been victorious over so few.

Another good question is why should the Baltic Coast with Szczecin and Gdansk have become the cradle of Solidarity and continue to be the hearth of resistance to the rule of the political military? Why not another region of Poland? A partial answer was given by a political officer in the Polish Navy. Describing his difficulties in party-political work he blamed the following factors: geography of the coast, relatively open frontier, daily contact with the potential enemy, travel to non-Socialist countries, direct contact with people of other nationalities, visits of foreign ships. To all this one must add the casual labor force in local factories (while waiting for jobs in the merchant navy), a large student population, well-paid jobs in shipping for ex-navy experts, and so on.[26]

It is not new that contacts with the West are blamed for making people think free. I am inclined to believe that in addition people who live with the sea are inclined more that way than others.

In the early days of Solidarity military publicists referred to the Gdansk and Szczecin area as the "Zone of radiation". They no longer do but the Baltic Coast of Poland continues to radiate the light of freedom. The light draws the full attention of all true Poles who see Gdansk as the home of Lech Walesa and his gallant fellow workers of the shipyard where Solidarity was born.

10
Intervention Forces of the Army
and the
Ministry of Internal Affairs

Contrary to the generally accepted view, only the top
leadership and a relatively small part of the army
were actively involved in the martial law intervention.
Its planning, organization, and direction were obviously
in the hands of the army but its execution was shared
with the State Security Forces subordinated to the
Ministry of Internal Affairs. It soon became known that
the latter were always used in actions where the workers'
resistance could be crushed only by armed force. In
these situations army units were merely covering the
backs of the militia units. This was so especially during
the early stage of martial law. Since then violent confrontations with the opposition have been reserved for the
security troops who seem to manage without army protection. The above division of labor was meant to safeguard "the good name" of the army.

There is a great deal of evidence that the close
links between the Polish Army and the State Security
Forces, which date back to 1945-48, developed in the
late 1970s into cooperation directed against the growing
political opposition. In 1981 the political military gained
full control of the State Security Service and Forces when
Jaruzelski made General Kiszczak, the army's top
security expert, minister of internal affairs, to whom
the civilian State Security Service and Forces are
subordinated (see Figure 1 in Chapter 1). The Army
Security Service played a major role in this development.

Martial law duties probably did not put any unexpected demands on the militarized security forces. By contrast, army units designated for martial law duties were given additional specialist and political instruction.

ARMY SECURITY SERVICE

The Army Security Service is known officially as the Army Internal Service (WSW). It was established by an order of the minister of defense (1957) and has two main functions: counterintelligence, that is, protection of the armed forces against enemy intelligence penetration; and military police duties in respect to army personnel, property, and traffic.[1]

In the last few years both these functions have been extended to cover also the civilian sector. Total strength could be several thousands. Head of the WSW is a normally a two-star general. A school for junior officers of the WSW at Minsk Mazowiecki trains specialists in crime investigation and prevention.

Considerable publicity was given to the work of the WSW outside the army in the second half of 1981. WSW patrols joined the militia in preventing hooliganism and antistate and anti-Soviet activities. When necessary they assisted the forces of law and order in restoring peace.[2]

When the government decided to involve the army in the fight against speculation (August 1981), the WSW became the organizer of the "battle of the marketplace." Apart from its own personnel, the WSW was able to use troops delegated for this purpose from the Internal Defense Troops. Thanks to this, the army was able to cover not only market and other trading places but also railway junctions and outer-city areas. Operations were controlled from special command posts that also served as centers for collecting information from the population.[3]

Seen in retrospect, the government decision was a decision taken by General Jaruzelski as prime minister. The purpose was to give some army and Internal Defense units an opportunity to become acquainted with their future areas of operation under the guise of fighting ordinary and economic crimes.

The contribution of the counterintelligence sector of the WSW was naturally more important than that of the uniformed Military Police. Counterintelligence in the Polish Army always was interpreted widely. General T. Kufel, head of the service, stated in an interview given in 1974 that WSW work was directed against those who enter into relations with political enemies, betray military secrets, or in some other way bring harm to the army and the country. Many fell, victims of the ideological enemy and his psychological warfare, unwittingly or by accident. That is why prevention was so important. In education and enlightenment work the WSW cooperated with commanders and the party-political apparatus.

The WSW acted as a kind of early-warning system that promoted active rather than passive security. Kufel added that in his view the most profitable investment in preventive security was ideological and political education and the creation of Socialist convictions and attitudes. Aggressive Communist education was the universal remedy for the majority of social ills by winning people's minds and hearts for Socialist values. It was also his view that the creation of ideological confusion, and ideological and political subversion, belonged to the same category of crimes as attempts to extract military and state secrets.[4]

In 1974, true to its name of an internal army service, WSW activities were concerned lnly with the army environment. A few years later, and certainly by 1978, its scope had widened to cover so-called enemy subversion in the civilian sector. There is some evidence of this development.

Among ten senior Polish Army officers (one general, nine colonels) who had been entered in the "Book of Honor" for 1982 for services connected with martial law, there were two colonels of the WSW. The citation for Colonel E. Bula said: "He directed and participated in detecting and liquidating centers of the anti-Socialist underground." The citation for Colonel R. Rybarczyk said: "He took part in the detection and neutralizing anti-Socialist forces and in the protection of troops from enemy influence."[5]

The above is evidence that the WSW was gathering intelligence on the anti-Socialist underground. The WSW was most likely the address in the army to which Regional Party Committees were obliged to send information about the local political situation in accordance with the guidelines issued by the Central Committee of the party (see Chapter 6).

Further evidence that the WSW has assumed a vital role in the army's actions against the political opposition can be gleaned from the career of General Kiszczak, minister of internal affairs and member of WRON. Kiszczak, who had spent most of his time in military counterintelligence, was from 1972 to 1979 head of military intelligence proper. From 1979 to 1981 he was head of the WSW, and from July 1981 minister of internal affairs. The latter move gave to Jaruzelski the control of the civilian State Security apparatus. More important perhaps was that with the imposition of martial law Kiszczak became a member of WRON, where he used his knowledge of who is who in Solidarity acquired in the position of head of the WSW to carry out its effective liquidation as an organization.

It appears that the WSW grew in importance at the expense of the civilian State Security organization. The role of the latter during the 1945-48 confrontation was praised in 1979:

> The State Security organs played a very important role in this fight. They uncovered the plans of the armed underground movement, its organization and structure, locations and collaborators. As a result, the control center of the reactionary forces were taken out or isolated from the population.

In the same article, P. Jaroszewicz, then prime minister, said that the Citizens' Militia and Security Service, faithful to their roots, were the first to take up the fight against home-grown reactionaries. [6]

No such claims have been made about the Security Service during the recent crisis. It may have been too scared to be effective, because like the party it was exposed to attacks from Solidarity. It could also be that the civilian State Security Service was not willing to provide information demanded by Jaruzelski because it would have implicated civilian party members. Jaruzelski therefore used his own WSW intelligence service.

INTERNAL DEFENSE TROOPS AND CITIZENS' MILITIA

Internal Defense and Frontier Guard Troops

The Internal Defense Troops (WOWewn) are a special category of troops destined for operations against subversion enemy groups on Polish territory. They may also be used for the protection and defense of important buildings and installations, for curing the effects of weapons of mass destruction. WOWewn are well-armed and equipped. They are based on certain regions of the country and bear their name. [7]

WOWewn are an integral part of the Defense of National Territory (OTK) and form one of the main elements of home-ground defense. They cooperate with other forces of the OTK system. WOWewn consist of units of a general military character and of specialized units—signals, bridge building, chemicals, and so on. [8] The estimated strength of WOWewn is about 14,000. The figure of 65,000 given in the International Institute for Strategic Studies' Military Balance 1982/83 is not likely to be correct. Their commander is a general (one-star) who reports directly to the chief inspector of OTK, General Tuczapski, who is a member of WRON.

WOWewn pride themselves in being direct descendants of the

Internal Security Corps (KBW), which acquired notoriety for their part in suppressing the right-wing underground in 1945-48. The KBW was at that time about 30,000 strong and was the army's main partner in imposing the Communist system on the Polish people. Until 1965 the KBW was subordinated to the Ministry of the Interior and had the distinct character of a uniformed political security police. It was renamed Internal Defense Troops when it was subordinated to the Ministry of Defense in 1965.[9] Several large units were put at the disposal of the Ministry of Internal Affairs. They are known as the "Vistula Military Units of the Ministry of the Interior" (Nadwislanskie Jednostki Wojskowe MSW).

Relatively little has been said about WOWewn and the Vistula Units' contribution to the martial law operations. Maybe WRON did not want to draw attention to their participation and they probably passed for normal army troops. However, they must have played a major role because that type of operation is their speciality and they have traditional links with the present leadership of the political army that date back to the early postwar period.

Similar in character to WOWewn are the Frontier Guard Troops (WOP). They also have the same tradition of fighting the right-wing underground in the 1945-48 confrontation. Subordinated to the Ministry of Internal Affairs until 1965, they then came under the Ministry of Defense. They operate in peace time under the Ministry of Internal Affairs. Their estimated strength is 18,000, organized in brigades, main frontier posts, and posts.[10] According to the military daily paper, during martial law soldiers of WOP together with Citizens' Militia units and the Security Service made a considerable contribution to maintaining order and in "preventive, protection and isolation actions." They also carried out ideological and political work with the population, concentrating their efforts on schools and teachers.[11]

Citizens' Militia, Mobile Militia Reserve, and
Voluntary Reserve

The Citizens' Militia (MO) is the full-time uniformed and armed Polish police. It was built up from scratch (1944) to eliminate any link with the prewar police. It consisted exclusively of left-wing elements. In the 1945-48 confrontation most of the 45,000-strong force helped the army and the Internal Security Corps to suppress the anti-Communist opposition. Its present organization and functions are defined in a decree of December 21, 1955. The organization structure follows the territorial-administrative division of the country. From the MO command in a town begins specialization of the services. The MO is part of OTK, which means that in war (and under martial law) it is regarded as a military formation responsible for maintaining law and order and helping the Internal Defense Troops fight an enemy on Polish territory.[12] Present estimated strength of the MO is 60,000 (the figure of 350,000 given in Military Balance 1982/83 probably includes the voluntary reserve), but this is bound to increase because early in 1983 it was decided to establish "district" MO commands as an intermediate link between town MO commands and regional MO commands.[13]

A new law about the office of the minister of internal affairs passed on July 14, 1983, made further changes. Regional MO commands have become Regional Offices of the Ministry of Internal Affairs and the same applied to district MO commands and town MO commands. Local lower MO offices and posts are subordinated to the new offices of the ministry.[14]

The obvious result of these changes will be that the numbers of security personnel and their networks of agents will be substantially increased and the Security Service will be brought that much closer to the ordinary citizen. Apart from that, reorganizations of that order offer scope for changes of personnel.

The Militia Motorized Reserve (ZOMO) are militarized militia units used as riot police. The second letter of the abbreviation stands for "Odwod," a reserve at the disposal of higher commands to meet unforseen contingencies. Mainly for this reason they must be motorized. Information on ZOMO is not officially published, and information published in the West is based on unofficial reports from Poland. One such report said that ZOMO strength was about 25,000, that it consisted mainly of convicted criminals who join to get a remission of sentence, a well-paid job, and suitable employment after a prescribed period of service in ZOMO. Their brutality is explained by the use of drugs.[15] A delegation of English writers and journalists was told at the offices of the government paper Polityka: "We have more than 200,000 people in the militia alone."[16] This could well be true and refer mainly to ZOMO, which has the capacity to prevent demonstrations in a large number of Polish cities scheduled for the same time.

One bit of official information implies that a conscript can choose to discharge his military service obligation by serving for two years in ZOMO.[17] Combined with special rates of pay and other privileges this can provide ZOMO with the required number of recruits. The same source refers to a special group of the MO that is said to be a commando-type elite unit, which one can join only by transfer from ZOMO. Secondary education is the minimum requirement.

The Voluntary Militia Reserve (ORMO) was formed in 1946 for

the specific purpose of helping the militia to fight the anti-Communist opposition. At that time ORMO had over 100,000 members. The present scope and organization are regulated by a special law of 1967. ORMO members have the rights of full-time militia men and wear uniforms while on duty. ORMO units are based in factories and localities. Separate units may be formed for special purposes: for example, traffic control on roads or crime prevention. In 1967 ORMO had about 300,000 members; present membership is supposed to be much smaller. Special committees made up of representatives of the party, militia, and local administrations exercise direct control. Overall control is in the hands of the Ministry of Internal Affairs.[18]

There were unconfirmed reports that during the period preceding martial law too many ORMO members had shown pro-Solidarity sympathies. Those who were considered politically reliable were used under martial law for auxiliary duties as ROMO (Voluntary Militia Reserve—as for ORMO).

Academy of Internal Affairs

Tradition is only one of the many links between the political army and the civilian Security Services. Cooperation exists on many planes, especially in the area of training of top-level cadres. It is interesting that the increase in ideological and political work in the army in the early 1970s was reflected in the State Security Service area. In 1972 three officer schools were established in the area of responsibility of the Ministry of Internal Affairs: the Officer School named after Jozwiak, the Higher Officer School named after Dzierzhinskij, and the Academy of Internal Affairs (ASW).

The declared aim was to improve the work of the Security Service and of the forces that maintain law and order.

The ASW trains the cadres for top positions in the Ministry of Internal Affairs. Graduates leave the academy with vast theoretical as well as practical knowledge that is needed to counter the threat posed by the enemies of Socialism. This commitment demands from the cadre and the whole personnel of the Ministry of the Interior, from its Security Service and militia, particular maturity and professional competence in defending the state against espionage and ideological and political subversion. In its education work the ASW exploits the rich traditions of the Security Service and militia dating back to the time when they fought the right-wing underground and built the foundations of the Socialist state.[19] According to another source, there is an agreement between the ASW and the Military Political Academy that provides for the exchange of lecturers and of experience in modernizing and expanding their respective teaching facilities. Both institutions hold joint scientific conferences and symposia. ASW students defend their doctoral theses at the Military Political Academy. [20]

Cooperation extends far beyond the two academies. For example, in 1974 the Chief Political Directorate of the army organized a joint conference for representatives of both academies and of officer schools and training centers of the Ministry of Defense and the Ministry of Internal Affairs. Twenty-three professors and assistant professors of the ASW are listed in a "Guide to Polish Science". [21]

SPECIALLY DESIGNATED ARMY UNITS

Colonel Professor J. Muszynski wrote in Wojsko Ludowe that for the defense of the threatened Socialist system the Military Council of National Salvation provided army units and its most faithful and best qualified cadres and that a part of the army left the barracks to take up the difficult and responsible duties of martial law. [22] At a conference of party members of Central Departments of the Ministry of Defense, General Siwicki, then chief of general staff, stated that the cadre of central departments had ensured precise planning and efficient execution of martial law tasks by specially designated units of the army. [23]

Units that were given much publicity in connection with their martial law operations came from crack divisions of the Polish Army, for example, the 1st Warsaw Mechanized Division, the 6th Airborne Division (Cracow), the 12th Mechanized Division (Szczecin), and the 10th Armored Division (Opole in Silesia); officer and other military schools have also been involved.

Even so, a major effort was needed to ensure that the chosen units contained only politically reliable personnel. To achieve this the political apparatus and commanders of the units employed the whole range of techniques that have already been described in Chapter 4. Teams were made up in such a way that even the smallest had an active party member.

Many army sources stressed the fact that the effective behavior of troops during the martial law operation was the result of solid preparatory work. One political officer wrote that in his regiment this course of events had been expected and preparations started long before December 13. This meant first of all that the formal division between "line" and political officers has disappeared. All officers, especially battalion and company commanders and officers of the Regiment HQ, were engaged in political work. Without their help the Political Department would have been unable to prepare the

troops for martial law duties. They organized a proper flow of
information that was transmitted speedily, honestly, and with
appropriate comments. The Party Committee of the regiment formed
a separate "agitation group," which comprised those officers from
the command HQ and the Political Department that carried authority
and possessed adequate political knowledge. They were briefed the
night before they went out to the troops with a uniform interpretation
of events. The meetings with troops were no longer the old type of
political information hours but true exchanges of views in a friendly
atmosphere. These meetings often exceeded the allotted time so that
all questions could be answered. The important thing was to establish
rapport and find a common language in order to convince. Daily
briefings of party youth organization activists were a separate
feature of this work. This was considered important since they were
spending all the time among the troops. [24]

It appears that party-political work with the troops involved in
the martial law operation has acquired certain new characteristics.
A senior political officer, member of the board of editors of Wojsko
Ludowe, summed up opinions expressed at a meeting of "front line"
party secretaries held in the Chief Political Directorate a few weeks
after the imposition of martial law. Martial law put before party
organizations in the army new concrete tasks: No more simulated
exercises but a deadly earnest situation with a real enemy and a real
threat to the security of the nation and to Socialism. It was necessary
to convince the troops that the home known as Poland was really
threatened and could burn down any moment, so that in their actions
there would be no hesitation and no doubts. In this the members of
the military party had been successful.

The key to success was a method of work known as "small form
of action," which meant that party members worked with small groups
of soldiers reaching every crew and every post with current information. Where possible they formed mixed party/party youth groups
as helpers. They explained the nature and the reasons for action.
They set the tasks and were able to appeal to feelings as well as
to minds.

Party members were not briefed, there were no full party and
no committee meetings, yet the system worked well. Party members
and the regular cadre stayed with the soldiers almost all the time.
They were able to monitor mood and react immediately. Political
officers, commanders, and party secretaries, freed from routine
duties like planning and making returns, were able to devote more
time to working straight with the men. [25]

A political officer described the work of a team of the Political
Section of the 2nd Mechanized Regiment of the 1st Warsaw Mechanized
Division prior to the imposition of martial law and during the first

five months of its duration. Three separate aspects of political
work were explained:

1. Ensuring that commanders, the party-political apparatus,
and party and youth party organizations were preparing the troops,
in the moral-political and psychophysical sense, for action in a true
combat situation as backup for the forces of law and order or for
direct action against open counterrevolutionary actions.
2. Active propaganda and frequent political information hours
mainly with the regular cadre, which in times of political tension
were held every day. Apart from that, short political information
sessions were held every day to give the troops a correct interpretation of the news that reached them by other means.
3. Organizing direct work with the troops. All officers of the
command HQ, of the political apparatus, and of the party committee
were given army and party orders to hold meetings with the regular
cadre, with serving conscripts and civilian army employees.
Political officers attended all meetings held in connection with
service or party matters, organized their own meetings in units,
and conducted individual talks with all soldiers. Newly inducted
conscripts were given priority.

With the imposition of martial law new methods of party-
political work had to be evolved for units that were sent into large
factories. With army units operating in an area covering several
regions, proper deployment of officers of the party-political apparatus and continuous reporting on the morale of troops and immediate
response were of paramount importance. The aim was to have at
least one political officer with a unit operating on its own. The
conclusion of the article was that thanks to the intensive and systematic ideological education work, all objectives had been achieved,
even with recent conscripts and called-up reservists who had taken
part in various protest actions. Military service has helped them to
calm down and accept WRON policy as the only right one.[26]
One source described the role of the Party Committee of the
12th Mechanized Division in the first days of martial law. The
division was "protecting" several factories at Szczecin, including
the shipyard. The secretary of the Division Party Committee related
to the Divisional Command information about the situation in the
shipyard that he had received from the civilian party secretary at
the shipyard. The committee meeting held at midmight surveyed the
situation in the field, took decisions, and allotted tasks. Members
learned about the newly issued rules on "party work under martial
law conditions," which aimed to increase party discipline and
accelerate decisionmaking. On the fifth day of martial law the

secretary of the Party Committee of the Pomeranian Military District came to talk to the troops. He said the army would prevent the over-throwing of Socialism but at the same time remove the deformations that had accumulated over the last decade.[27]

FIELD OPERATION GROUPS

Field Operation Groups (TGO) are army personnel made up into small teams and prepared for special nonmilitary duties in the civilian sector. They are an improved version of similar teams that were used by the provisional Communist government to win the first elections to the Polish Seym in January 1947 (see Chapter 1). They played a key role immediately before and during martial law and were deployed after the lifting of martial law. In the arsenal of the political military they have become one of the means of political coercion.

The decision to deploy TGO was taken by General Jaruzelski, presumably in his capacity as prime minister. It was approved by the Council of Ministers on October 23, 1981. The reasons for this measure were explained to the Polish people in a TV address by General T. Hupalowski, who was minister of administration and environment.

On October 26, 1981, TGO were sent out to over 2,000 towns and villages. Their brief was to assist organs of local administration and economy in the fulfilment of their functions. In addition they were to assist and "inspire" political, social, and professional bodies and other organizations in their economic and social functions and to cooperate with them in satisfying the most urgent needs of the people; improve the system of supplies, trade, and services for the population; cut out waste, mismanagement, and speculation; help to maintain law and order; and finally deal with most urgent local problems and with complaints from the population.

According to Wojsko Ludowe, TGO were able to improve matters in all the above respects. They also amassed suggestions and postulates that gave the central authorities a fairly objective picture of the situation on the ground and served as source material for analysis and for preparing appropriate functional, structural, and personnel improvements. On November 23, 1981, that is, after less than a month, General Jaruzelski decided to withdraw TGO temporarily. Before they left TGO organized meetings for summing up their work and they drew up a list of matters that had not been dealt with. The heads of TGO submitted their reports at region level and took part in meetings with political and administrative authorities of the region to sum up work done at region level. Collective reports from regions were sent to the Council of Ministers for study.

TGO withdrawn from fieldwork retained their readiness to take up the next tour of duty in the same localities. This began on December 10, 1981, that is three days before the imposition of martial law, ostensibly for checking implementation of decisions taken during the first tour.

In the meanwhile a new type of TGO was being formed. These were destined for regional towns and large conurbations, ostensibly to prepare them for the coming winter. On November 26, 1981, over 150 of these new groups, known as Urban Operation Groups (MTGO), were sent out to all 49 regional towns and 44 large towns. MTGO had 10-15 people and were therefore larger than TGO, which had 5-6 people. Depending on the size of the town, there could be 20 or more groups in one place. MTGO were reinforced with officer-specialists from service branches of the army like communications, quartermaster, supply, health, motor transport, and other technical services.

A third type of operation group, known as Military operation-inspection Groups (WGO-K), was formed when Jaruzelski became concerned that discipline and productivity in state enterprises, including defense industries, were rapidly falling. After appropriate training these groups were sent to selected enterprises on November 23, 1981. WGO-K consisting of 3-5 officers each covered one or more factories. They worked together with the management, political and social organizations, and with representatives of the work force. Any irregularities that worried the workers were reported to the appropriate administrative or economic bodies. On December 8 and 11 a second batch of WGO-K was sent to factories and this time also to the next higher level, to offices of branches of industry.

Next Jaruzelski established a Central Operation Group (CGO) for the coordination of the work of all TGO, MTGO, and WGO-K and for analyzing their reports. Military District Operation Groups (OGO) were formed to coordinate the activities of all groups working in the area of a military district and to produce comprehensive reports for the CGO. The OGO were assisted by the Military Staffs of Regions (WSzW), who looked after the groups in regions.

Heads of groups were given a "Guide for the Head of Group" containing all the information needed for the proper execution of duties. In addition the Chief Political Directorate issued to the groups special instructions on political and propaganda work to be carried out within the area of their responsibility. This was to be done in conjunction with local party, party youth, and other organizations.[28]

With the imposition of martial law the heads of the various operation groups became commissaries of the National Defense Committee (KOK) known also as plenipotentiaries of KOK. That meant that they were transformed into a key element of the military administration under the overall control of Jaruzelski's Military

Council of National Salvation. The personnel of the groups remained
as office and other support for the commissaries.

The Polish people at first really believed the official propaganda
that the various operation groups were a genuine attempt on the part
of Jaruzelski's government to alleviate the burdens of the crisis in
the coming winter. The imposition of martial law dispelled any such
illusions. Having carried out a kind of diversion, TGO established
bridgeheads in the civilian sector prior to the army's main assault
that came with martial law. The various operation groups, some
20,000 army personnel placed in key points, well in advance of the
main operation and well acquainted with the situation on the ground,
played a crucial role in the martial law operation. And in addition
there were the 33,000 army personnel employed in the civilian
sector in various defense-linked posts (see Chapter 6 and Figure 3).

WOOING ARMY PENSIONERS

The decision to form the Association of ex-Regular Army
Soldiers (ZBZZ) was taken on February 12, 1981, the day after
General Jaruzelski became prime minister. The founders were a
group of retired officers well connected with the political military.
ZBZZ was not formally constituted until June 1981, but it obtained
the status of a "higher utility organization" in April 1981. It was to
be expected that ZBZZ would be 100 percent behind the political
army in its confrontation with Solidarity. The manner of the support
was described in an interview with General (ret'd) B. Marchewka,
deputy chairman of ZBZZ in March 1982. He said that from the first
day of martial law thousands of retired soldiers performed duties
with groups that had been protecting army and state buildings. From
the beginning of 1982 they were explaining the facts of martial law to
young people in schools. They worked in antispeculation commissions,
with teams of military commissars, and with military operation
groups in towns and villages. They also sat on special courts that
tried martial law offenders. Many members were earmarked for full-
time positions as "deputy directors for defense matters" in schools.[29]

ZBZZ members were told in advance that they would be
rewarded for their services. Thus, according to one source, a few
days before the constitution meeting, on June 12, 1981, the Founding
Committee had signed an agreement with the Ministry of Defense, in
which the latter guaranteed second careers, improved pension rights,
and provided better living conditions. For example, members were
to be employed as "consultants and experts" in army units in the
field of training and education or commissioned to carry out research
and write up the history of individual regiments. They were also

to research the economic conditions of retired army personnel
and their families.

In another part of the agreement the ministry committed itself
to consult the main board of ZBZZ on planned legislation concerning
the rights of former soldiers, to include representatives of ZBZZ in
the Council of the Ministry for living conditions and in the Pensions
Commission of the ministry Finance Department. Special attention
was to be given to the matter of updating some earlier pensions.
Welfare was to be improved by granting access to army messes,
clubs, canteens, rest homes, and cultural and recreation facilities.[30]

General Marchewka, in the above-quoted source, also said
that members of ZBZZ proved by their attitudes and dedication that
they deserve better treatment than they had before. They wanted to
be remembered not only when the Socialist fatherland was in danger.
He gave the assurance that all the individual claims were being
effectively processed.

According to another source, in September 1981 ZBZZ signed
a cooperation agreement with the 2.5 million-strong KOR-LOK
organization (see Chapter 6), which secured for ZBZZ members
employment as instructors in defense training.[31]

In June 1982 the membership of ZBZZ reached 22,000, but at
least double that number was forecast. In the beginning ZBZZ groups
were attached to local army units, but gradually the national and
regional network was established.

The first chairman of ZBZZ was Colonel (ret'd) Roman Les; the
secretary was Colonel (ret'd) A. Jamrozinski. Both had been political
officers since the times of the Polish Army in the Soviet Union and
therefore were colsely linked with the political military. Colonel Les
was made member of WRON. It was not clear whether this was because
of the chairmanship of ZBZZ or his doctorate in economics, which made
him the only member of WRON with some knowledge of economics.
Until his retirement on health grounds in 1975 he worked as lecturer
in the Department of Economics of the Military Political Academy.
It was Colonel Les who said that there were no retired officers
because the majority of them worked somewhere. They ran self-
defense units based on localities and factories and worked in schools
as teachers of defense subjects.[32] Generals Jaruzelski, Tuczapski,
and Baryla, three prominent members of WRON, attended the founding congress of ZBZZ. In a speech made on this occasion Jaruzelski
said that just as during the war and the period of consolidating the
people's rule, retired officers, junior officers, and NCOs of the
Polish Army were now again in the foremost front line.[33]

On the main board of the ZBZZ is Colonel (ret'd) Brailowski,
who also happens to be chairman of the National Council of Former
Members of the Soviet Army. This organization has about 10,000

members with groups in 35 regions of the country. It was started in 1970 and became a component of ZBoWiD, the veterans' and combatants' association. Like ZBZZ it fully supports the policies of the political military.[34]

It is curious that the political military should have gone to all this trouble to secure support from a few thousand ex-servicemen when they should have been able to count on hundreds of thousands of serving Polish Army and Security Forces personnel. Several possible reasons spring to mind. The date of the decision suggests an element of panic. Early in 1981 Jaruzelski had a small revolt in the army on his hands and probably welcomed some help from the "old guard" who, like himself, owed everything to the system that was in peril. But army pensioners had been badly neglected under Gierek. Hence the deal on pensions and second careers to repair the damage and also to indicate to personnel still in service that under Jaruzelski they would be taken care of in retirement. Finally, one should not forget that in 1981 the top political military were rapidly approaching retirement themselves and this would have made them more interested in postarmy-life conditions. As it happened, however, they were able to make better provisions for themselves when they became top dogs of the system (see Chapter 12).

11
Martial Law: Warnings, Scope, and Machinery

Judging by the absence of contingency planning by leaders
of Solidarity, all preparations for martial law and warnings
issued by the political military passed unnoticed. The
first, it seems, were hidden under the veil of "military
secrets," the second were not taken seriously because the
political military always spoke in the name of the party, not
in the name of the political army. The party everybody
knew, was on the run.

Before but mainly after the imposition of martial
law the political military was trying to justify the army's
intervention. Some aims were revealed in the process.
The true objectives like the need to restore the Warsaw
Pact logistic infrastructure in the "Polish corridor" and
to neutralize the opposition to their plans of political
domination were carefully hidden from view. Yet the extent
of that opposition within the civilian party and state administration and even within their own military party must have
given them sleepless nights. I think these reasons rather
than the Solidarity threat to the system dictated the scale
of the martial law operation and the extensive measures
taken under the cover of martial law and after.

Many elements of the martial law machinery have
become permanent features of Polish public life through
new legislation. It was said that the institutions and
procedures "proved themselves" under difficult conditions
of martial law. Since they have not solved any of Poland's
basic problems, it must be assumed that their role was
to carry the political military to the top and to ensure
that they do stay there.

WARNINGS AND JUSTIFICATION

At the 9th Party Congress (July 1981) General Jaruzelski spoke as head of government and commander of the Polish armed forces. In his first capacity he said that a state can function only in conditions of law and order. Anarchy attacks the basic interests of the nation. There are limits that must not be exceeded. The state authority would be forced to fulfill its constitutional obligations, should the situation warrant such a course and so save the state from collapse and the nation from catastrophe.

About the army, he said that during the current difficult period it did not even wince, retained cohesion and discipline, always ready to defend the fatherland and its Socialist achievements. The army was a great armed force that would do everything to serve the nation in a peacetime emergency. The Polish people and the party had confidence that, as in the past, the Army would not fail them. He added that he hoped that party members who were also members of Solidarity would activiely oppose extremist elements of Solidarity that were hostile to the party and caused damage to Socialism. It should be made clear to all that people's rule, the power of the Socialist state, will not be surrendered. There should be no illusions on that score and no playing with fire. The call "Let Poland be Poland" means that in present times Poland must be Socialist.[1]

General J. Baryla was more explicit in his speech at the congress. He assured the comrades that the army would defend Socialism as it would defend Poland's independence, that it would not accept anything that strikes at the Polish reason of state and the foundations of the system. Those who incite others against the existing system, against the party, against existing alliances, especially the Polish-Soviet alliance and the Polish-Soviet brother-hood-of-arms, should not count on forbearance. It was the army's duty to strengthen the alliance, which was the basic condition of Poland's security.[2]

Both these warnings must have come as a surprise to delegates at the congress. In the "party program theses" prepared for the congress by the Congress Commission there had been no reference to any special role or obligations of the army in the solutions of the economic and political crises. Furthermore, the Congress Resolution did not confer any such special duties on the army. Yet the political army having inspired subsequent warnings by the Party Central Committee and its Political Bureau used them as justification for the army's intervention.

The primary source of the warnings is all too apparent. They reflect the credo of the political army. And so, in the Resoulution of the 11th plenary session of the Party Central Committee, it says:

- Poland was and will remain a Socialist country

- Friendship with the Soviet Union is the conerstone of Poland's foreign policy

- Poland will continue to build the political and military cooperation within the Warsaw Pact framework

- Poland is prepared to continue cooperation with other social and economic systems.[3]

On September 16, 1981, the Political Bureau of the party issued a declaration that the decisions of the Solidarity Congress at Gdansk, which began on September 5, 1981, broke the 1980 agreements and replaced them with a political opposition program that was directed against Poland's interests and led to confrontation and bloodshed. It was, the declaration said, a program of KSS-KOR and KPN and not of the workers in Solidarity.[4]

The 4th Plenary Session of the Party Central Committee (October 16-18, 1981) repeated the charges and addressed to the leadership of Solidarity six specific demands: observance of the Constitution and laws, cutting links with enemies of Socialism, stopping all strikes, cooperation with the government, respect for alliances and action against anti-Soviet propaganda, and respect for Poland's defense requirements, The resolution also stated the urgent need to renegotiate the Gdansk agreements.[5] The last warning before the imposition of martial law was issued by the 6th Plenary Session (November 28, 1981). The resolution said that measures would be taken against those who attack the party and the state.[6]

The first tangible warning of imminent major army operations was the deferment of release from conscript service of those who by October 6, 1981, would have completed 24 months of service. They were told about it only a few days earlier. No future date of release was given but soldiers were granted additional pay and privileges— for example, the chance of promotion above the rank of corporal that was hitherto restricted to regular soldiers. On October 23 came the deployment of Field Operation Groups.

Fratricidal War

Attempts to justify the army's intervention were made on various planes and from various angles. The first theme was that martial law prevented a fratricidal war. This was intended to counter the effect on public opinion of the loss of lives and brutality shown in

Wojsko Ludowe stated categorically that had the drastic decision of
the night of December 12-13, 1981, not been taken, the country
would have been deep in a fratricidal war. This apparently emerged
from documents seized in various offices of Solidarity. Imposition
of martial law was choosing a lesser evil. A war and its consequences
would have been felt for decades. The army's strength, organization,
and authority among the Polish people were used to strengthen
independence and respect for the state and eliminate anarchy and
disruption. [7]

The first proclamation issued by WRON said that the fatherland
was in mortal danger and that antistate, subversive, and anti-
Socialist forces had brought society to the brink of civil war. Colonel
M. Leczyk, the historian, wrote that in December 1981 Poland found
itself face to face with a fratricidal war. One Pole threatened another
with gallows, some people blinded with hatred of Socialism were
prepared to destroy the common home, burn down places of work,
and destroy all structures of social and political life. Streams of
Polish blood, human lives, ruin, and new graves, did not seem a
high price to pay. The Polish Army wrote another chapter of its
history, this time how it saved the country from fratricidal war. [8]

There is no evidence whatsoever that Solidarity and the rest
of the opposition ever planned this kind of confrontation. Unconfirmed
reports say that the evidence quoted was organized provocation.

The Polish Corridor

The need to restore Poland's defense capacity was a more
genuine justification for martial law. According to an article in
Wojsko Ludowe the high credibility of the Polish Army remained
unaffected by the political and economic crisis but Poland's defense
depended also on a number of nonmilitary factors, like geographical
position, external political links, international position, economic
situation, social and political situation, and scientific and technical
potential. Of all these only the first two elements remained unaffected.
Everything else has suffered deterioration, namely social discipline,
functioning of state administration, material production, transport
and communication, law and order, relations between professional
groups, supply of consumer goods, cooperation in industry, not to
mention the new social structures (Solidarity) with aims that were
incompatible with the interests of the state and nation. The result of
it all was a fall in Poland's international position and of its credibility
as a political and economic partner. It would be nonsense to maintain
that Poland's defense capacity did not suffer.

Admittedly, the article goes on, under the defense umbrella of the Warsaw Pact Poland has a better chance to solve its internal problems. Poland's frontiers are to some extent protected by the Joint Forces of the Warsaw Pact. At the same time one should bear in mind at least two important factors. First, even a temporary weakening of the defense capacity of Poland has a negative effect on the whole of the coalition because each member is expected to fulfill certain assigned tasks within the alliance. Second, Poland has toward its allies very concrete and time-scheduled obligations. Inability to meet the commitments would greatly affect the defense capacity of the coalition, apart from undermining Poland's reliability and credibility. The main thing, however, was that the balance of forces in Europe would be affected, thus endangering peace.[9]

The above extraordinarily frank admissions (for a serious Soviet bloc publication) were made by Colonel (diplomaed) Ireneusz Ruszkiewicz, deputy-chief editor of Wojsko Ludowe since 1977 and member of the board of editors at least since 1973. The article was written in connection with the 26th anniversary of the Warsaw Pact. Five months later the same admissions were repeated in another Ruszkiewicz article written in connection with the 38th anniversary of the Polish People's Army. There was one small difference. By then not two but one of the elements of defense capacity remained unchanged, namely Poland's geographical position.[10]

Colonel Ruszkiewicz ceased to appear as member of the board with No. 9, 1982 issue of Wojsko Ludowe. It had been noticed, much too late, that his remarks were an open admission of weaknesses in the logistic infrastructure of the Warsaw Pact in Poland.

STATE OF NEAR-WAR—A TYPE OF MARTIAL LAW

It appears that the English term "martial law" would in Polish conditions cover two different situations. They are defined in the Small Military Encyclopedia and are quoted here in full to bring out the difference and its implications. A state of emergency ("exceptional state" in Polish)

> is a situation resulting from a decision by higher state
> authorities (head of state, prime minister) that brings
> various limitations of political and personal freedom in
> connection with a dangerous internal situation caused by
> acts (sometimes with the use of arms) political demon-
> strations, terrorist actions, strike waves, attacks on
> police, and other acts that threaten the security of the
> state and public order. The state of emergency may
> bring suspension of public meeting rights, freedom of

speech and movement, curfew, inspection of documents and means of transport, summary court proceedings, extension of powers for organs of state administration, police and law enforcement agencies, use of the army for riot control, and other measures not used in normal conditions. It can apply to the whole or a part of the country. . . .

On the state of near-war (Stan wojenny in Polish) the entry says:

In accordance with the Constitution the Council of State may introduce the state of near-war on the whole or on a part of the country's territory and proclaim full or part mobilization (call-up). Introduction of state near-war is as a rule linked with a declaration of a state of war. The state of near-war may be introduced by a law or decree that describes in detail the legal consequences. It may, inter alia, bring a suspension or limitation of some citizens' rights, internment of aliens, military courts and summary proceedings, higher penalties for crimes affecting defense and security, taking over the powers of administrative organs in areas threatened or directly affected by enemy action, duty to remove the effects of air attacks, personal and material war contributions, evacuation of people and belongings from threatened areas.[11]

Thus the first difference was that there were provisions in Poland's Constitution for a state of near-war but not for a state of emergency. This came in very handy because the state of near-war (which we shall continue to call martial law) gave the political military the wide powers they needed to effect the political takeover of the country. Such powers would not have been available under a state of emergency. Furthermore, although Article 33 of the Constitution foresaw the introduction of martial law for reasons of defense and for reasons of state security, there were no statutory provisions that explained the effect and consequences of martial law. Thus the political military had a free hand drafting the provisions to suit the 1981 stiuation. These were issued as a "Decree on Martial Law" in confunction with a resolution of the Council of State on the day martial law was introduced. One should perhaps add that the Polish term for martial law carries the notion of facing a firing squad when orders are not obeyed. This must have had an effect on the troops used in the operation.

After the lifting of martial law an amendment to the Constitution brought in provisions for a state of emergency. The new rulers may feel that these would be adequate for some future situations.

MARTIAL LAW INSTITUTIONS

The various martial law institutions are described in detail because most of them suitably adjusted and updated progressed into the postmartial law era.

Control and management of affairs of the country under martial law was vested in the following institutions:

- Military Council of National Salvation (WRON),

- Country's Defense Committee (KOK) and its military commissaries (also known as plenipotentiaries of KOK),

- Regional Defense Committees (WKO),

- Inspection Commission (from the Inspection Department of the army).

Military Council of National Salvation

WRON became the supreme authority in the country. Its composition and the personal background of its members are given in Appendix A. In its first proclamation on December 13, 1981, WRON said that with the backing of the armed forces and the expected support of all patriotic and progressive social forces it was determined to ensure internal order and the country's security, that it was a temporary organ that would function until the situation was brought back to normal. It was not limiting the competences and not taking over duties from any existing state organ. Its aim was to snuff out the coup against the state, stabilize the situation, and ensure and enforce by legal means the effective functioning of organs of administration and of the national economy. WRON declared that it stands by Poland's political and defense alliances and honors international agreements and obligations concluded by the government of the Polish People's Republic. [12]

According to Colonel Z. Czerwinski, chief editor of Wojsko Ludowe, in its plans and actions WRON followed the basic line adopted at the 9th Congress of the Party (July 1981). The latter, he wrote, had correctly analyzed the causes and the consequences of mistakes made in the political and economic sphere and drew proper conclusions. In practice that meant overcoming all the bad things that date back to the era before August 1980 as well as to the Solidarity era. [13]

A chronicle of events throws some light on the functioning of

WRON. In the whole of 1982 WRON held 14 meetings, whereas in the early days of martial law, that is, in the first days of December 17, 1981, it held 7 meetings. A variety of subjects was covered: functioning of the state administration and of the economy, repressive measures against the opposition, building of national concord, education of the young, gradual lifting of restrictions, and so on. Public relations were not neglected and there were separate meetings with representatives of workers, peasants, and the womenfolk. The modus operandi was simple: WRON issued binding instructions to the authorities concerned and military commissaries of all levels supervised implementation. Here are three examples:

1. Meeting of December 16, 1981: WRON instructed the government to make a "survey" of all staff employed in state administration, to dismiss at the recommendation of commissaries all who were found to be inefficient or corrupt and to inspect the management of enterprises that had been militarized under martial law. The criterion of suitability for a post was security of the state (that is, political reliability).

2. Meeting of September 1, 1982: WRON obligated Regional Defense Committees to take appropriate and decisive steps to ensure peace and public security; asked the prosecutor general to complete the investigations against members of KSS-KOR and send them for trial; asked law enforcement authorities and the judiciary to take proceedings against people causing disturbances; asked the ministers of science, higher education, and standard education to investigate the unworthy behavior of adults and students and to take suitable measures.

3. Meeting of September 12, 1982: WRON asked the Seym to speed up the bill on procedures against adults who avoid work or schooling, increase penalties in the law on speculation and in parts of the Criminal Code concerning bribery; it asked the law enforcement authorities and the judiciary to apply stiffer penalties for normal and economic crimes.[14]

In his martial law introduction speech General Jaruzelski said that WRON would be dissolved when the rule of law had been restored and the civilian administration and elected bodies had begun to function normally. Although neither Jaruzelski nor WRON itself in its proclamation linked WRON with the duration of martial law, it was in fact dissolved when martial law was lifted in July 1983.

This does not necessarily mean the end of this institution. Colonel-Malina wrote in Wojsko Ludowe that the suspension or even lifting of martial law would not automatically create a case for eliminating the existing elements of control over Polish political and economic life. It appears that it will be necessary to continue the activities of WRON until, speaking in general terms, the country gets out of the crisis completely and all the functions of the constitutional bodies are strengthened. Experience in the defense sector suggested that WRON would be transformed into a highest constitutional authority responsible for defense matters and become a State Defense Council that would be a suitable solution covering both peace- and wartime conditions. The above comment did not represent a personal view of the writer. The article in question was published under the general heading "From the Discussion at the 4th Ideological Conference of the Polish Armed Forces," which took place in November 1982.[15] The idea was implemented in November 1983 (see Chapter 12).

National Defense Committee and its Plenipotentiaries

The position of the KOK in Poland's defense system and its role in peacetime are described in Chapter 1. Under martial law its role was increased beyond recognition mainly because it controlled thousands of the political army's chosen personnel who imposed Jaruzelski's version of "military" government.

On the first day of martial law the KOK issued an order that militarized key parts of the state administration and of the economy. A comprehensive list included central organizations of railways, road transport, postal, telephone, and telegraph communications, broadcasting and television, units of the communications protection service, oil products distribution, some power generation plants, port facilities, industrial freight services, fire-fighting services, enterprises and sections producing special goods (for defense and allied needs), local communication services, and other organizations. Employees of the above organizations and institutions were "called-up for service" and their civilian contract of service was suspended. The order also contained specific provisions that personnel serving or called up for service in Civil Defense were considered to be on active service.[16]

With the imposition of martial law, heads of the Field Operation (TGO) already deployed before martial law became military commissaries (plenipotentiaries of KOK) and assumed supervision and inspection duties. More important were the commissaries of the KOK appointed to ministries, certain central offices, military districts, regions, towns and town districts, town-villages, and certain enterprises and party offices. The commissaries, numbering over 2,000, were supported directly by some 5,000 mainly regular army personnel. Various martial law legal acts gave the commissaries extensive powers. They were directly subordinated to the chairman of the KOK, the prime minister, and the Chairman of WRON—that is, to General Jaruzelski, who held all three positions.

The role of commissaries was to remove the threat to Poland's security and defense capacity, in particular to secure the needs of the armed forces, ensure the proper functioning of transport, signal communications, power supply, and pipelines. They were to militarize certain sectors of the economy, ensure social discipline and observance of martial law regulations, and the supply of essential goods to the population. They were to combat speculation, waste, and mismanagement and to ensure that information transmission was kept within the law.

In order to achieve the above goals commissaries were assisting their own organizations to fulfill their functions and coordinating work with other organizations. It was their duty to provide the state authorities with current and reliable information on the area of responsibility. They were also expected to dissolve tensions in factories and to create the right conditions for the introduction of economic reforms.

In January 1982, after barely one month of operation, the functioning of the system of commissaries was checked out. The aim was to examine the effects of their work and the response of the population. This was done in 25 regions at region level and below. In May 1982 the system was reorganized. It was said this was made possible by the progressing stabilization. The following changes were made:

- Small teams of three to four army personnel with competences of military operation groups were formed to cover five villages and the small industries in them; they had their own means of transport and were led by commissaries of the KOK.

- Commissaries and operation groups in regional towns and large urban complexes were retained but were reduced in size to two to four officers.

- At region level separate supervision and inspection teams consisting of 10-15 officers with their own means of transport were formed and put at the disposal of the regional commissary, and covered the whole region in two subgroups, one urban and one rural.

Summing up the information on commissaries of the KOK it has been stated that "the assistance given by the officer corps to directing and management bodies of the state brought visible good results and enhanced the authority of the armed forces and that General Jaruzelski had referred to army officers as the mobile reserve of the People's Rule."[17]

It appears that the Field Operation Groups that were no longer needed after the May 1982 reorganization were not fully disbanded. They were sent out again on November 23, 1982, to inspect the functioning of administration at lower levels. The inspection covered most towns and villages all over Poland and was completed by December 12, 1982.[18]

In the first phase, before May 1982, commissaries headed operational groups in 1,059 enterprises and 1,064 localities. After May 1982, 528 commissaries and their teams covered 830 enterprises. In addition there were the commissaries in ministries and central offices and the separate supervision and inspection groups that worked for the commissaries in regions. It has been stated that the system of commissaries proved to be a most efficient instrument of supervision of the administration.[19] With the lifting of martial law, nearly 8,000 commissaries ended their duties and were withdrawn.

In early spring 1982 General Jaruzelski ordered a special operation, "Spring 82," in which officers of the army technical services and quartermaster and civilian specialists worked together with the TGO. It was reported that 976 teams inspected state, cooperative, and individual farms in 1,700 villages. The teams investigated the use of land, distribution of means of production, condition of agricultural equipment, purchase/delivery procedures of agricultural products, services to agriculture, and so on.[20]

The work of military commissaries and of TGO was widely publicized in the official press, especially military publications. Reports of their activities also represent a unique source of information about the depth of the Polish crisis and its extent. They prove beyond any doubt that devastation on that scale could not have been brought about by a band of indolent and corrupt "former" leaders. It is the result of the system. Telling examples of this are two reports on the situation on the land[21] and one on the ecological situation in the industrial region of Silesia.[22] The reports carry the message that superficial administrative measures taken by the army were not likely to have lasting effect.

Regional Defense Committees

Regional Defense Committees (WKO) were part of Poland's defense system (see Chapter 1). Under martial law their role was enhanced because they assumed directing powers over the regional and local administration authorities and a strict coordinating role in respect to all other organizations, especially economic enterprises located in the region. The WKO comprises the key personnel of the region. The head of the military staffs of the region who always was a prominent member of the WKO has in many instances been appointed commissary of the KOK for the region and supervised WKO activities. Under martial law the WKO became responsible for law and order, satisfying the basic needs of the population, proper functioning of administration, and continuity of industrial production. [23]

It appears that General Jaruzelski was not satisfied with progress made in the first six months of martial law. At three successive meetings of WRON, on August 20, September 1 and 12, 1981, the WKO were instructed to take drastic steps aimed at improving the situation in regions. [24]

An earlier quoted source suggested that the WKOs with the wider terms of reference given to them by WRON in August and September 1981 should continue for some time after the lifting of martial law. They have developed ways and means of dealing with social and political problems, with matters of law and order, speculation and economic crimes, improvement of administration and of the economy, including assistance to agriculture and provision of goods and housing for the population. The same applies to the institution of commissaries of KOK who, in a modified form, adapted to the changing political and economic situation, could fulfill a useful role while the country is trying to beat the crisis. The lifting of martial law would not create conditions for an automatic removal of all elements of control over the administration used under martial law. [25]

Numerous press reports about WKO sessions held after the lifting of martial law confirm that the WKOs are concerned with all aspects of life in a region in the same way as did the Regional Party Committee in the days when the party was still fulfilling its leading role.

Inspection Commission

The inspection slant of martial law institutions was further reinforced by bringing in the Inspection Department of the Armed Forces. A full account of this activity was given in the army daily at the end of 1982. From December 1981 to February 1982 a large number of officers of the department underwent practical training for the new role of inspecting the civilian sector. The Warsaw region served as a guinea pig. In March 1982 General Jaruzelski ordered a specially formed commission to carry out full inspections in individual regions. By the end of 1982 ten regions had been inspected and in three of them a second inspection was made to check on implementation of recommendations of the first inspection. On average 120-130 people are involved in one inspection. Of that number 60 percent were military personnel from the Inspection Department. The remainder were civilian inspectors of ministries and central offices.

The commission was accompanied by a team from the Central Audit Commission of the party, which took note of the findings that were of concern to the party.

An inspection lasted on the average two weeks. It covered ten sectors that had the greatest influence on the administration and economy in the region and on the conditions of life of the population. The day after an inspection a signal was sent to General Jaruzelski. General W. Mroz, head of the Inspection Department and chairman of the commission, said that the aim of an inspection was to form a composite picture of the situation in the region, showing cause and effect links that if properly analyzed and evaluated can indicate main lines of necessary action. Full-scale inspections of this type have never before been made in the civilian sector. They always had been narrow and fragmentary.

In this way a new system of inspection in the public sector came into being. Its uniformity could help to obtain a full picture of the situation in the country, bring to light the causes of existing shortages and shortcomings, and prevent their occurrence in the future. Furthermore, since inspections have established negligence in the fulfillment of duties, it makes sense to bring into the civilian sector the army principles that "everybody has a range of duties, carries them out well and reports the fact; he is then checked out in an inspection." Unless the same system is introduced in civilian life the incredible waste of time, of human abilities and qualifications, of means and materials, continues. It was General Jaruzelski himself who introduced the concept of "reinspection" when he said at one time that an inspection is finished when it has been established that conclusions and recommendation of the first part of the inspection had been implemented.

The author concluded by saying that the Inspection Department of the armed forces rendered a great service to the national economy by evolving the methodology of full-scale inspections of regions that probably will become a permanent feature of state administration.[26] He was right about that. A few months later the Ministry of Defense handed the inspection commitment over to the Ministry of Administration, Regional/Local Economy, and Environment Protection where a Chief Inspection Commission had been formed for this purpose. It is a copy of the Commission of the Inspection Department described above. According to a newspaper report, when the new commission began its work on the next region in line a group of officers from the Inspection Department of the armed forces acted as advisers.[27] Thus another of the martial law institutions was carried over into the postmartial law era.

Love of inspection jobs is characteristic of the political army. General T. Hupalowski, minister of administration since 1981, replaced in April 1983 General (of Security Service) M. Moczar as chairman of the Supreme Chamber of Control (NIK). Hupalowski, a member of WRON, thus became the supreme inspector in the country, making room for General Oliwa, another member of WRON who as minister of administration will be in charge of the new Chief Inspection Commission.

There is a simple explanation. The most tangible result of inspections was the sacking of incompetent, corrupt, or politically unreliable people. The political military was interested in that but even more in the resulting vacancies (compare Chapter 12).

12
Consolidation of Political Power

The political military used the state of martial law to
destroy the organization structure of Solidarity. This was
given widest publicity in Poland and abroad. That they
also used martial law provisions to eliminate a substantial
opposition to their policies in the civilian as well as the
military party is not so well known, although this involved
large-scale purges in both bodies. Having contained the
immediate threat to Soviet control in Poland the political
military set about consolidating its position. The always
obedient Seym produced legislation that strengthened the
Soviet-Socialist character of its rule and provided a
framework for a nationwide personnel policy. This helped
the placing of its own people in key positions and to secure
influence on any other important appointments. This was
perhaps the only area in which the political military could
count on some support from the Polish people.

CIVILIAN COMMUNIST PARTY NOT AN ASSET

Military sources never miss an opportunity to imply that the
army has saved the party from extinction. According to one source,
martial law found the party disarmed, incapable of action, and completely off balance. Party organizations were unable to control opinion
in factories and even in their own ranks. Many could not show that
they served any useful purpose, The party was unable to carry the
burden of its own faults and defend itself against attacks by internal
and external enemies. Martial law brought the stabilization that gave
the party a chance to renew itself, restore its links with the working

191

class and the people, and get rid of members who were ideologically neutral or alien.[1] The army weekly repeated the popular saying that of the four components of the name Polish United Workers' Party, not even one was true.[2]

The low morale of the civilian party during the early stage of martial law caused a propaganda vacuum that had to be filled by the military party. According to a lead article in the army weekly magazine, members of the military party were the first to go to schools, factories, steel works, mines, and other places of work as emissaries of the "party in uniform." They explained the legality of decisions of WRON, the program of the party, the need to fight the enemy, and the line of national revival and concord. They explained who was behind the ideological subversion directed by the West against Poland and the Socialist countries.[3]

The scale of this activity was described in a military daily paper. In 1982 the regular cadre of the Warsaw Military District "participated" in 6,395 meetings with the young of school age that were attended by 420,000, in 2,300 meetings with teachers attended by 47,000, and in 894 meetings with workers attended by 78,000.[4] Another source stated that activists of the military party of the Silesian Military District conducted party-political work in 207 large enterprises, and members of party youth in the army helped the civilian youth organization in 44 factories.[5]

Even party members of central departments of the MON found the time to meet with workers in factories and with students and teachers in schools. Their presence helped to calm the atmosphere, discourage the opposition, give confidence to the civilian party, improve the feeling of security, and counter various forms of "social pathology."[6]

At the Party Conference of the Warsaw Military District (February 1983) General W. Oliwa, member of WRON, urged activists of the military party to give fullest support to the party and government through "enlightenment actions" in factories, universities, and schools.[7] Army activists were asked to give a hand in rebuilding civilian party organizations in factories. But one secretary of a Party Committee of a military district complained that the party organizations in factories expected the army to do the job for them. He said that the army could not take on so many new duties and forever stand in for others. As the situation in factories began to stabilize, cooperation with the civilian party needed to be put on a different footing. Another party secretary of the same level stated that there were signs of physical fatigue and psychological weariness resulting from excessive duties. Many officers were engaged in duties outside the army, in factories, institutions, or state administration offices. Those who remained with units had to

accept additional duties. Having to remain on duty for 12 hours a day
must have a bad effect on ideological education work. [8]

At the 4th Ideological Conference of the Armed Forces (November 1982) General J. Baryla, Head of the GZP and member of
WRON, said:

> So far we have been able to restore the party's leading
> role in the state as guaranteed by the Constitution, but
> its guiding role in society is still not being adequately
> fulfilled. To be able to do this, to command the people's
> hearts for good, the party needs unity and cohesion
> in its ranks. It needs to regain credibility. This process
> will take a long time and calls for a huge effort because
> there are still many obstacles in the way.

Among the obstacles, according to Baryla, were on the one
hand liberal and rightist tendencies, "post-Solidarity reflexes,"
nationalist and chauvinistic echoes, and on the other hand ultra-left
pseudorevolutionary slogans. Against this background the party in
the army gave a splendid example when it achieved internal integration
in such a diverse organism as the army. The fact that so many
"Communists in uniform" have been elected to central and regional
offices of the (civilian) party testifies to their growing authority.
Proof of this is that many officers are engaged in drafting documents
of key and strategic importance to the party and the country. [9]

While the political military claimed that they were restoring
the party and its authority, party membership was falling faster than
ever before. In February 1983 Trybuna Ludu published a long report
on the activities of the party in 1982. It contains a statement that in
1982 the party lost 352,500 members and acquired 7,600 members.
It says that the majority left in the first quarter of 1982, that is, in
the first few months of martial law. If one were to apply the same
rate of loss to the first 17 days of martial law in December 1981, the
total loss of party membership to the end of 1982 would be at
least 400,000. [10]

Another source says that from July 1980 to the end of 1982
some 800,000 people left the party or were removed from it, bringing total party membership down to 2,340,000. [11] The figures mean
that about the same number left the party during the 16 months of the
Solidarity era as during the 12 months of martial law. More significant
than the numbers themselves is that they included a very large part
of party directing personnel. At the 7th Plenary Session of the
Central Committee (February 24, 1982), the first after the imposition
of martial law, General Jaruzelski declared: "Since December 13,
1981, due to resignations and decisions of party authorities, there
have been personnel changes: 311 secretaries of committees of the

regional and first level, 249 secretaries of factory committees,
1,856 secretaries of Party Primary Units and Subunits."[12]

All this happened in under two months of early martial law and
could not have happened normally because it would have been
impossible to organize party meetings of various levels at which
existing officeholders could be deposed and new ones elected. The
political military knew how to overcome such trifling formalities.
The secretariat of the Party Central Committee and the Political
Bureau met on December 19 and 22, 1981 respectively, to be
informed post factum about their role under martial law.[13] In
practice this meant that they approved a document prepared earlier
by the polical military known as "Instruction on management of party
affairs under martial law." The Instruction suspended some provisions
of the party statute, thereby limiting party democracy, by suspending
party elections and increasing the rights of higher executive organs
of the Party. For example, the secretariat of a Regional Party
Committee was given the right to dissolve Party Primary Units (POP)
when the latter acted against ideological principles embodied in the
statute or against resolutions of higher authorities of the party.[14]

Trusted party members, placed earlier in key party positions,
armed with the Instruction, and suitably guided by military commissaries attached to party offices, purged the civilian party in record
time. The extent and level of the purge justified a fashionable
description "the same Party and yet not the same." It could not be
the same because the said purge was already a second crisis in the
civilian party leadership. In the same address to the 7th Plenary
Session, General Jaruzelski stated that the elections that preceded
the 9th Party Congress resulted in an almost complete change of
leadership because they involved 80 percent of the personnel of
regional party commitees, over 65 percent of town, village, and
factory party committees, and 50 percent of secretaries of POPs.
In the party apparatus 53 percent of the full-time personnel were
replaced in the 18 months following August 1980. All these changes,
Jaruzelski said, were the biggest in the whole history of the postwar
Communist Party.[15]

This was followed by the biggest drop in party membership
ever. As has been said earlier, under martial law up to the end of
1982 the party lost about 400,000 members. From figures given in
an interview in November 1983 by General T. Dziekan, head of the
Personnel Department of the Party Central Committee, one can
deduce that in the first ten months of 1983, there was another sharp
drop in party membership.[16] Thus under the management of two top
political military leaders—Kania and Jaruzelski, first secretaries of
the party from September 1980 and October 1981, respectively—party
membership was reduced from over 3 million to less than 2 million.
Jaruzelski tried to console the comrades gathered for the 7th Plenary

Session by reminding them that in July 1944 the Polish Communist Party had about 20,000 members and its ally, the left-wing Socialist Party, 8,000 members. The lesson for today, he said, was that the role of the party depended on its quality, not numbers.

Giving the figures Jaruzelski confirmed once more that it could not have been the Polish Communist Party that imposed the Soviet-Socialist system in Poland but the Polish People's Army backed up by the Red Army. Thirty-five years later, when the system had to be defended, the same situation obtained.

PURGE IN THE MILITARY PARTY

Political developments in the civilian party were as a rule reflected in the military party. It would not have been normal if the big purge in the civilian party had no counterpart in the military party. Figures for the latter were not published separately for the simple reason that they would give away the extent of opposition to General Jaruzelski's war against the Polish people. Yet a percentage figure published for quite a different purpose is in this respect very helpful. A member of the board of editors of Wojsko Ludowe wrote in October 1983 that 64.3 percent of officers belonged to the party.[17] The previous percentage given before the imposition of martial law was 85 percent. Relating these percentages to a total of 64,000 officers one gets about 13,000 officers expelled from the military party. This has serious implications because unlike in the civilian party, loss of party membership in the army is tantamount to professional death. That is why one can say that the officers had been expelled.

Before one can draw any conclusions from this development one needs to understand the background. There is some information as to who were the main victims. It was provided by General Jaruzelski himself when he said:

> We remenber the very difficult situation in which the last elections to party office were held. They were the main reason for the exchange of party cadres, the rotation of generations, the distinct rejuvenation of activists. But some of these young, well-meaning, and keen people lacked the necessary knowledge and experience. Others had no moral fiber and probity. In the ideological confusion in some party organizations control fell into the hands of weak people who did not follow the party line and were unable to resist the influence of anti-Socialist forces.[18]

What happened at the spring 1981 party elections and why has been described in Chapters 7 and 8. At that time many line officers opposed the political officers' politicization of the army. Later that year they probably opposed the political military in its preparation for martial law. They did not follow the party line and had to be punished and deprived of any influence when the imposition of martial law made this possible.

By that time their enemies, the political officers, had made their come-back. The political military could not move without them. An article in Wojsko Ludowe contained this statement:

> Martial law has shown that that those who thought that the political apparatus would never again become important were mistaken. Martial law also demonstrated to the faint-hearted the tremendous importance of party-political work and the urgent need to extend its front by involving all who can be useful. Political officers can rightly be proud of their record and have no real ground for worry when they are criticized by dilletantes. [19]

The reason for this change in fortunes was given earlier when it was claimed that martial law was for the political apparatus, the party, and party youth activists a real test of operating in conditions that closely resembled combat. What hitherto was fiction-like and imaginary became stark reality. The tasks of protecting law and order in large conurbations and dealing with criminal elements were as real as the threat and the hidden enemy. In these actions the political apparatus tested its own capacity and learned a great deal. [20]

The political military used the "Instruction on management of party affairs under martial law" to quickly regain control over the military party. A part of this process was the accelerated purge of opponents. Some political officers had reservations about the method. One wrote:

> In the first weeks of martial law the system of running the Party by orders has proved very effective. A great many matters that had been a burden to the party were speedily settled, especially those that emanated from misinterpretation of democracy. It was simple—steps were taken against the guilty, others were only reprimanded. Quick and clear decisions were made. That was so in the first few weeks but now it should not be necessary to use commissary powers in party work. People say it can be harmful. [21]

A Division Party Committee secretary said that in the early part of martial law running the party by orders was widespread and this was understandable. Now, however, these powers should be used only in exceptional circumstances and wherever possible the rules of the party statute should be followed. He wondered whether in some cases commissary powers were not used to remove secretaries who were merely difficult.[22]

The application of commissary powers in the army in connection with martial law is clear evidence that <u>the political military faced at that time a substantial opposition within the army</u>. That the opposition was made ineffective and even its existence not allowed to leak out shows that the political military proceeded against army personnel even more ruthlessly than against the civilian population.

Party Control Commissions as Political Vice Squads

The above commissary powers were emergency measures adopted to restore quickly the ideological orthodoxy, political reliability, and organizational unity of the party. The commitment belongs normally to so-called party control commissions. Their role is to guard the statute and program of the party and to step in when party members deviate from them ideologically or politically and violate accepted legal and moral codes. The civilian party has its Central Party Control Commission (CKKP) and regional and local commissions. The party in the army has its own Party Control Commission of the army and commissions in military districts, arms of service, and lately also in divisions or their equivalent.

A report on activities of party control commissions for 1982 says that commissions of all levels handled 19,500 matters of individual party members and examined 12,500 letters and complaints from party members and nonparty people. Activities directed against party unity and violating party rules were responsible for 72 percent of expulsions and for 46 percent of party punishments. They were also the subject of 6,000 admonition talks held with party members. Other expulsions, punishments, and admonition talks related to moral offenses and breaking professional discipline. Apart from adjudicating in matters of individual members, control commissions inspected party organizations and acted on information obtained from organs of state control, offices of state prosecutors, and from the Inspection Department of the army. Under the heading of prevention measures an additional 12,500 warning talks were given. In general, the commissions cleared fully 1,100 comrades.[23]

Party control commissions reinstated some party officials who, it was said, had been treated unfairly when they were removed from

office in the spring 1981 party elections. Colonel Z. Czerwinski
had this to say:

> In the name of cleansing the party and restoring the
> credibility of its authorities many good and experienced
> party workers among the full-time cadre and voluntary
> activists were removed in one go, in one massive
> operation. Their only sin was that they had been active
> before August 1980 and erred together with the rest of
> the party acting on orders of an indolent leadership.
> They left party office and work. Something ought to
> be done that this is not for ever. [24]

Useful information on the work of party control commissions
of the army was given in an interview by Colonel Stefan Rutkowski,
chairman of the main control commission of the army. [25] The most
important item was that after the 9th Party Congress party control
commissions in the army were brought down to division level. This
was a most important development because it drastically increased
the number of commissions. Until then there were only seven
commissions—the main commission and one each for the three
military districts and arms of service. By introducing them at
division level their number was increased ten times or more. This
build up meant that the political military had decided to carry out a
political health checkup of all party officials and members who were
suspected of pro-Solidarity sympathies before and after the
imposition of martial law.

Another important change was that according to the new party
statute party control commissions were no longer subordinated to
party committees of the same level but functioned alongside them
independently. This enabled the commissions to take action
irrespective of the party member's position in the army or party.

Colonel Rutkowski said that from the very beginning the
commission proceeded against party members who succumbed to
enemy ideologies, adopted passive attitudes to anti-Socialist
propaganda, and neglected their service and party duties. About
the role of the commissions under martial law he said:

> In accordance with the "Instruction on management of
> party affairs under martial law" issued by the Political
> Bureau and Secretariat of the Party Central Committee,
> control commissions together with party authorities
> intervened more boldly in matters that influenced poli-
> tical and moral attitudes of party members and indirectly
> the level of combat readiness. Immediate response to

every breach of party discipline, to acceptance of alien
opinions, and to activities not allowed by the party
statute restored among the troops the party's credibility.

For party's credibility among the troops read "fear from the
political military," because according to Rutkowski under martial
law the area of education and warning talks was extended and the
party was cleansed of people who had adopted two-faced attitudes
in political matters. Finally steps were also taken against people
who abused their position for private gain or did not look after
public property for which they were responsible.

When inspecting party organizations the commissions found
cases of unjustified tolerance. Some party members were of the
opinion that in conditions of Socialist renewal and national concord
one's world outlook was a private matter of an individual and they
did not react when comrades were giving in to the church. Party
authorities and the control commissions could not ignore this,
especially when a comrade held an important position in the army
and the party. Rutkowski added that he could not understand those
who all their lives professed a materialistic outlook and then,
suddenly, late in life turned to religion. Some regular soldiers
changed like that when they retired. On this a clear stand would
be taken.

Rutkowski also said that whereas one could understand that
before the imposition of martial law and soon after some comrades
suffered from ideological confusion and could not withstand enemy
pressure, one would today have to be more demanding as regards
those comrades who still remained passive because they could not
or would not understand the seriousness of the situation.

In general he was of the opinion that effective prevention
depended on close cooperation between the control commissions,
party committees, and POPs which should compare notes as regards
behavior of party members and candidates and implementation of
party resolutions and recommendations.[26]

Reorganization of the Military Party

The intensive work of Party Control Commissions was accompanied by a substantial reorganization of the military party and its work
methods. This is reflected in two instructions issued in summer
1982. One, the "Instruction of the Central Committee of the Party
on tasks, competences, and organization structure of Party Political
Boards and Party Organizations in the Armed Forces" replaced two
instructions on the same subject issued in August 1980, that is, before

the emergence of Solidarity. A veteran member of the board of
editors of <u>Wojsko Ludowe</u> stressed aome aspects of the new
instruction:

- Issued under the signature of the Party Central Committee it
  enjoys higher authority than previous instructions.

- The aim is to ensure full unity of actions in party-political
  work.

- The role of the party-political apparatus was redefined in
  light of experience of the previous two years.

- The leading role of the party in respect to the army was
  reaffirmed and the military party remains its integral part.

- Commanders and other leading personnel have a duty to take
  part in political work and combine this with their service
  duties.

- Party-political organs are brought down to regiment level.

- Party members have the right and duty to react to improper
  behavior of party members and candidates, especially as
  regards ideology, party and professional ethics, party and
  service discipline, and so on.

- First secretaries of all levels are subordinated to the political
  deputy commander in service matters and to the 1st secretary
  of the next higher committee in internal party matters.

- The collegium of the GZP has been widened to include the
  chairman of the party control commission of the army and first
  secretaries of party committees of military districts and arms
  of service commands. [27]

The second document is "Guidelines on propaganda and agitation
training of party members and candidates" (agitation, it was explained
elsewhere, is propaganda that plays on emotions). General Baryla
explained that changes were dictated by internal army needs but also
by the sociopolitical situation in the country and in the world. Most
study programs of WUML and at other party courses were given a
new content. This would help a deeper understanding of the role of
the army in building a Socialist society and in overcoming the crisis.
Knowledge of the laws of economic development and of the functioning

of a socialist economy is needed more than ever before. It is the
army's duty to defend the party and to rebuild its authority. Workers
of the ideological front must go outside the army, work among the
people, take up the dialogue with various environments. [28]

The combined effort of all these elements of the military party
eventually brought many sinners back to the fold. One political
officer wrote that in the post-August 1980 atmosphere party members
who demanded changes in the party and even in the army and often
ingnored the basic principle of democratic centralism. On the whole
this phase was now over. One was able to bring people back to earth
and give their thinking a realistic dimension. [29]

SPEEDY LEGISLATION BY AN OBEDIENT SEYM

Totally ignoring the fact that none of Poland's laws passed
since World War II have any legality since they have not been
approved by freely elected representatives of the Polish people, the
political military attaches the greatest importance to a formalistic
observance of existing laws. Since the imposition of martial law its
propaganda never ceased to stress the absolute legality of martial
law itself and of the measures that followed from it. This pseudo-
legality was the weapon most often used against the political opposition
that was all the time accused of lawlessness.

It did not suffice that the existing laws were slanted in favor of
the political military. Everything was done to ensure that they could
be manipulated and produce a quick result. For this purpose large
numbers of army lawyers were trained and necessary steps were
taken to integrate them with the state judiciary and state prosecutors.
Arrests, internments, trials, and imprisonments of Solidarity and
other opposition leaders were the visible fruit of the cooperation.

However, the political military have realized that in the long
run manipulative interpretation of laws was less effective than having
laws that were geared to achieving political objectives. This would
be important in the postmartial law era. That is why already under
martial law they embarked on a program of legislation that helped
them to consolidate their hold over the Polish people. The general
disciplinary character of the legislation made it a suitable instrument
for subjugating the civilian sector in much the same way as service
and party discipline were used for regaining control in the army and
party discipline for establishing control over the civilian party.
Only this can explain the large volume of legislation passed by the
Polish Seym in 1982 and after.

In the first nine months the Seym passed 38 laws that had been
tabled by the government. There were also laws proposed by the

Council of State and individual Seym members. The average number of laws passed during a four-year term of any previous Seym was 40.[30]

The first session of the Seym (January 25-26, 1982) approved the four basic decrees of the Council of State on martial law dated December 12, 1981. One month later the Seym passed nine laws concerning the elements of economic reform, like planning, prices, statistics, financing of state enterprises, taxation of publicly owned enterprises, foreign trade, banking, the statute of the Polish National Bank, the office of the minister for prices. The remaining laws can be grouped around the following subjects:

- key occupations (civil servants, miners, dockers, farmers)

- "social pathology" (speculation, work avoidance, juvenile delinquency, alcoholism)

- jurisdiction (civil law and civil law procedures, penal law, councils for defense, State Tribunal and Constitutional Tribunal)

- education and culture (National Council of Culture, Culture Development Fund, minister of culture and arts, Main Council of Science and Higher Education)

- workers' rights (law on trade unions, on unions for agricultural workers, on private farmers)

In addition the Seym carried on work on a large number of projects of new laws.

According to the same source the above legislation represents a consistent effort to form a strong legal framework for a reconstruction of the political, social, and economic order along the lines of the 9th Party Congress. The laws on economic reform in particular prepared the ground for eliminating the direction of the economy by order and allocation and replacing it by one based on incentives and economic mechanisms.[31]

Before the imposition of martial law, official propaganda maintained that there was nothing wrong with the Socialist system, only with the people who administered it. This line has obviously been dropped because the new legislation introduced a great many changes. The new line that has gradually emerged was contrary to what people thought: that there never was in Poland too much Socialism but too little and that this was the cause of all the trouble. The new legislation was meant to correct that.

The law on trade unions passed on October 8, 1982, is a good example. The first effect of this law was that Solidarity was outlawed and any activity carried out in its name became illegal. The obvious aim was a further fragmentation of the still-active elements and their gradual extermination. Other provisions of the law may yet turn out to be more important. For example, any new unions may be built up only by stages: after December 1982 they may begin to operate at factory level; after December 1983, at national level as single unions; after December 1984, as federations of trade unions. This arrangement has a purpose. Already in the spring of 1983 union organizations at factory level were getting together to form provisional founding committees for the union organization of the next, the national, level. This process gives the political military ample warning on who aspires and is being put forward to play a role in the national union. The same will happen in 1984 when the founding bodies for the interunion federations or a central trade union organization will be formed. Should the program or the composition of the provisional bodies create misgivings, registration would be refused and the organization would not come into being. <u>The political military can now safely predict that another Solidarity will not emerge</u>.[32]

A new employment policy provides another example. During martial law many thousands of Solidarity supporters lost their jobs after being declared politically unreliable. Unofficial sources stated that in the first few months some 40,000 people lost their jobs. One of the laws in the "social pathology" group gives the authorities the right to direct people who had been out of work for more than three months to specific jobs or labor units. There were many who could not get new jobs because employers were reluctant to take on people labeled as rebels. A decree of the council of ministers (August 1983) ruled that until the end of 1985 no job may be taken in any of 15 specified regions—and no employment offered—without the consent of an official labor exchange. The decree applied to the most industrialized regions of Poland and was an instrument of a new labor policy aimed at alleviating a labor shortage. It also offered opportunities for discrimination on political grounds since the same regions were known Solidarity strongholds. The 15 regions named were: Warsaw City, Bielsko, Bydgoszcz, Czestochowa, Gdansk, Jelenia Gora, Katowice, Cracow, Lublin, Lodz, Olsztyn, Poznan, Szczecin, Wroclaw, and Walbrzych.[33]

One law of great importance was passed in November 1983 as an amendment to the law on universal defense obligations (1967). It brought in radical changes at the top of Poland's defense structure. The KOK, hitherto only an organ of the Council of Ministers for defense matters and during martial law an instrument of WRON, has become the supreme authority in matters of defense and securtiy and in practice the supreme state authority. From the Seym debate on

the law it emerged that the KOK now has the power to propose the
introduction of a state of emergency, state of martial law, general
mobilization, and state of war. It becomes the "administrator" when
such states are declared. The rules on composition of the KOK were
also changed. The chairman is now appointed by the Seym and his
deputies by the Council of State.

The competences of Regional Defense Committees (WKO) that
are directly subordinated to the KOK have been increased accordingly.
They have assumed administration and supervision functions in
defense and security matters in regions and in practice coordinate
all aspects of life in the regions.

The amendment established the institution of "supreme commander of the armed forces," which did not exist before. The
chairman of the KOK is the supreme Authority of the armed forces
in peacetime. The Council of State promptly appointed General
Jaruzelski Supreme Commander of the Armed Forces in wartime.
The above changes in the defense structure brought the Polish system
more in line with other countries of the Warsaw Pact. [34]

It was no surprise that the obedient Seym appointed Jaruzelski
as chairman of the KOK and that General Florian Siwicki, No. 2 in
the hierarchy of the political military, succeeded him as minister
of defense. The rumors that a post of president would be created for
Jaruzelski were discounted earlier but a journalist wrote that he
knew from reliable sources that the presidency idea has not been
dropped for good and that the accepted view in Seym and Council of
State circles was that this would happen when the situation in the
country returns to full normality (whatever this term may mean in
Polish conditions). [35]

In general it can be said that the 1983 amendment to the law
on universal defense obligations wrapped up nicely all the legislative
efforts by the political military to transform martial law into a
militarized administration. It is characteristic of the system that
the composition of the KOK, the top body of this administration, is
to be kept secret.

JOBS FOR THE BOYS

Legislation that changed many existing organization structures
has yet another great advantage: It provides natural and innocuous
reasons for large-scale changes of personnel. This, we already
know, was an important objective of the political military.

In his address to the 7th Plenary Session of the Party Central
Committee (February 1982) Jaruzelski said that the harmonious
cooperation of party authorities, state administration, and army was

a necessary precondition for solving existing problems in a speedy and proper way. Jaruzelski's personal experience was that the greatest degree of cooperation between the three elements is achieved when they are combined in one person, as in his case when he simultaneously held the posts of first secretary of the party, prime minister, and minister of defense. Many in the political military followed his example when as army officers and party members they placed themselves and their supporters in key civilian posts.

In his speech Jaruzelski outlined a nationwide personnel policy:

> We are making a start on a personnel policy and a personnel management system for the whole country. We have rejected the bad practices of the past, including the bureaucratic and formalistic approach to "nomenklatura" but we are retaining the active role of the party in matters of personnel. . . . There will be a uniform procedure as regards selection and appointments, training and career development, systematic appraisal of performance and there will be no secrecy.

Jaruzelski added that for the first time there would be annual staff reviews in ministries and regional and local administrations. They would be modeled on army procedures. For directing posts of all levels very strict requirements would apply: acceptance of Socialism, professional competence, organization abilities, individual culture, and unblemished moral standards. Intellectual qualifications alone would not be sufficient for such posts.[36]

The term "nomenklatura," which has no English equivalent, has never been officially defined. It is generally accepted that it refers to lists of posts and positions held by party authorities of various levels. Appointment to a position that appears on the list cannot take place without prior sanction by the party authority concerned. The system came under heavy attack during the Solidarity era as being open to unlimited abuse. It should be noted that Jaruzelski does not propose to abolish it but only to correct its "bureaucratic and formalistic" application and that political reliability is still the main criterion of suitability for directing posts.

Implementation of the above policy started immediately after the imposition of martial law. On December 16, 1981, WRON instructed the government to carry out reviews of all staff employed in state administration and to dismiss at the recommendation of commissaries of the KOK all who were found inefficient or corrupt. The stated reason for this measure was security of the state.

These reviews went under the name of "verification," a type of investigation of the state employees' behavior during the Solidarity period by specially appointed teams of investigators. In January 1982 the army daily wrote that martial law had created ideal conditions for carrying out true and effective verifications of officials of the party, employees in the state administration and the economy, in education, press, radio and television, and in many other areas of public life.

The director of the Department of Local Administration stated in an interview that verification of personnel will consider qualifications and "social values" (that is, political views). A civil servant is obliged to give a written undertaking that he will work for the future of a Socialist Poland and that he will treat his job also as a civic service to the state and its people.[37]

Verifications of personnel employed in state organs and institutions were carried out with the participation and under the supervision of army personnel. The reviews that had been carried out by October 1982 revealed numerous weaknesses in personnel policy or, to be more precise, an absence of a policy. The findings were used to take immediate and important decisions on personnel. They also help to evolve new principles of a personnel policy in respect to state employees.[38] It is difficult to imagine that the army could find enough suitable personnel for this enormous operation. The statement probably meant that there were provisions for the army to participate when army interests were involved.

A professor of economics at the Military Political Academy wrote early in 1983 that considerable numbers of the regular army cadre have been given jobs in the civilian sector, including the national economy. This confirmed the usefulness of the qualification obtained in military schools. Trained economists were needed not only in the army but in the country as a whole.[39]

The vacancies filled by army personnel came from staff reviews and other types of inspections. One press report said that under martial law (December 1981–December 1982) there have been 889 changes in regional and local state administration posts. Directing posts accounted for 17 percent of that number and included 14 regional governors (voyevodes), 51 deputy regional governors (voyevodes), and 34 presidents of larger towns.[40] The total number of changes in central level posts, that is, of ministers, undersecretaries of state, directors of central offices and their deputies, directors general, were not given. In the second half of 1982 there were 29 changes in these posts that, it was stated, was a slowing down compared with the first half of the year.[41]

The military daily reported that during martial law up to January 25, 1983, 107 people who had held directing positions were tried for offenses like theft of public property, mismanagement, taking bribes, abuse of authority, or neglect of duties. Of these, 70 were sentenced, 27 found not guilty, and 6 cases were dismissed.[42]

It appears that the political army has an in-built facility for creating vacancies. A report to the Council of Ministers stated that from March to November 1982 inspections by the Army Inspection Department and Field Operation Groups resulted in dismissing 179 people from posts in state administration. Among them were 2 voyevodes, 2 deputy voyevodes, and 44 directors. The Presidium of the government obligated ministers and heads of central offices to check out the implementation of recommendations resulting from the inspections with representatives of the Army Inspection Department.[43] Bearing in mind that the Army Inspection Department inspected in that period only 10 out of 49 regions of Poland, many more vacancies will have arisen by the time the whole of Poland has been covered.

Two appointments made under martial law were almost certainly linked with the deployment of army regular personnel in the civilian sector. General Zygmunt Zielinski, head of the Personnel Department in the Ministry of Defense since 1968, retained that position when appointed secretary to WRON. In the latter post Zielinski, the "walking who-is-who in the Polish Army" undoubtedly played a key role in personnel moves resulting from martial law. Zielinski had two other great assets: He was a member of the Central Party Control Commission and, having graduated from the Ryazan Officer School, also a member of Jaruzelski's inner circle. General T. Dziekan, until December 1981 deputy head in the Chief Political Directorate of the Army, became head of the Personnel Department of the Central Committee of the party. In that capacity he dictated policies and issued instructions to personnel departments of any organization or institution in the country. He would have countered any opposition to sackings of high officials who would have been important party members.

At the 13th Plenary Session of the Central Committee (October 1983) General Dziekan submitted for approval of the Central Committee a document entitled "Principles of Personnel Policy of the Polish United Workers' Party." One part of it was "Procedures for appointments to directing posts (in the state)." General Dziekan said that the document is the result of nearly two years of work in which army experience in personnel matters had been taken into account.[44]

In 1983 a Postgraduate Training Center for Administration Employees was established in Warsaw. Staff under age 35 with five years' experience in administration work attend a course of 18 months' duration. There is a two-stage selection and a stiff entry examination. Students take an oath before admission.[45]

In his speech in the Seym made in connection with the lifting of martial law General Jaruzelski declared: "The regular army cadre yielded great many political and state functionaries who in the most difficult period proved their idealism, organization talent, and solid qualifications. They can continue to serve the country in civilian posts."[46]

The political army had the necessary manpower resources to fill posts in the civilian sector that were essential for consolidating its political position in the country. First, it had political officers who since 1970 had been produced in numbers far exceeding the internal needs of the army. Furthermore, after ten years of continuous political training these officers were overqualified for average political posts in the army and more suited for jobs in the civilian sector. For many political officers, posting outside the army after years of service in the political apparatus and well before the normal term of service expired provided a welcome beginning of a second career. Second careers were also an obvious objective of many "line" officers after normal or early retirement from army service.

The implementation of the above personnel policy was greatly helped by the fact that this was one of the few areas in which the political military could to some extent count on the support of the Polish people. The reason was that by and large the people who were being replaced were incompetent, corrupt, and discredited. The elite of the political army were in every respect superior to the "aparatchiki" of the civilian party.

13
Post-Martial Law Problems

Martial law was suspended on December 18, 1982, and
finally lifted on July 22, 1983. For the average Pole it
meant that after the 585 long days of the Jaruzelski
war came "occupation" (an analogy to the German occupation of Poland during World War II). To this day
members of the Citizens' Militia and State Security are
commonly called "Gestapo." The main factor of the
post-martial law era is that although Solidarity as an
organization had been crushed, Polish people's resistance to the rule of the political military continues. They
are fully aware of this and brace themselves for a long
haul. They do not consider that Underground Solidarity
poses a serious threat and their real worry is that they
are unable to win over the minds and hearts of the
people, especially of the young. An all-out effort to
establish the Patriotic Movement of National Salvation
as nationwide broadly based support for their policies
has not brought tangible results. The main weakness of
their approach to solving Poland's problems is that they
always deal with symptoms, not the root causes of
the ills.

NATION'S RESISTANCE CONTINUES

General Siwicki, addressing the Seym in connection with the
suspension of martial law, said that it brought about positive thinking,
especially in the matter of supreme interests of the Socialist state.
WRON helped the process of stabilization but the road to full normal

life in Poland is long and difficult. The opposition has not surrendered its weapons, has not ceased hostile actions. The social and economic situation is still serious. Malpractices, breaking of the law, of moral and social justice norms have not yet been eradicated. Positive processes that started under martial law needed the army's support to survive. For the time being the army would maintain a low-profile presence in the interest of defense and Socialism. Having saved the country it was the army's duty to contribute to its revival. By retaining commissaries of the KOK in ministries and regional offices, in institutions and, in a number of enterprises, the army would assist the functioning of state administration and of the economy and in this way ensure that normalization processes were not disturbed. The rest of Siwicki's address was an attack on the United States with its declared aim to achieve political and military domination over the Soviet Union and the Socialist countries.[1]

The government daily Rzeczpospolita published in February 1983 a full-page article by General Baryla entitled "After Suspension of Martial Law—Time for National Concord, Time for Battle" (whereby the "time for battle" is in three-times bolder print than the "time for national concord"). According to Baryla, confrontation is inevitable because the opposition has developed the concept of the underground state. This implied "obstinate negation, passive resistance, and "internal emigration" as means to immobilizing the neutral middle ground of society." The opposition may try to infiltrate legal organizations and associations. The coming months and years would be a battle for the Socialist beliefs of the Polish people. It would be fought in all spheres of life and the weapon would be reasoned argument, not force. In this process the army would continue to play an important role by maintaining law and order.

The article contains the extraordinary remark that during martial law the army learned how to integrate the regular cadre with the troops.[2] What is more, two senior political officers wrote that the political battle had consolidated the regular cadre itself, which had begun to feel stronger ideologically and as an organization. The army was aware that the struggle for the Socialist character of Poland was being fought on many planes with varying intensity. There should be no halt that could dull vigilance and encourage the enemy to renew its activities. The army could not withdraw to a political rest camp. This was because the process of erosion caused by the mistakes of the last decade and the counterrevolutionary activities after 1980 was so deep that many years would be needed to make Poland strong, well-governed, and just. The army had an important role to play because of its organization and structure, its ideological and moral cohesion, and the qualifications and experience of its cadres.[3]

In connection with the lifting of martial law the official press agency release said that representatives of the state authorities handed to the military thank-you letters, medals, and so on, and declared that the experience of working with the military would be used in further work for society. It added that with the progressing normalization of life in the country the organization/intervention-type role of the army would give way to an inspiration role accompanied with passing onto the civilian sector what is best in the army.

The same issue of the army daily contains an interview with General Tuczapski, a top political military personality. He said that there were two dangers: from the opposition who were capable of revival and were waiting for suitable conditions, and from tendencies to return to discredited forms of direction and management in the state administration and economy. The army would be on guard against them because "although the protecting umbrella spread over the authorities during martial law is removed, the army would, should this be necessary, use other forms of action to give help and support." Tuczapski said that officers who served as commissaries of the KOK and in Field Operation Groups should use their knowledge of the area to give informal support. They should maintain contacts with factories and offices in which they operated to be able to explain government and party policies and to inform the managers about matters that worry ordinary people. He concluded by saying that the army was now in the second line but basic issues were still its concern.[4]

THE YOUNG A MAJOR SOURCE OF WORRY

From the large volume of material in the military press and publications one sees that the young and their attitude to the Soviet-Socialist system are a cause of worry to the political military. One of their well-known political writers said that this was unavoidable. He wrote that workers in their mass, especially the young ones (every second worker was in that category) have begun to think politically and would not and were not able to accept decisions that are vital to them in a passive way. Any hope that this trend could be put back, and there are people who still think so, is as unfounded as hoping that people who have mastered the alphabet would give up reading.[5] This is a problem the political military must face as the new rulers of the country, but every intake of conscripts and of candidates to military schools brings it close to home.

A political officer wrote that the events of 1981 and 1982 had shown that a large part of the younger generation was too easily affected by enemy centers of ideological subversion. They lack a historical perspective in thinking and are guided by emotions. They had been for years in the center of interest at the Institute of Social Studies of the Military Political Academy because an early recognition of their attitudes and behavior followed by appropriate corrective ideological education measures during their conscript service affects the results of training and education. Sociological studies carried out by the institute on a sample of conscripts in 1982 have shown that the majority had been exposed to a greater or lesser degree of propaganda by external and internal anti-Socialist forces. The main aim was to make them lose hope of a better future, make them believe that they were a generation of lost chances, and that Polish society was dominated by the old. These influences were not seriously opposed and there were shortcomings in political education in secondary and higher schools and in places of work.

It was not surprising that to many young people Socialism is an abstract idea. They have not been given the most elementary social and political knowledge. Only 21 percent were aware that the abolition of private ownership of means of production, big industry, banks, and of large agricultural estates was one of the main conditions of social justice.[6]

During a discussion among political officers it was said that some conscripts who in civilian life did not bother to show their religious feelings were now displaying religious badges in a demonstrative manner. One must be prepared that some conscripts before joining the army would have been briefed on how to behave.[7] The young with secondary school education come under even heavier criticism. A political officer, not a regular officer, wrote that his experience as university lecturer was that university students simply do not know the meaning of Socialism. The same applied to a large part of society. One would have to start from scratch. He quoted Jaruzelski that the crisis in the minds of the young would not be solved by the forces of law and order. It is not only the anti-Socialist attitudes but also nihilism, apathy, and selfishness.[8]

The above situation is of great importance since candidates for officer schools are recruited from that social stratum. Colonel (now Maj.-Gen.) M. Wlodarski, deputy head of GZP responsible for military schools, wrote in Wojsko Ludowe that entry examinations to officer schools revealed deformations in the understanding of history, disorientation in world outlook, and decline in respect for authority and the value of work. There were signs of return to bourgeois ideology and many other symptoms of "social pathology." There was a vast field here for military scientists of such disciplines as history, political economy, philosophy, sociology, and political sciences. They ought to transmit knowledge well supported by arguments that were relevant to the current situation and political solutions.[9]

When even the crack 12th Mechanized Division could not avoid
the intakes of hostile conscripts one must conclude that the problem
was universal and deep-rooted. Colonel (now Major General) H.
Szumski, division commander, complained about the Solidarity-
infected intakes of conscripts since the autumn of 1980. Then quoting
research carried out in the army he wrote that conscripts called up
in 1982 displayed big doubts about the value of conscript service,
demonstrated a low level of political culture, dislike of political
instruction, disapproval of martial law, susceptibility to information
emanating from the Solidarity Underground and other nonauthorized
sources, and finally succumbed to the political influence of the
church. It required a great effort to turn that lot into soldiers. Even
then the efforts of commanders and the political apparatus were not
always rewarded. Solidarity activities were glorified and the
authorities were blamed for causing martial law, for the moral and
economic crisis, and for the difficult start in life for the young.
It was sad that the young did not see the destructive hand of the
Underground and its links with the international anti-Polish and
anti-Communist front. [10]

The above "unperfumed" account of the situation in the division
(an expression much favored by political officers) is in sharp contrast
to the publicity in the popular military media given to the division
about the same time. The army daily published an article by Colonel
Szumski as commander of a division that distinguished itself in the
execution of martial law duties. The article is full of praise for the
troops and there is no hint of internal difficulties. [11] Furthermore,
Colonel Szumski has been entered in the Army Book of Honor for
1982. The citation said that his units were a model of discipline,
combat readiness, and political reliability, which qualities had been
demonstrated during the martial law operation. [12] The latter could
be true if it is applied to units of the Division that had been hand-
picked for the martial operation.

Ideological and Pragmatic Solutions

It has been noticed that the political military would normally
try to solve its problems by approaching them from the ideological
as well as the political/practical angle. The latter would include a
definite political army interest. This can be illustrated in attempts
to deal with the young.

On the ideology plane it was decided to correct the historical
awareness of young Poles. At the 4th Ideological Conference of the
Armed Forces (November 1982) General Baryla stated that the
enemies of Socialism exploited the shortcomings of official history

with its many taboos. History has become the object of a sharp political battle. The army had escaped ideological erosion thanks to the courageous tackling of key historical issues during ideological and political instruction hours. [13] He inferred that the army would make its history teaching a model for the rest of the country.

The Scientific Council of the Ministry of Defense, together with the Military Historical Institute, held at the end of November 1982 a symposium that was attended by military and civilian academics, history teachers of primary and secondary schools, and journalists and publicists who write about history. General Baryla, who chaired the meeting, said that the army leadership attached great importance to raising the awareness of history in today's Poland, especially among the young. The time had come to create a national program for teaching history that would embrace most of the population. The aim would be to resolve all the controversies and polemics about Poland's history in line with the interests of the working class, the nation, and Socialism. When political convictions begin to be based on the knowledge of facts, people would resist being led by the nose by political gamblers. [14]

Colonel K. Sobczak, commandant of the Military Historical Institute, in his long address at the symposium made it quite clear that when the political military start rewriting history and fixing history teaching programs, Polish military history would be brought to the fore. To prove that the political opposition wanted to negate one part of Poland's contribution in World War II he quoted a survey of ten best-known periodicals during the Solidarity era that had shown that out of 400 articles of a historical content there had been only two about the battle of Lenino and none about the Polish People's Army and the left-wing resistance. He was convinced that no other part of history had the same effect on young people as military history, which binds them to the state and makes them feel responsible for its security and fate. [15]

The same Colonel Sobczak was later present at a course of instruction for political officers on the subject of "shaping of the historical awareness of young people, including Army personnel" held in March 1983 at the Training Center for Political Officers at Lodz. It was stated there that due to lack of honest knowledge of history the young were guided by a simplified view of values and authority. Speakers stressed the value of military history for the teaching of history in the country. Colonel Sobczak informed the course about steps that are being taken in that direction at the Military Historical Institute. [16] That piece of information shows that by March 1983 teaching of new history reached the operational level.

From the discussion on the subject of history one can deduce that the political military will try to sell to young Poles patriotism rather than Marxism-Leninism. But it would be a special brand of patriotism because, according to General Baryla,

> teaching of history must go together with education in internationalism, which is a must in our policies. . . . In the ideological confrontation the enemy tries to undermine the bases of Poland's Socialist existence, tries to sow discord between the states and armies of the Warsaw Pact. His attack is directed against our fundamental values—the alliance and cooperation with the Soviet Union and the Polish-Soviet brotherhood-of-arms. The defense of principles of internationalism is our first priority and is synonymous with the Polish "reason of state."[17]

An example of political/practical actions was the establishment of a militarized Youth Labor Force. By a decision of the Council of Ministers of December 16, 1982, the 26-year-old Voluntary Labor Youth Organization (OHP) was turned into a military organization subordinated to the minister of defense through the head of Civil Defense of the country. The declared aim is to educate Polish youth through work, schooling, and organized activities.[18] The OHP (the old name is retained) will have two streams, one consisting of units of the old voluntary type and the other of Civil Defense units in which conscripts discharge their military service obligation. Common for both streams is work for the sectors of the national economy most affected by the crisis, that is, building, communications, and food production.

According to the military weekly about 100,000 young people who are not employed and not studying and are to some extent lost will find in the OHP a new chance to fulfill their life ambitions through work and learning. In both streams physical work will be combined with ideological and political education, acquisition of general knowledge, and learning a trade. They will be given defense training.[19]

The forming of the new military OHP is an expansion of provisions made in September 1980 whereby a substitute military service was introduced and made available to a number of organizations, including the OHP.[20] The main difference between the earlier and the latest decree lies in the numbers. They suggest that in addition to the declared aims, the move was intended to mop up "socially maladjusted" youngsters, that is, those who take part in antigovernment demonstrations or are guilty of nonpolitical crimes. By diverting the undesirables from the army and placing them in labor units under strict military discipline the political military obtained the means of subjecting them to intense ideological and political indoctrination. They are now controlled by the Chief Political Directorate of the army, whereas in the original 1980 (pre-martial law) provisions the GZP was not directly involved.

Members of the OHP enjoy the rights of military personnel but are also subject to army discipline, including jurisdiction of military courts. Yet they are not called soldiers but <u>junak</u> (member of a labor unit). In November 1983 the OHP had about 15,000 members.[21] It probably has not developed as fast as was expected; the reason could be financial since the OHP is not on the Ministry of Defense budget.

PATRIOTIC MOVEMENT OF NATIONAL REVIVAL

The political military knew that the party, although still numerous, could not mobilize for them the necessary support within society. They decided to form a new organization or movement with the principal objective to gain the confidence of the Polish people. It started in January 1982 as "spontaneous" Civic Committees of National Salvation (OKON), which as the name suggests had the same aims as the Military Council of National Salvation. By June 1982 there were over 7,000 local OKON units and they needed an organizational structure. This took the form of coordination councils of the OKON that then developed into a nationwide Patriotic Movement of National Revival (PRON), organized on the usual territorial pattern with central, regional, local, and factory levels.[22]

A declaration that contained the ideological and organizational principles of PRON was subnitted for nationwide discussion in February 1983. PRON was established as a national level organization at its 1st Congress in May 1983. The high hopes that the political military pinned on PRON are reflected in a correction to the Constitution made when martial law was lifted in July 1983. PRON has taken the place of the moribund Front of National Unity (FJN), the institution that has been winning general elections for the Communist Party in Poland ever since 1956. The new Article 3 of the Constitution makes PRON "a platform for uniting the patriotic forces of the nation for the good of the Polish People's Republic."

The official propaganda claim that PRON is a spontaneous healthy reaction of all patriotic Poles to the nation-saving role of the army is unfounded. PRON is a legitimate baby of the political military and babies, by nature, are not spontaneous.

General Jaruzelski used the Seym platform to promote the idea. In a speech in the Seym on July 21, 1982, he said: "PRON may become our great historic chance and an important stepping stone to higher forms of Socialist democracy. . . . Within the movement all classes, social strata, and sections of society could be represented better than ever before." In another speech (October 1982) he said that it was his wish that PRON would embrace all that was patriotic, honest, creative, and consistent with the interests of the Socialist state.[23] Jaruzelski does not seem to realize that to a true Pole the first three are incompatible with the Soviet-Socialist state he has in mind.

General Baryla said at the 4th Ideological Conference of the Armed Forces that thousands of regular soldiers, reservists, and civilian army employees were actively engaged in PRON.[24] Two senior political officers wrote that political work in the civilian sector meant first of all participation in consolidating PRON's organization structure and that involvement of the army in PRON arose from the growing conviction that national conciliation would be achieved through PRON.[25]

The political military used its domination of the party to promote PRON, even though this was not in the interest of the party. In March 1982 the Political Bureau issued a directive that obliged party authorities and organizations to give the organization (known at that time as OKON) all the necessary assistance. At the Party Ideological Conference (August 1982) General T. Szacilo of the GZP stated that only open enemies of Socialism should remain outside national concord.[26]

WRON decided early in 1982 to use the vast machinery of the FJN to build up PRON. One of the reasons was that prior to martial law over a thousand regular Army officers worked for the FJN. The FJN consisted of the party (PUWP), the United Peasant Party (ZSL), and the Democratic Party (SD). Before every general election the three parties came together to fix the single list of candidates and so it was possible to keep up the pretense that Poland was not a one-party state. The substantial presence of ZSL and SD members in the Seym (25 and 9 percent of the total number of MPs, respectively) never had any practical significance. They were led by the nose by the "leading" Communist Party.

In addition to the three parties the FJN comprised public associations that aspired to parliamentary representation. Among them were three nonparty groups representing lay Catholics. In July 1982 the permanent Commission of Cooperation of the three parties and representatives of the smaller groupings signed a declaration about the aims of PRON. A provisional National Council of PRON formed in September 1982 was the organizing body until the congress, when a proper National Council took over.

Political and social associations that helped with the imposition

of martial law were quick to declare their support for OKON (PRON).
In March 1982 ZBoWiD asked its members to join in the activities
of OKON. In June 1982 the 22,000-strong ZBZZ declared that its
members regarded work for OKON as their principal duty. The
party youth organization (ZSMP) joined as a body in September 1982.[27]
So did 75 other organizations, which makes these declarations of
accession quite meaningless.

The massive effort of the political military to make PRON into
its power base outside the army has not given the expected results.
In February 1983 PRON membership reached 230,000, which is very
small for a mass organization. For the army weekly it was a lot
"considering that not long ago PRON was considerd an insignificant
collection of 'collaborators,' an object of tasteless jokes and a
target for combined attacks by Radio Free Europe and underground
publications in Poland."[28] At the time of the 1st Congress, PRON
was reported to have nearly half a million members organized in
10,300 units. This explains the rather modest claim made by the
deputy chief editor of Wojsko Ludowe that

> PRON is today already an authoritative advocate of
> national concord that is being achieved by dialogue and
> discussion between various organizations and social
> forces whose common denominator is acceptance of the
> present Constitution and of the supreme interest of
> the Socialist state. In a relatively short time it has
> become a respected exponent of the patriotic and pro-
> Socialist public opinion.

he then repeats the feeble propaganda line that martial law was
suspended and later lifted altogether because of the appeals by PRON
to the Seym, the Council of State, and to the government.[29]

ASSESSMENT OF UNDERGROUND SOLIDARITY

Since the imposition of martial law the political army has
conducted an open war, at first against the suspended and after
October 1982 against the outlawed Solidarity. The state's whole
repression machine went into action with daily arrests, trials,
imprisonment, and also with intimidation and blackmail. General
Stachura, deputy minister of internal affairs, gave an account of the
achievements for 1982: 677 illegal conspiratorial groups were
unmasked and eliminated, including 360 facilities for the production
of illegal literature, 1,196 items of duplicating equipment, and 468
typewriters were confiscated; also about 730,000 leaflets, 34,000
brochures and publications, 11 radio transmitters; 150,000 warning

talks were given; altogether 10,131 people had been interned and 3,616 persons were arrested to be tried for political offenses; the Citizens' Militia used fire-arms several times; and 813 militiamen and soldiers were injured.[30] General Stachura did not give the number of killed and injured among the political opposition.

It is not easy to reconcile the above data with a fairly detailed description of the political underground and its activities presented in three articles in Wojsko Ludowe in 1983. They were written by Colonel L. Wojtasik, head of the Propaganda and Agitation Department of the GZP. The information given under this heading is based on the first of these articles.[31]

The underground had no clear strategy and no united organization. Attempts to form one were not systematic. There was no agreement on ways and means of achieving the stated objectives. The organization pattern was a visible sign of the overall weakness. Attempts to form various organizations were often meant to create the impression that the underground was well-developed, active throughout the country, and embraced the whole of the people. The existence of ostensibly different programs was to create the impression of political and ideological pluralism. The whole thing was an improvisation that, with the help of information services of Radio Free Europe, was to serve the propaganda inside the country and justify material help from the West. The main components of the political underground are: All-Poland Resistance Committee of Solidarity, Provisional Coordination Commission, regional organizations, secret factory commissions, interfactory organizations, horizontal groupings (Interregional Defense Commissions of Solidarity, Solidarity Fights, Movement for Freedom, Justice, and Independence), and All-Poland Resistance Committee of Farmers.

The All-Poland Resistance Committee of Solidarity was formed early in January 1982 by 20 leaders of Solidarity who had not been interned. Its aims were to coordinate Solidarity activities until the lifting of martial law, release all internees, and start negotiations between the authorities and the Solidarity leadership with Lech Walesa as its head. In February 1982 the committee issued instructions on forming four-person Solidarity groups of social resistance (KOS) that would operate independently from one another but on instructions from the committee. For this the committee formed an editing team for a KOS bulletin.

In April 1982 the committee became affiliated with the Provisional Coordination Commission (TKK). TKK was formed on April 22, 1982, by Solidarity representatives from Gdansk, Lower Silesia, and Central and Southern Poland. The founders declared that the TKK would act in place of the suspended National Commission of Solidarity. The move sprang from the realization that martial law would be a long affair and that the Underground Solidarity must adjust to that situation.

The TKK coordinated protest actions all over Poland with the help of Polish-language broadcasts by Western stations. It was also busy publishing information and activating its supporters. In July 1982 it published a program document entitled "The Underground Society," which advocated general resistance to the authorities. The composition of the TKK changed as members were arrested. In January 1983 its members were Z. Bujak, W. Hardek, B. Lis, J. Pinor, and E. Szumiejko.

After the establishment of the central TKK, Regional Coordination Commissions (RKK) were formed in various regions, most of them in the second half of 1982. As a rule the RKK worked independently from the central TKK but cooperated with the latter when their protest actions were part of a nationwide action. RKK work with interfactory commissions to coordinate activities in a region. They also give direct assistance to factory commissions in matters like publishing, supply of information, training of printers, and so on. The rebuilding of the old Solidarity regional structure so that it could be controlled from one center did not materialize, mainly because of lack of popular backing.

The establishment of secret commissions in Factories (TKZ) was slow in spite of constant appeals from the RKK to form them in all factories where they did not yet exist. The Gdansk Regional Commission, for instance, declared that the most important task of the moment was to rebuild the factory structures of Solidarity. The appeals were backed up by examples of tasks and of organization models for factory organizations. The instructions aim to destroy morale of the work force and through that the production results of a factory. The following advice on conspiratorial activities was given: "Base activities on well-known and trustworthy people, use cover names in discussions even with most trusted people [because of bugging], avoid doubling of functions and crossing of contacts—for example, the printer must not himself distribute the material, the printing place must not be used for meetings—do not talk about one's own or other people's work."

Interfactory organizations were to remedy the lack of response in individual factories. They were made up of more aggressive members of Solidarity. The Warsaw Organization had representatives from 63 Warsaw factories. When the leaders of that organization were arrested in December 1982 (after seven months of operation), it was found that it consisted of members of the board of the Mazowsze Region of Solidarity. It was also established that the organization carried out and coordinated subversive activities into which young people were often drawn. A similar group in Gdansk, whose leaders were arrested in January 1983, was disseminating false information in order to create public unrest and also preparing terrorist actions. Several such groups functioned in Wroclaw, where they organized active resistance against martial law provisions. The objective of "spectacular actions" was to break the impasse that the underground has reached in factories.

The so-called "horizontal structures" were manifestations of differences among the leaders of the political underground of how best to achieve Solidarity objectives. They sprang up in various parts of the country and most of them never developed beyond a program declaration stage. A few made a limited impact. The Interregional Commission of Defense of Solidarity issued in September 1982 a program declaration calling for national concord on terms made public a few months earlier by the Social Council to the Primate of Poland. This was unacceptable to the authorities because it would have meant a modification of Socialism that in the end would lead to its liquidation. The "Soldarity Fights On" group issued its first bulletin under that title in July 1982. The group advocated confrontation with the authorities wherever possible. Since a frontal attack was clearly unthinkable, it recommended continuous guerilla actions that, if conducted with stubborn determination, were to lead them to victory. An information network was to be developed because information and propaganda were considered important weapons. The confrontation with the authorities would take various forms, beginning with passive resistance and not excluding terrorist actions. The group was publishing the newspaper Solidarity Fights On that, it was hoped, would get nationwide circulation and in the future was to be published in languages of neighboring countries. The group was responsible for clandestine radio broadcasts.

The Movement for Freedom, Justice, and Independence announced its existence in August 1982. It called for the formation of the elements of an underground society and underground state in the form of self-government, at first at the basic level, in factories (as trade unions), in professions, and in all other fields, and later at locality, town, and regional levels. Self-government evolved in this manner, according to the authors of the declaration, would have a right and duty to speak on behalf of the people and would become the framework of an underground state. The aim was a free and democratic Poland achieved by stages through protest actions, resistance, and other activities—for example, political, ideological, and historical self-education; publishing and publicizing; participation in underground work of Solidarity and of other organizations.

The horizontal organizations were the means by which the leadership of the political underground tried to gauge the popularity of any particular conception or approach and they were not meant to function as separate organizations.

Forming underground organizations in the countryside was on

the whole not successful, thanks to the clear and consistent agricultural policy adopted by the government. In spite of that, in August 1982 the All-Poland Resistance Committee of Farmers (OKOR) announced its program declaration. It was critical of government policy and demanded the restoration of "Solidarity of Individual Farmers," of "Rural Solidarity," and "Peasant Solidarity." It declared cooperation with the TKK and asked farmers and agricultural workers to show support through protest actions and resistance (by-passing official food purchase points and delivering straight to consumers) and giving help to victims of martial law.

Colonel Wojtasik concludes his articles in Wojsko Ludowe saying that the huge propaganda effort and expense did not produce sufficiently cohesive and developed underground organizations.[32] It should be noted that the articles had been written before the May 1982 Solidarity demonstration.

14
Relations with the Church Hierarchy

The political military must try to close the enormous gap
that exists between the official (legal) position of the
church, which limits the fulfillment of its proper mission,
and its true power and influence in the country, which
keep expanding. Since we already know the preference
and capacity of the political military to solve its problems
by creating suitable statutory provisions, we may assume
that attempts will be made to reach an agreement that
would appear to legalize the gains made by the church
but in practice would limit its role and standing. After
all it would be the controlled state security authorities
and the judiciary who would decide what the bishops
and clergy would and would not be allowed to do. A
good illustration of what can be expected from the
political military is the position of the church inside the
army with the all-pervading antichurch propaganda and
the wholly fictitious role of army chaplains.

OFFICIAL POSITION OF THE CHURCH IN THE STATE

The official position of the church in the state is described in
detail since I assume that the political military will make it the
starting point for the negotiations on the new legislation because it
would give them ascendancy in that matter.

General Jaruzelski made his attitude known at the 7th Plenum
of the Central Committee, the first after the imposition of martial
law. He stated that state-church relations would as in the past be
decided in the spirit of the Constitution and that he was for the

continuation of a useful dialogue that could reduce the differences and increase the area of mutual understanding.

Article 82 of the Polish Constitution says: "1. The Polish People's Republic guarantees freedom of conscience and religion to all its citizens; 2. The church is separated from the state." The official interpretation of these principles was given in Wojsko Ludowe in 1979. It is presented here in an abridged form.

More than one-half of the Polish population are believers and members of one or another denomination or religious organization that functions in Poland. The decisive majority of believers belong to the Catholic Church. A correct church policy is one of the basic conditions for the normal functioning and building of a Socialist State. The aim must be to regulate church matters on the basis of Marxist-Leninist methodology in concrete social and political conditions.

Separation of church and state means that religion is a private matter of an individual. The role of churches is to satisfy the religious needs of the people and nothing more. They do not have any influence on political authorities and do not fulfill any of the state's functions. In relations with the churches the state is guided by the need to guarantee its own safety, law and order, rights of other citizens, education, health, and welfare of citizens, friendly relations with other nations, and any other important interests of the state and the rest of society. The practical consequences are:

- Churches are to keep away from all political, social, economic, cultural, educational, and so on, activities of the state.

- The state does not interfere with the religious work of churches if it does not affect security and public order.

- There is to be equality of all citizens and equality of denominations irrespective of territorial influence or membership.

- There is prohibition of material support of churches by the state, except for historical building of merit.

- There is acceptance of the principle that the sole reason for the work of churches (in Poland) is the right of individual citizens to freedom of conscience and of religion.

The church-state separation stems also from the nature of Marxism-Leninism. The state is on its territory the only holder of authority and cannot share it with anybody. It determines the scope of authority of all social organizations. State-church relations cannot be based on equality and still less on supremacy of the church.

The latter cannot have any legal or political autonomy except in strictly religious matters.

The state provides the conditions that allow the citizen to exercise his religious rights but he must not abuse these rights against the interests of the state.

Because Poland is a secular state it is not acceptable that a person who represents state authority in administration, economy, education, and so on, would demonstrate his participation in religious ceremonies. The same applies to regular soldiers, militia functionaries, teachers, and others, who by the mere fact of taking the job have declared a certain attitude that cannot be in conflict with the nature and interests of the state.

The law demands that organizers of secular meetings notify the authorities in advance giving time, location, and purpose of the meeting. The authorities have the right to refuse if they endanger public order. Services and other meetings that take place in consecrated buildings are given a favored treatment and are not supervised by the administrative authorities.

The Office for Denominational Affairs is the highest state organ in these matters. It is directly subordinated to the prime minister and consists of four departments: general, Roman-Catholic, other denominations, and religious orders. Its comptences include denominational statistics, coordination with other government departments, legal matters, projects of laws regulating relations with the state, supervision of regulations on religious matters, rights and duties of priests and auxiliary personnel, rules governing individual denominations with their institutions and establishments, personnel matters, endorsing various applications from religious bodies, registration of religious bodies and supervision of their activities.

Under the Central Office there are Regional Offices for Denominational Matters. They are specifically responsible for church appointments, supervision of priest seminaries (together with the regional education authorities), coordination with other regional offices, building of churches, and church property matters.

One of the most important rights of the state is permission or refusal to operate in a given area. Another is influence on appointments. The state has the right to oppose an appointment or demand removal from a post. Persons appointed to church posts take the following oath: "I solemnly swear to be faithful to the Polish People's Republic, to observe its laws, and not to undertake anything that would bring it harm." (Given in bold print in the original text.)

According to a law of 1961, schools are secular institutions and teaching of religion in schools is not allowed. The same law gives the Ministry of Education control over teaching activities and over other work with the young. Some church representatives would want the state to be neutral in the matter of education, but this is clearly not acceptable. The churches in Poland apparently have facilities that are not available in bourgeois countries.[1]

However, the state was never able to enforce the above limitations of activities of the Catholic Church in Poland. One can see this clearly in extracts from a series of articles in Wojsko Ludowe published in 1974:

1. There are no serious points of disagreement on the line between Warsaw and the Vatican. The main obstacle to continued dialogue is the reactionary, anti-Socialist attitude of the church hierarchy in Poland. They violate the legal order, act against the constitutional principles of the Socialist state, continually mix religion with politics, and interfere in public life. Futher negotiations will depend on the will and ability of the Holy See to put an end to it.[2]

2. Reactionists in the leadership of the episcopate use all legal and illegal means to foment a political offensive aimed to impose, by force if they can, religious beliefs on the young and at the same time prevent the growth of the materialistic outlook and of secular tendencies. The aims of the hierarchy are well understood by the enemies of Poland who all the time use pseudoreligious arguments for psychological and ideological subversion, which includes inciting the Catholic clergy to anti-Socialist activities.[3]

3. In spite of the unquestionable freedom of religion in Poland, a fact appreciated by the Vatican, the Polish bishops incessantly produce new, mostly demagogic, demands so that they could assume an important political role in Poland. This goes against the constitutional principle of church being separate from the state and against the secular nature of Polish laws and policies. The hierarchy has opposed the practice of taking an oath of loyalty to the state. In 1974 they tried to forbid parish priests to take the oath. Cardinal Karol Wojtyla, the archbishop of Cracow (now Pope John Paul II) used the St. Stanislas celebrations, suggesting in his homily that also in present-day conditions lay authority had no right to impose on the church authorities any political orientation.[4]

4. And finally a verbatim comment by the author of the above-quoted extracts:

In the course of the last 30 years of Socialist Poland the political tactics of the reactionary faction of the episcopate varied according to the situation and current conditions. However, the substance of the policy that rejects any possibility of the Catholic Church adapting to the requirements and rules of the Socialist system remains unchanged.[5]

References to "reactionary factions of the episcopate,"
"extremists of Solidarity," or "some comrades erring" are an
accepted form of Communist writing, a kind of pars pro toto
expedient that is used when the whole truth is too unpalatable. There
is no doubt that the above attacks were aimed at the whole Polish
episcopate.

The attacks on the Polish bishops in the first half of the 1970s
makes their total absence in the second half (at least in serious
military sources) more noticeable. One can even find statements
that since the middle of the 1970s the church stood on a Socialist
foundation and did not compete with the state.[6]

Since the episcopate never accepted the privacy of religion
concept and always demanded recognition that the church had a role
to play in public life with a greater say in education and freedom of
information (access to the mass media), the ceasing of attacks can
only mean that the political military did not look for trouble in
this area.

ROLE OF ARMY CHAPLAINS

Ceasing open attacks on the Catholic Church hierarchy did not
mean a truce. Throughout the 1970s the political apparatus of the
army tried to counter the influence of the church in the army by
making atheist indoctrination, which went under the name of "forming
a scientific world outlook," an integral part of the ideological and
political indoctrination program. There is evidence that as with
many other great efforts in the ideological and political field the
effects of antichurch activities did not come up to expectations.

Against this background it is difficult to explain the need for
the institution known as "army chaplaincy." It is also difficult to
understand the total absence of information on army chaplains in the
media controlled by the Chief Political Directorate, to whom the
army chaplains are directly subordinated. Is there nothing in their
work that could be of interest? If there is not why do they exist? An
entry in the Small Military Encyclopedia "explains":

In the Polish People's Army military chaplains come under
the Ministry of Defense as regards administration and
under the church hierarchy as regards jurisdiction. At
their head is the dean general of the Polish Army.
Contrary to chaplains in capitalist armies who have
political functions, chaplains in the Polish People's
Army perform only religious functions in garrison
churches when desired by soldiers and their families.[7]

An organization order issued by the Commander-in-Chief of
the Polish Army in October 1944, which, still in force, fixed the
following established posts for the army chaplaincy:

Dean General	with rank of Brigade General
Deputy	Colonel
Head of Office	Major
Dean of Army	Colonel/Lt. Col.
Vicar of Army	Captain
Priest of Corps	Major
Deputy	Captain
Priest of Division	Captain/Major
Chaplain of Brigade	Captain/Major
Chaplain of Regiment	Captain

If all posts were filled according to that establishment, the number
of army chaplains would be considerable. In reality, for many
years the total has been in the region of 35. They belong to a
separate corps of "Officers of Chaplaincy." Dean general of the
Polish Army since 1964 is Rev. Colonel Julian Jozef Humenski,
editor of the monthly Army Chaplain, which has a restricted internal
circulation. In a book entitled Always with the Nation published in
connection with the 35th anniversary of the Polish Army, Humenski's
contribution refers to the service of army chaplains during World
War II and nothing else. He describes the memorable day of July,
15, 1943, when the colors of the 1st Kosciuszko Division were
blessed and the first military oath was taken during an open-air mass
by Rev. Major Wilhelm Kubsz, the first chaplain of the division. In
those days the central army daily paper Zolnierz Polski had a
religious supplement. 8

General Jaruzelski prides himself to be an upholder of the
traditions of the Polish Army, not only of the Polish People's Army.
The noble role that army chaplains played in Poland's military
history is an essential part of the army's tradition. The political
military not only did not uphold that tradition but actively soiled it
in a most cynical manner. The entry in the Small Military Encyclopedia is wrong in two points: military chaplains have been politically
active since 1948, and they do not come under the jurisdiction of the
church hierarchy. The connection between the two facts is explained
in a full special study on the subject.

A papal decree issued in 1948 that was to regulate the jurisdiction of army chaplains was rejected by a number of serving
chaplains. They subsequently became the core of the "Patriotic
Priests" movement, which had been formed by party and government
authorities for the infiltration of the church organization and agitation

against individual bishops and the episcopate as a whole. They were regarded by the latter as renegades who tried to reconcile their priestly duties with Communist policies and ended up as servants of the system. They were active in organizations like ZBoWiD, the Peace Committee, the Polish Red Cross, and above all in the Lay Catholics Association "Caritas," another state-sponsored organization. The Conference of Polish Bishops held in June 1978 warned the whole clergy about the activities of "Caritas." The Bishops described "Caritas" as an instrument of permanent disinformation of Catholic opinion in the country and abroad about the true position of the church in Poland and as a political organization concerned mainly with the Communist indoctrination of priests. It should be added that the association is directly subordinated to the Office for Denominational Affairs and has its own "Caritas" Publishing House. It is not surprising that in a document published under the auspices of the church hierarchy in October 1978 it says that army chaplaincy is a fiction and that the term serves no other but propaganda purposes. Matters were not made any easier by the fact that many army chaplains had disagreements of a private and personal nature with the hierarchy before they landed in the group. [9]

The above situation and the linked question of the status of garrison churches make the institution of army chaplains an important issue in the proposed new law on the status of the church. If and when a solution is found it will be an excellent barometer for indicating the climate of future church-state relations. The reason for saying this is that the army chaplaincy is in practice an outpost of the Chief Political Department.

THE POPE'S "DIVISIONS" IN POLAND

All who comment on the situation in Poland inevitably stress the spiritual role and strength of the Catholic Church as a major element in the confrontation between the people and the system imposed by the political military. The material base of the church, its organization and human resources, are hardly ever mentioned. Yet they are substantial. In 1982 there were 21,059 priests, including 5,117 priests in 39 religious orders; 7,225 people being trained for the priesthood; 775 new priests ordained, and 1,755 entered seminaries for priests (about 200 more than in any of the three preceding years). [10]

Religious instruction (an internal matter of the church) was given in 19,000 religious instruction points. In 46 seminaries 6,700 men are currently trained for the priesthood. Apart from the seminaries there are four papal faculties, one nonstate Catholic University, one Academy of Catholic Theology. There were about 10,000 monks and 28,000 nuns. New churches are being built, adding to the 14,000 existing churches.[11]

The Catholic University at Lublin (KUL), which had survived the Hitler and Stalin eras in Poland, continues as the main center of catholic thought in the country. The scope, size, and caliber of this institution is reflected in its organization and staff. In 1981 the university had four faculties: christian philosophy with 23 chairs (professorships), social sciences with 35, canon law with 8, and theology with 34. In addition there were eight interfaculty establishments. There were over 90 professors and assistant professors and about 105 scientific workers with doctor's degrees. Corresponding figures for the Academy of Catholic Theology (ATK) in Warsaw were: faculty of christian philosophy with 7 chairs, of canon law with 8, and theological faculty with 17. In addition there were five interfaculty facilities. The staff consisted of about 55 professors and assistant professors and of over 70 scientific workers with doctor's degrees.[12]

In 1983 KUL had 2,700 students, lay and clergy, over 300 scientific workers, and as many other staff. Every year about 400 M.A.s, 40-50 Ph.D.s, and about 10 assistant professors qualify here. Over 70 percent of Polish bishops first graduated here and so did the great majority of teaching staff of priest training colleges. KUL's economic independence from the state allowed it to maintain its freedom of thought and to make a big contribution to the development of Polish culture. At all times, even during the Stalinist period. an unfalsified history of Poland was taught here. There were no taboo subjects and the names of famous Poles, like Czeslaw Milosz, were not removed from history or literature textbooks.[13]

The most influential regular catholic publication is the literary-philosophical weekly Tygodnik Powszechny, published in Cracow. Ever since it reappeared after a few months' break due to martial law it has been heavily censored. The editor adopted the practice to indicate the censor's intervention by quoting in the affected space the reference of the law on censorship of July 31, 1981. The political military seems to be concerned about the influence of the publication. It was attacked in the weekly called Argumenty, which said that its intellectual catholicism was only a facade for political Catholicism and that its ideology was hiding behind religion.[14] It turned out that the authors of the attack were two regular contributors to Wojsko Ludowe.

In 1982, which was the 600th anniversary of the Jasna Gora monastery, over 5 million people visited the shrine of the Black Madonna, 2 million more than in 1981. The number included 6,791 pilgrim groups that were led by their parish priests.[15] According to government sources, 6.6 million people attended masses and meetings with Pope John Paul II during his 1983 visit to Poland. According to a catholic source the Vatican paper <u>Osservatore Romano</u> produced a 56-page commemorative copy of its Polish edition containing all the pope's sermons with addresses directed to him. A consignment of 160,000 copies was shipped to Poland.

There are contentious opinions as to what the pope's divisions would be ready to fight for. The influential Paris monthly <u>Kultura</u> stated in a lead article:

> The church is an invaluable ally in the fight for independence. Hundreds if not thousands of priests will one day be given a right place in the nation's history. But the church fights in the first place for preserving its special position in a Communist country that is part of the Soviet bloc. This forces the church to seek compromises with the party.[16]

This is a Polish pessimistic view compared with one that emerges from the communiqué issued after the 195th Plenary Session of the Episcopate at Jasna Gora on August 25, 1983. This communiqué says that the Holy Father has outlined a long-term religious and social life program for all Poles. It demands the right of the nation to independence and the right of the people to be masters of their destiny. It calls for return to renewal based on an honest implementation of the agreements of August 1980 and to a dialogue with the people. It stresses the need for patriotism, moral values, and respect for human labor. The bishops expressed regret that the authorities missed the chance for national concord created by the pope's visit and condemned the repressive legislation introduced in July 1983 in place of martial law. To prevent a further growth of social unrest the authorities should listen to the just demands of the people expressed by its genuine representatives (implying that PRON and the new trade unions did not qualify for that role). They should restore genuine trade unions and organizations for creators of culture. The bishops call for pluralism of trade unions, a principle that had been removed already from the new trade union law. They want all Clubs for Catholic Intellectuals (KIK) to be able to resume activities. Finally the Bishops spoke of the need to repair wrongs where this is still possible, apply a general amnesty, reemploy people who had been sacked for their convictions, and readmit university students.

The introduction part of the communiqué deals with the pope's visit, which was declared an unqualified success because it strengthened and united the nation.[17]

SOME WELL-TRIED TACTICS

The demands contained in the communiqué were not new. They had been presented earlier, after each tightening of the Jaruzelski clamp, and were ignored. Perhaps the bishops believed that by putting them once again all together and exploiting the impact of the pope's visit they might obtain some concession for the Polish people and the church itself. Time will show whether they were right.

My view is that when General Jaruzelski agreed to the visit he had taken everything into calculation and was confident that he could deal with the aftermath of the visit. Compared with the early part of martial law this was child's play. Since martial law he acquired some support from the PRON movement, the new trade unions, and remnants of the civilian party, and even from lay Catholic organizations. He could now also use the new legislation against the active political opposition.

At the end of June 1983, soon after the pope's visit, PRON issued a declaration that the visit was an opportunity for a positive dialogue in which different points of view did not exclude concurrence in matters that for the Polish people are of basic importance.[18] In September 1983, J. Dobraczynski, head of the National Council of PRON, said in an interview that PRON had the same aims and aspirations as the church. The church could help in the process of moral renewal. PRON was expecting that help.

Zenon Komender, chairman of the lay Catholic Association "Pax," said at a meeting of representatives of regional "Pax" organizations that because PRON has been sanctioned by the Constitution it was the duty of all "Pax" activists to support PRON in all its activities. "Pax" was trying to create social conditions that would allow the alleviation of the effects of the temporary regulations (which replaced martial law). Komender stressed the fact that the "course on confrontation" that has surfaced in connection with the Gdansk agreements anniversary was a sign of irresponsibility and of absence of positive ideas.[19] Komender, said to be Jaruzelski's friend from school days, was appointed minister of internal trade and services in October 1981 and after declaration of martial law was made chairman of "Pax," in place of R. Reiff, one of the few members of the Seym who openly opposed martial law. Komender is now also deputy prime minister.

The situation in the country was discussed at the end of August 1983 at the plenary session of the management board of the Christian Social Association (ChSS) under the chairmanship of K. Morawski, head of ChSS. It was agreed that in order to overcome existing difficulties all Poles had to show civic responsibility and produce good work. Confrontation tendencies were to be opposed.[20] Morawski has been made a member of the Council of State. Finding jobs in advance of services to be rendered seems to be a strong point of the top political military who used "Pax," ChSS, "Caritas," and perhaps other Catholic lay organizations for weakening the church from within.

According to a report that came out of Poland via Underground Solidarity the Propaganda Department of the party (controlled now by the political military) formulated a whole range of tasks aimed at neutralizing the effect of the pope's visit.[21] If true, the report would herald a planned drive against the church in which an "enlightenment campaign" would be the dominant background factor. It would closely resemble the drive by the political army mounted after the imposition of martial law, which has been described earlier (see Chapter 11). The only difference would be that the church, not Solidarity, would now be the prime target (see Appendix F).

Enlightenment campaigns have a long tradition in the army. It is worth recalling one directed specifically against the church that was described in Wojsko Ludowe:

> In Spring 1966 at the request of the authorities the army
> took part in actions linked with celebrations of "One
> Thousand Years [Millenium] of Existence of the Polish
> State." Over 16,000 regular officers and NCOs were
> sent into action. They covered about 37,000 villages and
> hamlets. Nearly 3.5 million people took part in meetings
> with these troops. In addition about 5,000 meetings
> were organized in various centers, mainly for the
> young, for the work force in factories, and for other
> social groups. There were meetings with priests in
> parishes. "One Thousand Years of the Polish State and
> History of Polish Arms" was the theme of the meetings
> of the population with lecturers from the army. It
> was presented against the background of the German
> problem and of church-state relations.[22]

The "input" of units of the Polish Air Force into the above action is given in fuller detail in Appendix G. There it says specifically:

> As is well known the Millenium celebrations were accompa-
> nied by improper actions on the part of the reactionary
> section of the clergy with Cardinal Wyszynski in the lead.
> Their aim was to torpedo initiatives of the party and
> government, to give the celebrations the religious char-
> acter of baptism of Poland, to split society into believers

234 / POLAND'S POLITICIZED ARMY

and nonbelievers, and to set one part of the people
against the People's Rule and Socialism. [23]

It is a small point but one that needs to be made. General Jaruzelski
was at that time chief of the General Staff. He must have been
involved in these "operations."

While using the stick of antichurch propaganda to deter the
church from actively supporting the political opposition, the
political military intends to offer the carrot of a new law that would
regulate the position of the church in Poland and give it greater
freedom of action providing it stays out of politics. As in the case
of other Jaruzelski legislation, such new law would legalize what
is acceptable to him and outlaw what he does not want to happen.
The interpretation of the new law, the decision of what is lawful and
unlawful in the activities of a priest, would rest with the judiciary,
which in light of the experience of the last few years, is a mere
tool of the political military.

General Jaruzelski treats this particular aspect of church-
state relations very seriously. In 1982 he replaced the head of the
Office for Denominational Affairs, J. Kuberski, a teacher by
profession, with Professor Dr. Adam Lopatka, an expert on theory
of state and law. Lopatka is well qualified for this very job. In 1981
he was director of the Institute for State and Law of the Polish
Academy of Sciences, chairman of the Scientific Council of the
Institute of Judiciary in the Ministry of Justice, professor at the
Institute for Fundamental Problems of Marxism-Leninism of the
Central Committee of the party. From 1978 to 1980 he was Poland's
delegate to the U.N. Commission on Human Rights and he is
generally steeped in the theory of human rights. If I were to offer
any advice to the Catholic Church hierarchy in Poland it would be:
Beware of Lopatka (Polish for shovel), even one loaded with gifts.

An appraisal of the present state of church-state relations by
the political military is given in Appendix H. It amounts to saying,
"Let's agree to disagree."

Conclusions

Various general conclusions can be drawn from the mass of factual information presented in this book. Some of these conclusions should help to correct misconceptions still common in the West about the Polish drama of the 1980s.

1. The whole Polish Army did not turn against its own people. It was its present leadership, with a part of the army on which they could rely politically. Elements outside the army played a major role as part of the informal political army.

2. The army leadership and its support in the army are not military in the Western meaning of the word but political military. They operate in a dimension that is totally unknown in armies of the West.

3. The party is still in control in Poland, not the army. The elite brought forth by the political military displaced the old party apparatus and took the reins of the party into its own hands. At lower levels there is conflict of interest between the civilian and military parties and their members.

4. Jaruzelski as leader of the political military does not represent Polish but Soviet interests. His Polish Army and patriotic postures are part of a carefully prepared legend. He is a political functionary, a "Communist in uniform."

These are sufficient reasons to draw a distinction between his lot and the rest of the Polish Army by adopting a more appropriate terminology—for example, political leadership of the army, political military, political army, military party, civilian party, comrade general, comrade colonel, major, and so on. The existing terminology is harmful to Western and Polish interests because it distorts the

current political picture of Poland and prevents clear thinking about
the new phenomenon of "militarized Communism," and it antagonizes
those elements in the Polish Army who are on our side.

Other conclusions could take the form of answers to pertinent
questions:

1. Is Jaruzelski's intervention a one of the kind affair or a
model that could be followed by other East European countries? The
very close integration of a national army with the Soviet Army and
the specific political condition of Poland have no counterpart in East
European satellites. However, it is certain that the Jaruzelski
techniques had been developed in the Soviet Union and are probably
not for export only.

2. How was it possible that Solidarity leaders, the church, and
the rest of the opposition in Poland did not expect this form of intervention and did not credit the army with a capacity to organize a
new administration in place of the one that practically collapsed?
The huge effort that went into the buildup of the political army
passed unnoticed mainly because it happened under the cloak of
military secrecy. Even the final preparations did not arouse suspicion because "these were the silly games the army played without
causing harm to anybody." But above all there was the image of
upright, young, handsome men who were made the pride of many a
father or mother and there was the warm feeling of affection for the
army as a trustworthy institution. Sadly, it was a case of nurturing
a viper in one's bosom (Polish proverb).

3. Can the political military succeed where the civilian party
failed? On the present track record, no, for several reasons:

● For at least a decade the political military practiced a system
of indoctrination whereby thousands of full-time political
officers forced many more thousands of part-time army party
workers to cooperate in political indoctrination of hundreds
of thousands of the remaining army personnel. The system did not
bring the expected results.

● By the time Solidarity appeared, General Jaruzelski had over
12 years of sole management of the army as minister of
defense. All that time, combat readiness (political reliability)
was top priority. When in the winter and spring of 1980-81 he
needed combat readiness to check the growth of Solidarity it
wasn't there. He eventually found it but only when he was able
to apply special martial law provisions against those in the
army who opposed him. Running a country is infinitely more
difficult than running an army.

• During the 24 months that the political military have been in power they have shown that they see Poland as a huge garrison where law and order and life in general would be maintained by regulations and discipline modeled on the army. Endless inspection would keep people on their toes. This is not the right treatment for the ills of Poland. Real incentives, not an improved "historical awareness," would make the Polish people work. But real incentives are one thing the political military cannot provide because they hold on tenaciously to principles of a centrally planned war economy.

4. Is the fighting role of the Polish People's Army compatible with its internal political role? It is a fact that the political army leadership has sapped the strength of the Polish Army. This is not only because major resources have been systematically diverted to building the political army (Jaruzelski's first indictment will be "fraudulent conversion of funds") but also because the political apparatus and the military party as institutions are sources of permanent organizational, political, and procedural conflicts within the army. The cumulative effect is that of a crippling cancer that affects the whole body.

5. Are there any redeeming features of the political military? Yes, one: They had the common sense not to let themselves be used by the Soviet Union in political-military adventures in the outside world.

Notes

Abbreviations of titles used in the notes:

Dz.U.R.P.   Dziennik Ustaw Rzeczypospolitej Polskiej (Poland's
            official gazette)
M.E.W.   Mala Encyklopedia Wojskowa (Small Military Encyclo-
            pedia)
P.O.C.   Przeglad Obrony Cywilnej (Civil Defense Survey)
W.E.P.   Wielka Encyklopedia Powszechna (General Polish
            Encyclopedia)
W.L.   Wojsko Ludowe (People's Army)
Z.P.   Zolnierz Polski (Soldier of Poland)
Z.W.   Zolnierz Wolnosci (Soldier of Freedom)

CHAPTER 1

1. Sroga, A., W.L. No. 10, 1973, pp. 98-99.
2. Rutkowski S., Zarys Dziejow Polskiego Szkolnictwa
Wojskowego, MON, 1970, p. 234.
3. Jamrozinski, A., W.L. No. 5, 1980, p. 44.
4. W.L. No. 4, 1977, p. 74; Konecki, T., W.L. No. 9, 1973,
p. 42.
5. Rutkowski, S., Zarys. . . , pp. 261-62.
6. W.E.P. Vol. 9, p. 357.
7. Jaruzelski, W., W.L. No. 1, 1972, p. 29.
8. Grechko, A., W.L. No. 11, 1973, p. 13.
9. W.E.P. Vol. 1, pp. 387-88, 637.
10. M.E.W. Vol. 2, 1970, pp. 96, 701.
11. Jaruzelski, W., 20 Lat PRL, 1964, p. 198.
12. W.L. No. 9, 1973, p. 58.
13. Leczyk, M., W.L. No. 3, 1982, p. 65.
14. Who is Who in Poland. Warsaw: Interpress Publishers,
1982, p. 295.
15. Jaruzelski, W., W.L. No. 4, 1982, p. 7.
16. Jaruzelski, W., W.L. No. 1, 1982, p. 8.
17. Jaruzelski, W., 20 Lat PRL, 1964, p. 208.
18. Dz.U.R.P. 1979, No. 18, p. 248.
19. M.E.W. Vol. 2, 1970, pp. 367-68.
20. Ibid.
21. Ibid.

22. Muszynski, J., W.L. No. 5, 1983, pp. 45-46.
23. P.O.C. No. 1, 1980, p. 40.
24. Monitor Polski, No. 23, 1980, item 107.
25. Z.P. No. 37, 1979, p. 7.

CHAPTER 2

1. Military Balance 1982-83. London: International Institute of Strategic Studies, 1982.
2. Jaruzelski, W., W.L. No. 1, 1976, p. 27.
3. Jaruzelski, W., W.L. No. 3, 1980, p. 6.
4. Sadykiewicz, M., Survey Vol. 26, No. 3, pp. 20-21.
5. Ciechanowski, A., W.L. No. 9, 1980, pp. 27-30.
6. Z.P. No. 41, 1979, pp. 6-7.
7. Jaruzelski, W., W.L. No. 10, 1973, pp. 17-18.
8. Wojcik, J., W.L. No. 5, 1972, pp. 60-62.
9. Jaruzelski, op. cit.
10. Zegnalek, K., W.L. No. 9, 1980, pp. 30-32.
11. Tomczak, E., W.L. No. 3, 1979, p. 67.
12. Brzezinski, S., W.L. No. 9, 1982, p. 54.
13. Kwiatkowski, Z., Z.P. No. 15, 1983, p. 5.
14. M.E.W. Vol. 2, 1970, pp. 708-09.
15. Konecki, T., W.L. No. 9, 1973, pp. 41-50.
16. Ibid.
17. M.E.W. Vol. 2, op. cit.
18. Tomczak, op. cit.
19. Honkisz, W., W.L. No. 4, 1977, p. 40-45.
20. Konecki, op. cit.
21. Honkisz, op. cit.
22. Glajzner, T., W.L. No. 7, 1977, p. 55.
23. Goralewski, M., W.L. No. 11, 1976, pp. 29-34.
24. Ibid.
25. Miller, Z., W.L. No. 9, 1982, p. 45.
26. Ratajczyk, L., W.L. No. 9, 1976, p. 121.
27. Polanski, W., W.L. No. 12, 1981, pp. 36-41.
28. Ibid.
29. Polanski, W., W.L. No. 9, 1976, pp. 14-20.
30. Bartosinski, B., W.L. No. 4, 1977, pp. 51-52.
31. Anysz, M., W.L. No. 9, 1982, p. 62.
32. Moryc, B., W.L. No. 4, 1977, pp. 67-68.
33. Doroba, Z., W.L. No. 11, 1975, pp. 57-58.
34. Tomczak, E., W.L. No. 11, 1980, p. 55.
35. Polanski, 1976, op. cit.

36. Doroba, Z., W.L. No. 3, 1976, p. 58.
37. Sawczuk, W., W.L. No. 9, 1976, p. 7.

CHAPTER 3

1. Sawczuk, W., W.L. No. 2, 1972, pp. 5, 10.
2. M.E.W. Vol. 2, 1970, pp. 570, 662-63.
3. Sadowski, S., & Janusz, T., W.L. No. 8, 1979, pp. 48-49.
4. Doroba, Z., W.L. No. 3, 1976, pp. 55-59.
5. Ibid.
6. M.E.W. Vol. 2, op. cit.
7. Rutkowski, H., & Wasilewicz, P., W.L. No. 6, 1980,
pp. 12-13.
8. Rutkowski, H., W.L. No. 8, 1980, p. 14.
9. Jaruzelski, W., 20 Lat PRL, 1964, p. 205.
10. Sawczuk, op. cit.
11. Glowczyk, A., W.L. No. 10, 1979, p. 33.
12. Czajkowski, S., W.L. No. 10, 1978, pp. 61-62.
13. Klobukowski, Z., W.L. No. 12, 1978, p. 26.
14. Skorodenko, P., Voyenno-distoricheskiy Zhurnal No. 5,
1983, p. 56.
15. Olszewski, I., W.L. No. 10, 1983, p. 62.
16. Janusz, H., W.L. No. 11, 1979, p. 84-85.
17. Maciejewski, K., W.L. No. 10, 1978, p. 108.
18. Janusz, op. cit.
19. W.L. No. 12, 1973, p. 9.
20. Maluta, R., W.L. No. 11, 1975, pp. 50-51.
21. Rzepecki, T., W.L. No. 11, 1979, pp. 46-48.
22. Maluta, R., W.L. No. 4, 1980, pp. 16-18.
23. Krajewski, Z., W.L. No. 12, 1978, pp. 34-37.
24. M.E.W. Vol. 2, op. cit.
25. Kacala, H., W.L. No. 7, 1973, p. 22.
26. Skrzypkowski, E., W.L. No. 7, 1973, pp. 15-16.
27. Rozbicki, Z., W.L. No. 8, 1979, p. 36.
28. Baryla, J., W.L. No. 1, 1981, p. 14.
29. Ruszkiewicz, I., W.L. No. 3, 1982, p. 25.
30. Yepishev, A., Kommunist No. 7, 1972.
31. Muszynski, J., W.L. No. 2, 1978, p. 51.
32. Jaruzelski, W., Nowe Drogi No. 5, 1975.
33. M.E.W. Vol. 1, 1967, p. 464.
34. Zachariasiewicz, P., W.L. No. 10, 1976, p. 31.
35. Yepishev, op. cit.
36. Sawczuk, W., W.L. No. 2, 1972, p. 3.

37. Siwicki, F., W.L. No. 12, 1975, p. 16.
38. Zachariasiewicz, op. cit.
39. Sawczuk, W., W.L. No. 10, 1978, pp. 4-8.
40. Kuberski, J., W.L. No. 10, 1978, pp. 9-10.
41. Urlinski, R., W.L. No. 1, 1981, p. 71.
42. Kuberski, op. cit.
43. Baryla, J., W.L. No. 7, 1983, p. 7.
44. W.L. No. 12, 1975, pp. 6-7.

CHAPTER 4

1. M.E.W. Vol. 2, 1970, p. 571.
2. M.E.W. Vol. 3, 1971, pp. 43, 254-55.
3. Matiocha, A., W.L. No. 12, 1979, p. 13.
4. Sawczuk, W., W.L. No. 2, 1972, p. 4.
5. Koczara H., W.L. No. 11, 1974, pp. 4-7.
6. M.E.W. Vol. 3, op. cit.
7. Kacala, H., W.L. No. 9, 1974, p. 57.
8. Poweska, S., W.L. No. 12, 1978, p. 31.
9. W.L. No. 10, 1976, p. 89.
10. Jura, W., W.L. No. 12, 1977, pp. 40-44.
11. Glajzner, T., W.L. No. 9, 1978, p. 12.
12. W.L. No. 3, 1976, p. 53.
13. Brodzinski, S., W.L. No. 11, 1973, p. 50.
14. Glajzner, op. cit.
15. Kostecki, A., W.L. No. 2, 1976, p. 37.
16. Rostowski, A., W.L. No. 2, 1979, pp. 43-46.
17. Krajewski, Z., W.L. No. 2, 1977, pp. 19-23.
18. Wojtasik, L., W.L. No. 8, 1981, pp. 73-77.
19. Krajewski, Z., W.L. No. 7, 1977, pp. 31-35.
20. Rostowski, op. cit.
21. Ibid.
22. Przelaskowski, R., W.L. No. 5, 1978, pp. 57-58.
23. Kwiatkowski, S., W.L. No. 4, 1978, pp. 48-50.
24. Przelaskowski, op. cit.
25. Krajewski, Z., W.L. No. 11, 1978, pp. 39-40.

CHAPTER 5

1. Polanski, W., W.L. No. 5, 1973, pp. 95-102.
2. Michalik, M., W.L. No. 9, 1976, pp. 90-97.
3. Olczyk, E., Staciwa C., & Michalczak J., W.L. No. 1, 1974, pp. 95-99.

4. Polanski, op. cit.
5. Michalik, op. cit.
6. Michalik, op. cit.
7. Olczyk, et al., op. cit.
8. Ibid.
9. Olczyk, E., W.L. No. 1, 1972, p. 91.
10. Michalik, op. cit.
11. Polanski, W., W.L. No. 12, 1981.
12. Olczyk, et al., op. cit.
13. Michalik, op. cit.
14. Olczyk, et al., op. cit.
15. Polanski, W., W.L. No. 10, 1973, p. 51.
16. Polanski, W., W.L. No. 12, 1981, op. cit.
17. Informator Nauki Polskiej, 1980/81, Warsaw, 1981, pp. 432-40.
18. Informator Nauki Polskiej, op. cit.
19. Olczyk, et al., op. cit.
20. Michalik, op. cit.
21. Olczyk, et al., op. cit.
22. Gesek, J. T., W.L. No. 18, 1981, pp. 56-60.
23. Baryla, J., W.L. No. 1, 1983, p. 10.
24. Wiatr, J. J., W.L. No. 2, 1983, p. 10.
25. W.L. No. 5, 1975, pp. 107-11.
26. The Europa Yearbook, 1980, p. 1015.
27. W.L. No. 11, 1975, p. 101.
28. Europa Yearbook, op. cit.
29. W.L. Nos. 2 and 7, 1973, No. 2, 1974, No. 2, 1975, No. 4, 1976, Chronicle pages.
30. Witczak, M., W.L. No. 2, 1975, pp. 57-59.
31. Tempski, Z., W.L. No. 10, 1978, pp. 18-19.
32. Zyto, A., W.L. No. 7, 1975, pp. 32-33.
33. Sawczuk, W., W.L. No. 6, 1978, pp. 4-10.
34. Zyto, op. cit.
35. Lutomski, J., Z.P. No. 47, 1979, pp. 18, 21.
36. Damski, Z., Z.P. No. 50, 1979, p. 18.
37. Sawczuk, op. cit.
38. Ibid.
39. Zyto, op. cit.
40. W.L. No. 6, 1973, p. 118.
41. W.L. No. 11, 1975, p. 101.
42. W.L. No. 1, 1976, p. 98.
43. W.L. No. 8, 1975, p. 89.
44. Z.P. No. 9, 1981, p. 13.
45. W.L. No. 2, 1975, p. 110.
46. W.L. No. 2, 1976, p. 100.

47. Zielinska, K., W.L. No. 10, 1980, pp. 47-49.
48. Z.P. No. 51-52, 1979, p. 37.
49. Z.P. No. 9, 1981, p. 13.
50. W.L. No. 12, 1975, p. 9.
51. Czerwinski, Z., W.L. No. 6, 1975, p. 37.
52. Szczygielski, S., W.L. No. 9, 1976, pp. 98-105.
53. Sawczuk, op. cit.
54. Zyto, A., W.L. No. 6, 1978, p. 18.

CHAPTER 6

1. Jaruzelski, W., W.L. No. 3, 1980, p. 7.
2. Grygiel, J., W.L. No. 7, 1980, pp. 24-26.
3. Kowalski, A., W.L. No. 8, 1980, pp. 17-18.
4. Kruk, W., W.L. No. 8, 1980, pp. 17-18.
5. Chodyla, Z., W.L. No. 7, 1980, pp. 26-28.
6. Wojnowski, E., W.L. No. 9, 1980, pp. 8-11.
7. Chodyla, op. cit.
8. Wesolowski, T., W.L. No. 9, 1980, pp. 6-8.
9. Grochmalicki, J., W.L. No. 9, 1980, pp. 4-5.
10. Kowalski, op. cit.
11. Szymanski, E., W.L. No. 8, 1980, pp. 20-23.
12. Jaruzelski, op. cit.
13. Witczak, M., W.L. No. 2, 1975.
14. M.E.W. Vol. 2, 1970, pp. 339-40.
15. Zbowidowcy, Ksiazkai Wiedza Warsaw, 1969, pp. 391-93.
16. Glowczyk, A., W.L. No. 9, 1979, pp. 54-55.
17. Jurek, M., W.L. No. 2, 1974, pp. 48-52.
18. Glowczyk, op. cit.
19. Jurek, op. cit.
20. M.E.W. Vol. 2, 1970, p. 183.
21. Glowczyk, op. cit.
22. W.L. No. 8, 1973, p. 119.
23. W.L. No. 5, 1976, p. 100.
24. W.L. No. 6, 1976, p. 92.
25. Monitor Polski No. 28, 1979, item 146.
26. P.O.C. No. 5, 1979, p. 6.
27. Bonczak, J., W.L. No. 9, 1979, pp. 88-89.
28. P.O.C., op. cit.
29. P.O.C. No. 5, 1981, p. 11.
30. M.E.W. Vol. 3, 1971, p. 624.
31. P.O.C. No. 9, 1979, p. 14.
32. Z.P. No. 50, 1982, p. 21.
33. Z.P. No. 46, 1981, p. 21.

34. P.O.C. No. 11, 1980, pp. 27-28.
35. Zembrzycki, Z., W.L. No. 5, 1978, pp. 56-57.
36. Z.P. No. 35, 1979, p. 8.
37. Z.P. No. 2, 1982, p. 7.
38. Bieniasz, S., W.L. No. 10, 1978, pp. 112-16.
39. Z.P. No. 4, 1979, p. 5.
40. Malinowski, S., W.L. No. 5, 1981, p. 60.
41. Jaroszewicz, P., W.L. No. 10, 1973, p. 9.
42. Jaruzelski, W., W.L. No. 1, 1972, p. 27.

CHAPTER 7

1. Walczuk, E., W.L. No. 4, 1981, pp. 52-56.
2. Ibid.
3. Ibid.
4. Olszewski, I., W.L. No. 12, 1981, pp. 42-45.
5. Ibid.
6. Boguszewicz, I., W.L. No. 11, 1981, pp. 266-68.
7. Olszewski, I., No. 4, 1981, pp. 27-28.
8. Wojtas, P., W.L. No. 6, 1981, p. 18.
9. Boguszewicz, I., W.L. No. 9, 1981, pp. 53-56.
10. Maluta, R., W.L. No. 7, 1981, pp. 43-49.
11. Walczuk, E., W.L. No. 4, 1980, pp. 12-15.
12. Maluta, op. cit.
13. Boguszewicz, W.L. No. 9, op. cit.
14. Maluta, op. cit.
15. Zdziech, M., W.L. No. 5, 1981, p. 12.
16. Chwilkowski, S., W.L. No. 5, 1981, p. 50.
17. Gaszczolowski, W., W.L. No. 8, 1981, pp. 63-65.
18. Molinski, J., W.L. No. 5, 1981, p. 51.
19. Iwaniec, W., W.L. No. 5, 1981, p. 51.
20. Bogusz, J., W.L. No. 5, 1981, p. 50.
21. Rozbicki, Z., W.L. No. 8, 1981, p. 57.
22. Mielczarek, R., W.L. No. 8, 1981, p. 59.
23. Szyszkowski, J., W.L. No. 8, 1981, pp. 66-69.
24. Gaszczolowski, op. cit.
25. Kujawa, J., W.L. No. 12, 1981, pp. 45-48.
26. Boguszewicz, I., & Kasprzak R., W.L. No. 2, 1982, pp. 66-68.
27. Boguszewicz, I., W.L. No. 2, 1981, pp. 52-55.
28. Olszewski, I., W.L. No. 7, 1981, pp. 49-52.
29. Walczuk, E., W.L. No. 7, 1981, pp. 53-58.
30. Rozbicki, Z., W.L. No. 3, 1981, pp. 42-46.
31. Wojtasik, L., W.L. No. 9, 1981, pp. 11, 37.

32. Zdziech, M., W.L. No. 8, 1981, p. 70.
33. W.L. No. 9, 1981, pp. 45-46.
34. Uliasz, Z., W.L. No. 9, 1981, pp. 50-51.
35. Slowinski, S., W.L. No. 9, 1981, pp. 46-47.
36. Hanczewski, J., W.L. No. 8, 1981, p. 61.
37. Zdziech, M., W.L. No. 11, 1981, pp. 55-57.
38. Kujawa, op. cit.
39. Apanasowicz, W.L. No. 10, 1981, p. 63.
40. Gluszko, T., W.L. No. 9, 1981, p. 58.
41. Dziewulski, A., W.L. No. 12, 1981, p. 50.
42. Uliasz, op. cit.
43. Kujawa, op. cit.
44. Wesolowski, A., W.L. No. 9, 1981, p. 48.
45. Slowinski, op. cit.
46. Wesolowski, op. cit.
47. Jankowski, J., W.L. No. 10, 1981, p. 52.
48. Wojtas, P., W.L. No. 10, 1981, p. 54.
49. Krzanik, K., W.L. No. 10, 1981, p. 63.
50. Kujawa, op. cit.
51. W.L. No. 4, 1981, pp. 22-23.
52. Jaroszewicz, P., W.L. No. 10, 1973, p. 7.
53. Walczuk, E., W.L. No. 6, 1981, p. 51.
54. Wojtasik, op. cit.
55. Rozko, Z., W.L. No. 12, 1980, pp. 37-39.
56. Olszewski, I., W.L. No. 6, 1981, p. 63.

CHAPTER 8

1. Jaruzelski, W., W.L. No. 11, 1980, pp. 24-26.
2. Michalik, M., W.L. No. 7, 1981, pp. 13-19.
3. Baryla, J., W.L. No. 1, 1981, pp. 13-14.
4. Maluta, R., W.L. No. 2, 1981, pp. 7-11.
5. Glowczyk, A., W.L. No. 2, 1981, pp. 11-15.
6. Zielinski, K., W.L. No. 2, 1981, pp. 18-20.
7. Olszewski, I., W.L. No. 2, 1981, pp. 15-18.
8. Maluta, R., W.L. No. 7, 1981, pp. 43-49.
9. Rozbicki, Z., W.L. No. 3, 1981, pp. 42-47.
10. Rozbicki, Z., W.L. No. 1, 1982, pp. 54-57.
11. Wojtasik, L., W.L. No. 8, 1981, pp. 73-76.
12. M.E.W. Vol. 3, 1971, p. 5.
13. Jaruzelski, W., W.L. No. 1, 1982, pp. 6-8.
14. Z.P. No. 6, 1982, p. 10.
15. W.L. No. 7, 1981, p. 38.
16. W.L. No. 12, 1981, p. 24.

17. W.L. No. 11, 1981, p. 9.
18. Z.W. June 30, 1981.
19. Skrzypkowski, E., W.L. No. 4, 1972, p. 87.
20. Trybuna Ludu, October 30, 1981.
21. Paluch, E., Z.P. No. 8, 1983, p. 14.
22. W.L. No. 12, 1981, p. 35.
23. Borgosz, J., W.L. No. 10, 1981, pp. 23-29.
24. Leczyk, M., W.L. No. 7, 1981, p. 41.
25. Bobrowicz, J., W.L. No. 11, 1981, pp. 91-96.
26. Jaruzelski, W., W.L. No. 8, 1981, p. 34.
27. W.L. No. 9, 1982, p. 3.
28. Jaruzelski, W., W.L. No. 4, 1982, pp. 6-21.
29. Fiedorow, A., W.L. No. 1, 1983, pp. 45-47.
30. Gasperowicz, M., W.L. No. 1, 1983, p. 47.
31. Jakubiak, B., W.L. No. 1, 1983, pp. 53-55.
32. Olszewski, I., W.L. No. 10, 1981, pp. 21-22.
33. Zielinski, K., W.L. No. 9, 1981, p. 49.
34. Olszewski, I., W.L. No. 7, 1982, p. 79.
35. Boguszewicz, I., W.L. No. 12, 1980, p. 51.
36. Rozko, Z., W.L. No. 12, 1980.
37. Bieniek, J., W.L. No. 8, 1981, pp. 71-72.
38. Maluta, W.L. No. 7, op. cit.
39. Wyruch, W., W.L. No. 3, 1981, pp. 11-12.
40. Skrzypiec, J., W.L. No. 9, 1980, pp. 57-61; No. 10, 1980, pp. 42-46.
41. Szyszkowski, J., W.L. No. 12, 1980, pp. 46-48.
42. Baryla, J., W.L. No. 8, 1981, pp. 36-37.
43. Zielinski, W.L. No. 2, op. cit.
44. Szyszkowski, J., W.L. No. 8, 1981.
45. Olszewski, W.L. No. 10, op. cit.
46. Koczy, K., W.L. No. 8, 1981, p. 58.

CHAPTER 9

1. Michta, N., Trybuna Ludu, September 15, 1981.
2. Krajewski, M., W.L. No. 11, 1981, pp. 17-21.
3. Michalik, M., W.L. No. 4, 1981, pp. 29-34.
4. Wojcik, P., W.L. No. 4, 1982, pp. 49-54.
5. Kwiatkowski, S., & Gluszko, T., W.L. No. 3, 1982, pp. 53-55.
6. Muszynski, J., W.L. No. 12, 1980, pp. 10-19.
7. Czerwinski, Z., W.L. No. 7, 1981, pp. 3-6.
8. Muszynski, op. cit.
9. Erasmus, and others, W.L. No. 4, 1981, p. 39.

10. Kossecki, J., W.L. No. 2, 1982, p. 22; No. 11, 1982, pp. 41–46.

11. Ochocki, K., W.L. No. 2, 1982, p. 19.

12. Kossecki, op. cit.

13. Wojtasik, L., W.L. No. 6, 1982, pp. 11–14.

14. Baryla, J., W.L. No. 1, 1983, pp. 7–14.

15. Jaruzelski, W., W.L. No. 3, 1982, p. 7.

16. W.L. No. 7, 1983, pp. 88–89.

17. Tydzien i Dziennik Polski (London), No. 42, October 22, 1983, pp. 1, 11.

18. Iwaniec, W., W.L. No. 8, 1982, pp. 24–28.

19. Pozoga, W., W.L. No. 10, 1981, pp. 12–13.

20. Maski, C., W.L. No. 7, 1982, pp. 95–99.

21. Wojtasik, L., W.L. No. 7, 1982, pp. 32–35.

22. Muszynski, op. cit.

23. Wojtasik, W.L. No. 7, op. cit.

24. Krajewski, op. cit.

25. W.L. No. 3, 1982, p. 19.

26. Waga, A., W.L. No. 2, 1983, p. 52.

CHAPTER 10

1. M.E.W. Vol. 2, 1970, p. 707.

2. Z.P. No. 41, 1981, p. 4.

3. Z.P. No. 36, 1981, p. 16.

4. Kufel, T., W.L. No. 1, 1974, pp. 35–39.

5. W.L. No. 12, 1982, pp. 6–9.

6. Tobiasz, J., W.L. No. 10, 1979, p. 95.

7. M.E.W. Vol. 2, 1970, p. 706.

8. M.E.W. Vol. 3, 1971, p. 528.

9. M.E.W. Vol. 2, 1970, p. 96.

10. M.E.W. Vol. 3, 1971, p. 528.

11. Z.W., February 18, 1983, p. 2.

12. M.E.W. Vol. 2, 1970, pp. 311–12.

13. Tygodnik Powszechny, February 27, 1983.

14. Z.W., August 16, 1983, p. 2.

15. Dziennik Polski (London), April 13, 1982.

16. Gazeta Niedzielna (London), December 18–25, 1983.

17. Z.P. No. 32, 1983, p. 20.

18. M.E.W. Vol. 2, 1970, pp. 482–83.

19. Tobiasz, J., Z.P. No. 40, 1979, p. 6.

20. Januszewski, M., W.L. No. 4, 1978, p. 53.

21. Informator Nauki Polskiej, 1980/81, Warsaw, 1981, p. 441.

22. Muszynski, J., W.L. No. 10, 1983, p. 9.

23. Siwicki, F., <u>Trybuna Ludu</u>, February 25, 1983.

24. Dunal, W., W.L. No. 8, 1982, pp. 39-40.

25. Olszewski, I., W.L. No. 2, 1982, pp. 55-57.

26. Porajski, H., W.L. No. 8, 1982, pp. 40-43.

27. Mitek, T., W.L. No. 6, 1982, pp. 39-43.

28. Bandosz, E., W.L. No. 12, 1982, pp. 17-20.

29. Z.W., March 17, 1982, p. 6.

30. Suwart, J., P.O.C. No. 2, 1982, pp. 32-33.

31. Z.P. No. 40, 1981, p. 5.

32. Z.P. No. 12, 1981, p. 2.

33. Z.P. No. 28, 1981, p. 14.

34. <u>Stolica</u>, No. 9, 1983, p. 12.

CHAPTER 11

1. Jaruzelski, W., W.L. No. 8, 1981, p. 34.

2. Baryla, J., W.L. No. 8, 1981, pp. 36-37.

3. Czerwinski, Z., W.L. No. 7, 1981.

4. Z.P. No. 7, 1982, p. 10.

5. W.L. No. 11, 1981, p. 3.

6. Z.P. No. 8, 1982, p. 9.

7. W.L. No. 1, 1982, pp. 1-5.

8. Leczyk, M., W.L. No. 3, 1982, pp. 63-64.

9. Ruszkiewicz, I., W.L. No. 5, 1981, pp. 13-18.

10. Ruszkiewicz, I., W.L. No. 10, 1981, pp. 3-7.

11. M.E.W. Vol. 3, 1971, p. 195.

12. W.L. No. 1, 1982, pp. 10-11.

13. Czerwinski, Z., W.L. No. 4, 1982, p. 67.

14. Jurek, M., W.L. No. 12, 1982, pp. 12-17.

15. Malina, Z., W.L. No. 2, 1983, pp. 53-54.

16. W.L. No. 1, 1982, p. 13.

17. Bandosz, W.L. No. 12, 1982.

18. Z.P. No. 50, 1982, p. 2.

19. W.L. No. 7, 1982, p. 10.

20. Z.P. No. 17, 1982, p. 5.

21. Masztanowicz, S., & Moryc, B., W.L. No. 1, 1982, pp. 58-66.

22. Walczuk, E., W.L. No. 10, 1982, p. 24.

23. Z.P. No. 6, 1982, p. 2.

24. Jurek, op. cit.

25. Malina, op. cit.

26. Makowiecki, W., Z.W., December 28, 1982.

27. Z.W., April 8, 1983, p. 1.

CHAPTER 12

1. Krajewski, M., W.L. No. 1, 1983, pp. 29-31.
2. Z.P. No. 12, 1982, p. 2.
3. Z.P. No. 10, 1983, p. 2.
4. Z.W., February 11, 1983, p. 3.
5. Z.W., February 17, 1983, p. 2.
6. Siwicki, F., Trybuna Ludu, February 25, 1983.
7. Oliwa, W., Z.W., February 18, 1983, p. 3.
8. W.L. No. 5, 1982, p. 47.
9. Baryla, J., W.L. No. 1, 1983, pp. 7-14.
10. Trybuna Ludu, February 11, 1983.
11. Tygodnik Powszechny, March 20, 1983, p. 1.
12. Jaruzelski, W., W.L. No. 4, 1982, .p. 6-21.
13. W.L. No. 12, 1982, p. 24.
14. W.L. No. 4, 1982, p. 3.
15. Jaruzelski, W., op. cit.
16. Dziekan, T., Polityka, November 11, 1983.
17. Olszewski, I., W.L. No. 10, 1983, p. 62.
18. Jaruzelski, op. cit.
19. Boguszewicz, W.L. No. 7, 1982, pp. 63-66.
20. Boguszewicz, W.L. No. 3, 1982, pp. 75-77.
21. Mitek, T., W.L. No. 6, 1982.
22. W.L. No. 5, 1982.
23. Z.W., February 17, 1983, pp. 1-2.
24. Czerwinski, Z., W.L. No. 9, 1981, pp. 12-13.
25. Rutkowski, S., W.L. No. 1, 1983, pp. 32-36.
26. Ibid.
27. Olszewski, I., W.L. No. 7, 1982, pp. 58-59.
28. Baryla, J., W.L. No. 11, 1982, pp. 6-8.
29. Kozlowski, E., W.L. No. 1, 1983, pp. 49-51.
30. Badowski, T., W.L. No. 12, 1982, pp. 20-24.
31. Ibid.
32. Badowski, T., W.L. No. 9, 1983, p. 14.
33. Tygodnik Powszechny, August 21, 1983, p. 1.
34. Rzeczpospolita, November 22, 1983.
35. Szokarski, S., Gazeta Robotnicza, August 15, 1983.
36. Jaruzelski, W.L. No. 4, 1982.
37. Skweres, J., Z.P. No. 11, 1982, p. 2.
38. Zwolinski, S., W.L. No. 10, 1982, pp. 11-16.
39. Grabowski, T., Z.W., January 21, 1983, p. 4.
40. Tygodnik Powszechny, February 6, 1983.
41. Z.W., January 27, 1983.
42. Z.W., January 29-30, 1983, p. 2.
43. Z.W., March 8, 1983, pp. 1-2.

44. Dziekan, T., Rzeczpospolita, October 15-16, 1983.
45. Rzeczpospolita, October 5, 1983, pp. 1-2.
46. Jaruzelski, W., Z.W., July 22, 1983, p. 3.

CHAPTER 13

1. Siwicki, F., Z.W., December 20, 1982, p. 3.
2. Baryla, J., Rzeczpospolita, February 9, 1983.
3. Jurek, M., & Badowski, T., W.L. No. 1, 1983, pp. 20-23.
4. Tuczapski, T., Z.W., August 16, 1983, p. 3.
5. Gulczynski, M., W.L. No. 11, 1983, p. 39.
6. Wojtylowicz, M., W.L. No. 2, 1983, pp. 61-63.
7. Porajski, H., W.L. No. 2, 1983, p. 55.
8. Jurczak, K., W.L. No. 5, 1982, p. 43.
9. Wlodarski, M., W.L. No. 3, 1983, pp. 45-47.
10. Szumski, H., W.L. No. 2, 1983, pp. 50-52.
11. Szumski, H., Z.W., December 31, 1982, p. 6.
12. W.L. No. 12, 1982, p. 9.
13. Baryla, J., W.L. No. 1, 1983.
14. Baryla, J., W.L. No. 3, 1983, p. 80.
15. Sobczak, K., W.L. No. 3, 1983, pp. 83-85.
16. Z.W., March 2, 1983, p. 3.
17. Baryla, W.L. No. 1, op. cit.
18. Monitor Polski, No. 31, 1982.
19. Z.P. No. 9, 1983, p. 9.
20. Monitor Polski, No. 23, 1980.
21. Z.W., December 12, 1983.
22. Kujawa, J., W.L. No. 12, 1982, pp. 31-35.
23. Ibid.
24. Baryla, W.L. No. 1, op. cit.
25. Jurek & Badowski, op. cit.
26. Kujawa, op. cit.
27. Ibid.
28. Z.P. No. 8, 1983, p. 2.
29. Badowski, T., W.L. No. 9, 1983, p. 14.
30. Tygodnik Powszechny, December 19, 1982.
31. Wojtasik, L., W.L. No. 4, 1983, pp. 25-31.
32. Ibid.

CHAPTER 14

1. Gellert, T., W.L. No. 8, 1979, pp. 24-28.
2. Krasicki, I., W.L. No. 5, 1974, p. 21.

3. Krasicki, I., W.L. No. 6, 1974, p. 32.

4. Krasicki, I., W.L. No. 8, 1974, p. 2-26.

5. Krasicki, I., W.L. No. 9, 1974, p. 32.

6. Erasmus, I., W.L. No. 8, 1981, p. 38.

7. M.E.W. Vol. 2, 1970, pp. 20-21.

8. Zawsze z Narodem. Warsaw: Interpress, 1978, p. 98.

9. Black, Johann, Militaerseelsorge in Polen. Stuttgart: See-wald, 1981, pp. 87-96.

10. Tygodnik Powszechny, January 23, 1983.

11. Z.P. No. 7, 1983, p. 21.

12. Informator Nauki Polskiej, 1980/81, Warsaw 1981, pp. 143-58, 363-69.

13. Gazeta Niedzielna (London), December 18-25, 1983.

14. Tygodnik Powszechny, September 4, 1983.

15. Tygodnik Powszechny, March 20, 1983.

16. Kultura (Paris), No. 9, 1983, p. 3.

17. Tygodnik Powszechny, October 2, 1983, p. 1.

18. Trybuna Ludu, June 30, 1983, p. 1.

19. Rzeczpospolita, September 8, 1983, p. 2.

20. Rzeczpospolita, August 31, 1983, p. 2.

21. Dziennik Polski (London), September 8, 1983, p. 2.

22. Jaworski, M., W.L. No. 5, 1983, p. 107.

23. Kolodziejak, Z., Wojskowy Przeglad Lotniczy No. 3, 1967, p. 4.

Appendix A

On December 13, 1981, supreme power was assumed by a Military Council of National Salvation, which consisted of a chairman and 21 high-ranking officers of the Polish Army.

Chairman

Jaruzelski, Wojciech: General of the Army, Minister of Defense (since 1968), Prime Minister (since February 1981), 1st Secretary of the Polish United Workers' Party (since October 1981), Member of Parliament

Members:

Siwicki, Florian: General, Chief of General Staff (since 1973) Deputy-Minister of Defense, Member of Parliament

Tuczapski, Tadeusz: General, Chief Inspector of Territorial Defense (since 1972), Deputy-Minister of Defense

Molczyk, Eugeniusz: General, Chief Inspector of Training (since 1972), Deputy-Minister of Defense, Deputy Commander of Warsaw Pact Forces

Janczyszyn, Ludwik: Admiral, Commander of the Navy, Member of Parliament

Kiszczak, Czeslaw: Lt.-General (now General), Minister of the Interior (since July 1981)

Hupalowski, Tadeusz: Lt.-General, Minister for Administration, Regional Economy, and Environment; former 1st Deputy Chief of General Staff (1973-81)

Piotrowski, Czeslaw: Lt.-General, Minister for Mines and Power Industry (since July 1981), former Head of Military Research and Technology

Baryla, Jozef: Lt.-General (now General), Head of Chief Political
    Directorate of the Polish Army, Deputy Minister of Defense
Oliwa, Wlodzimierz: Lt.-General, Commander of Warsaw Military
    District, Member of Parliament
Rapacewicz, Henryk: Lt.-General, Commander of Silesian Military
    District, Member of Parliament
Uzycki, Jozef: Lt.-General, Commander of Pomeranian Military
    District, Member of Parliament
Krepski, Tadeusz: Lt.-General, Commander of Polish Air Force
Lozowicki, Longin: Lt.-General, Commander of Air Defense Troops
Janiszewski, Michal: Maj.-General (now Lt.-Gen.), Head of Prime
    Minister's Office
Jarosz, Jerzy: Maj.-General, Commander 1st Warsaw Mechanized
    Division
Makarewicz, Tadeusz: Colonel, Commander of a (unspecified) unit
Garbacik, Kazimierz: Colonel, Chief of Regional Military Staff
Les, Roman: Colonel (retired), Chairman of Union of ex-Regular
    Soldiers
Wlosinski, Jerzy: Lt.-Colonel (now Colonel), Commander of an
    Internal Defense Troops Unit (Warsaw Region)
Hermaszewski, Miroslaw: Lt.-Colonel (now Colonel), Polish
    astronaut
Zielinski, Zygmunt: Lt.-General, co-opted Secretary of the Council,
    Head of Department of Cadres in the Ministry of Defense
    (since 1968)

Appendix B

Every year one of the divisional exercises "in Methods" is devoted to the role of the political apparatus during tactical exercises. The two-day exercises consist of seminars, lectures, information service, and practical training in the field. During the exercises officers of the political apparatus were given concrete tasks.

Among the more important problems tackled during the exercises were: conducting a political reconnaissance, establishing and maintaining contact with the political apparatus of neighboring units, directing the political work in own units, procedures to be followed after encircling large numbers of enemy troops, political activity on entering allied or enemy territory, counteracting subversion and psychological warfare of the enemy, eliminating psychological and moral effects of weapons of mass destruction, preparing propaganda material, recording of broadcasts, and so on.

Some attention was given to preparing and keeping the "map of political operations" on which basic information is shown in a much abridged form with the help of the special signs of the political apparatus and a graphic presentation of data.

In the Political Department of the division and in Political Sections of regiments two basic sets of documentation are kept:

- An "Alarm Instruction," which gives the outline of work and the duties of political officers during the various stages of increasing combat readiness.

- Documentation that describes the scope of work for the Political Department and Political Sections during the preparation and conduct of tactical exercises (or combat), namely during attack, defense, and movement; it describes the duties of individual officers and contains some information on enemy and own troops.

The documentation is kept in a special plastic cover and fits into a briefcase with writing and drawing materials. Every political officer has in addition a workbook in which his duties are described and samples of documents used in his work are given together with auxiliary materials. The documentation helps the officer to work independently, without additional explanations or instructions after he has acquainted himself with the tactical situation and objective.

In garrison conditions officers of the Political Department work in three groups, each looking after a sector of the department's work: party, organization, propaganda. When the division starts exercises or combat there are only two teams: one with the Command Post, the other with the Quartermaster Command Post. The first team consists of the head of the Political Department, his deputy, three senior political instructors (for organization, propaganda, and special propaganda), one senior instructor for party matters assigned by the Party Committee of the Division Command, and two instructors (for organization and propaganda).

The first team is responsible for planning, directing, and organizing the whole of the political work of the division on exercises. The second team is auxiliary in character. Its composition varies according to the situation. It consists normally of the secretary of the Party Committee, one instructor for party records, one instructor for culture and education, and sometimes also one instructor for technical means of propaganda. The team maintains party records, organizes the distribution of press and propaganda materials, conducts party-political work among the personnel of the Quartermaster Command Post, and organizes a film exchange base and a propaganda equipment repair point.

It is a rule that at every stage of the exercise or combat one to three groups are madeup from among the personnel of the Political Department for the performance of special duties, for example,

- a group that supervises the conduct of political work, living conditions, and performs other duties if and when they arise

- a group directly involved in propaganda work among troops during halts in operations

- a group that becomes part of an evacuation and rescue unit when weapons of mass destruction are used.

Unlike the first two groups, which are formed as needs arise, the third group has a more specialized and permanent character. It has at its disposal a loudspeaker system and its officers are provided with tape-recorded instructions, appeals, and propaganda material.

Working in a group does not preclude sending individual officers to units of the division for special duties, like strengthening the Political Section of a regiment that is in an exposed position. Officers keep in touch with one another at all times.

The system as described above gives the head of the Political Department the facility to concentrate his actions where most needed. It also allows him to keep some officers in reserve for emergencies.

By contrast the deployment of political officers of a Political Section of a regiment is not governed by any fixed rules except that they are attached for a given period to units that have suffered heavy casualties or have received fresh reinforcements.

Source: Based on Wojsko Ludowe No. 2, 1974, pp. 53-58.

Appendix C

Meetings of Party Primary Unit (POP) committees took place once or twice a month. Two or three subjects prepared in advance by the secretary of the POP committee were discussed. The subjects were usually taken up later by the full meeting of the POP. The subjects belonged to one of four groups: (a) ideological-political, (b) command and directing, (c) training and education, or (d) internal party matters (organization and personnel matters).

During the two-year term of office the total nember of meetings held by the eight POP committees was 294. Of these, 142 meetings were devoted to subjects of group (d), 73 to group (a), 71 to group (c), eight to group (b).

During the same term of office, 164 full meetings of POP were held, making it 0.85 per POP per month. Of these, 79 were devoted to group (d), 46 to group (a), 25 to group (c), 14 to group (b). Group (d), which occupied almost as many meetings as the remaining three groups together, covered the following subjects: admission of new members and candidate members of the party; assignment of jobs, missions, and tasks and reporting on their execution; inquiry into ethical or moral offenses of members; matters concerning the current report-election campaign; degree of implementation of own resolutions and of tasks emerging from the party congress and Central Committee sessions.

A meeting normally ended with resolutions or motions on the subjects discussed. Passing of resolutions was followed by assigning specific jobs to individual members. During the two-year term of office, 577 tasks were assigned to 463 people, which meant that a member was given only two jobs a year whereas there should have been six, including one of longer duration. Regular NCOs and conscript personnel of the POP did not have jobs assigned to them on the assumption that they could not do much. About 30 percent of jobs were not done or were completed after the deadline.

Long-term assignments were to organize and run a group of self-improvement courses for soldiers with low training marks; give systematic help to the regiment's youth organization and report back to the committee every three months; assist the Executive Committee of the Military Families Association (ORW) with planning and work and report back on the activities of the organization, and run an instruction group on party matters.

Short term tasks were to organize a question and answer evening for the unit on an international topic; study the documents of the last Central Committee Plenum and give a lecture on the subject; organize a meeting with workers of a nearby factory in connection with an army anniversary; and hold a meeting with new party members and candidates about the role and duties of a party member in the army.

The POP of the regiment HQ is officially subordinated to the Party Committee at the regiment Command like any other POP in the regiment. In practice, subordination has become cooperation because both party bodies deal with matters concerning the whole regiment.

Source: Wojsko Ludowe No. 2, 1973, pp. 28-34.

Appendix D

Feliks Dzierzhinskij (1877-1926) came from a Polish landed-gentry family. From his early youth he was involved in revolutionary activities against Tsarist Russia. He was arrested six times, spent 11 years in prison, and was twice deported to Siberia. He was a friend of Lenin. In 1917 he organized and became head of the ignominious Tsheka, the first Soviet state security organization, the forerunner of the GPU (State Political Directorate) later to become the KGB. He ran the GPU until his death in 1926, at the age of 49.

Dzierzhinskij combined GPU duties with those of minister of communications (railways), minister of internal affairs, and chairman of the Supreme Economic Council. In the latter capacity he earned the name of father of Soviet heavy industry. The above four organizations had one thing in common: they handled large numbers of people, first as suspects of counterrevolution then as political prisoners and labor camp inmates. This was the origin of the ingenious conveyor belt that for decades has been solving Soviet political and labor problems in a systematic and organized way.

In the GPU Dzierzhinskij surrounded himself with Poles. His deputy, W. Mienzhinskij, succeeded him as head of GPU. At one time there were about 400 Poles in high positions in the central and regional organs of the Soviet state security service. It is curious that in the early years of the Soviet state a band of Poles was allowed to run the state security service. One can only assume that they were able to bring to the job a degree of detachment that might not have heen easy to find among Russians of that period.

In 1920, during the Soviet-Polish War, Dzierzhinskij was a member of a revolutionary committee of Poland that functioned as a provisional government on Polish territory already occupied by the

Red Army. The aim of the committee was to establish a Polish Soviet Socialist Republic. It formed a people's militia, handed over all factories to factory committees, and started to call up Poles for service in the 1st Polish Red Army.

The Soviet offensive was beaten back by Polish Forces under Jozef Pilsudski. Poland did not become the 17th Soviet socialist republic.

_____

Sources: W.E.P. Vol.3, 1963, p. 254; Vol. 11, 1968, p. 750; and J. Bobrowicz, Wojsko Ludowe No. 11, 1981, p. 96.

Appendix E

Solidarity is an association with a diverse political character and a complex professional composition. Intended perhaps originally as a trade union, it absorbed millions of people, mainly nonparty people whose interests and aspirations center on living conditions. But there is a significant number of Party members and of those who represent Social-Democratic, Christian-Democratic, syndicalist, and even anarchist attitudes. The bulk are workers but there are also hundreds of thousands of technical and nontechnical intelligentsia who are employed in state administration, the economy, education, trade, transport and services, and there are self-employed persons and individual farmers.

Solidarity is diversified also as regards world outlook as it embraces the range from believers to freemasons and atheists. When one adds diverse moral, ethical, and behavior standards Solidarity forms a picture of an organization that is varied ideologically and politically. . . .

Already at inception Solidarity was penetrated by various advisers, experts, and consultants who offered their services. They come in the main from KSS-KOR and included Jacek Kuron, Adam Michnik, and Karol Modzelewski, well know since the events of 1968. Having lost at that time, they reappeared with a much enhanced reputation in 1976, a great deal more political experience, and a determination to become the ideological leaders of Solidarity, In this way KSS-KOR obtained a chance to realize its own political

---

*President of the Higher School of Social Sciences of the Central Committee of the PUWP

aspirations, which in general terms aimed at transforming the Polish socialist system into a Social-Democratic model with anarchist and syndicalist undertones. Whereas the leaders of the Confederation of Independent Poland (KPN), led by Leszek Moczulski, who had some influence in Solidarity, were not hiding that their objective was over-throwing the Communist system in Poland and creating a bourgeois-democratic state, KSS-KOR leaders were backing a process of evolutionary changes that would lead to a gradual change of the existing political order. . . .

It would be wrong to regard all the advisers and experts who formulate the program, current tasks, and tactics of Solidarity as a uniform group who try to use the massive trade union movement for overthrowing the Socialist system and building their own political careers. They [the advisers and experts] represent various trends and concepts that have appeared and have been developing for months in Solidarity, leading to controversy, tensions, and to increasingly more apparent discord. . . .

It is known, for example, that among the leaders of the National Coordination Commission of Solidarity and at the regional level there are, broadly speaking, two conflicting lines: one stands for cooperation with the party and government in order to obtain for Solidarity certain advantages and influence, the other opposes cooperation and is for creating elements of a new political system through gaining control over workers' self-government in factories, predominance in elected regional and local councils, in cooperatives and consumer associa-tions, and later in the Seym.

Up to the 9th Party Congress, in Solidarity on the whole the tendency prevailed that the conflict should be settled through negotiation and some modus vivendi with the authorities reached. Already at that time, however, attempts were made in some regional organizations to achieve things by force. Most likely a part of Solidarity activists expected that the congress will take a course favorable to them, that is, produce if not a split in the party then at least its weakening. Against this hope after the congress the party grew in strength and its Central Committee assumed a greater worker and peasant character than ever before. The congress resolutions, the new statute, and the discussion created a basis and conditions for the party's revival in the spirit of Marxism-Leninism and for a gradual regaining of confidence among workers and society.

The government also worked more energetically because it had a ready conception of economic reform to which Solidarity had no alternative. It turned out, however, that these important preconditions for undertaking more effective steps in dealing with the crisis not only did not get the understanding and support from a section of Solidarity activists, but on the contrary, and surprisingly, produced a wave of actions that were directed against the party and government.

Instead of working with the authorities to serve the true interest of the nation in overcoming the shortage of food and goods through more effective work, greater discipline, and frugal management of the rapidly dwindling material resources, some adventure-seeking and irresponsible leaders of some regional and factory organizations of Solidarity started actions to create great tension in the country that threatened a confrontation of incalculable consequences. . . .

To sum-up: The anarchist and syndicalist stream in Solidarity nurtured ideologically by KSS-KOR with Kuron and Michnik at the helm strives to undermine further the position of the party and government by saying that they are unable to stem the crisis and that Solidarity is the only force that can do it because at its first congress it would present a "program of democracy for the state" and for improving the economy. In the same way as Moczulski and Szeremietiew of the KPN, some "radicals" of Solidarity uphold among the naive the illusion that they have a ready prescription and wonder medicines for all the nation's illnesses. All that was necessary was to give them power! In this way the point has been reached that Solidarity is assuming the character of a political organization determined to take power.

Source: Extracted from Trybuna Ludu, September 15, 1981.

Appendix F

The Propaganda Department of the party prepared a list of tasks designed to counter the effect of Pope John Paul II's visit to Poland in June 1983:

1. Acquaint party activists and members with the political assessment of the visit through lectures and meetings.
2. Start an ideological and political offensive.
3. The 13th Central Committee Plenum would arm the party ideologically.
4. The Party would soon prepare a declaration dealing with religion, denominations, and politics together.
5. Make a thorough analysis of the Pope's pronouncements and prepare for a possible offensive by the clergy.
6. Categorically oppose the theory of evolutionary changes in Poland.
7. Start an enlightenment campaign on church-state relations.
8. Categorically deny the possibility of the authorities reaching an agreement with the opposition.
9. Ask members and activists to prepare an interpretation of the pope's pronouncements.
10. Forestall the opposition in presenting an interpretation to the country.
11. Continue to decry Lech Walesa.
12. Analyze the attitude of the young during the visit and draw conclusions.
13. Argue for the introduction of the "knowledge of religions" subject into secondary and higher schools.
14. Establish actions explaining the attitude of the church to workers' movements.

15. Establish actions in support of the PRON mass organization.
16. Oppose attempts by the church to penetrate social organizations.
17. Prevent church organization formed for the visit to become permanent.
18. Make a thorough analysis of the political situation in towns visited by the pope.
19. Oppose attempts to introduce crosses into schools and review the church building program.
20. Maintain regular contacts with bishops and parish priests in order to combat social plagues and promote correct attitudes to work.
21. Categorically oppose hostile actions of priests and the use of churches as a platform for lay people.

Source: Text published in Bulletin No. 151 of Underground Solidarity for the Mazowsze Region, reproduced in Dziennik Polski (London) September 8, 1983, 3, p. 2.

Appendix G

The main political campaigns of 1966 were the celebrations connected with "A Thousand Years of Existence of the Polish State." Many regulars and their families, plus conscripts and civilian army employees, took part in large-scale political and cultural actions. The activities of air force personnel reached far beyond the gates of barracks and embraced large sections of the civilian population.

In units the aim was to popularize Polish history, especially the progressive and revolutionary traditions of the Polish Army and to prove that the People's Poland is the rightful heir to the achievements of that one thousand years. . . .

As is well known the Millenium celebrations were accompanied by improper actions on the part of the reactionary section of the clergy with Cardinal Wyszynski at the helm. Their aim was to torpedo initiatives of the party and government, to give the celebrations the religious character of baptism of Poland, to split society into believers and nonbelievers, and to set one part of the people against the People's Rule and Socialism.

These efforts of the Polish episcopate ended in failure. The Polish people, including a great many believers, stood with the authorities. Naturally, the activities of Wyszynski and part of the clergy were bound to have some effect in air force units. Because of that, commanders, the political apparatus, party, and party youth organizations had to consider the complexity of the situation and in order to counter signs of enemy propaganda had to arm the cadre and conscript soldiers with arguments and at the same time not lose sight of the important ideological education objectives contained in the guidelines issued by the Central Committee of the party and the Chief Political Directorate of the army.

The participation of regular and conscript personnel in the various actions and celebrations served as a kind of political exam and a test of the ideological attitude of air force personnel. . . .

Propaganda lecture tours among the rural population were one form of activity that deserves to be highlighted. The action embraced almost all Polish villages. An army officer was present at every village meeting. Officers of the air force gave 2,700 lectures, which were attended by 250,000 people. Teams of doctors, technical-repair specialists, and artists also took part. They saw 7,000 patients and carried out repairs to the value of 100,000 zloty. For comparison one should mention that the previous year during a campaign in connection with the 20th anniversary of the end of the war, air force officers held 340 meetings in which 75,000 people took part. . . .

The main themes of the meetings were the achievements in rural areas and defense matters, including the role of the air force in Poland's defense system. The meetings provided the opportunity to explain difficult matters and correct false opinions that had been spread by politically hostile centers. Here belonged the enlightenment work carried out by the air force cadre in connection with the famous address from Polish bishops to the German bishops [on reconciliation]. The officers treated this matter seriously and with deep inner commitment. Their work and attitude were highly praised by the party Central Committee. . . .

An additional and separate contribution was made in the Poznan Region where on November 26 and December 3, 1966, officers of the air force command and of some air force units "serviced" 250 meetings that were attended by about 24,000 people. In October 1966 in connection with Army Day celebrations, air force personnel organized 730 meetings with the civilian population that were attended by about 100,000 people. . . .

Altogether about 500,000 people took part in the above-described actions organized by the air force for the benefit of the civilian population.

Source: Extracted from Wojskowy Przeglad Lotniczy, No. 3, 1967, pp. 3-9.

Appendix H

The benefits to the nation and the state of the pope's visit, in our view, are manifold:

1. The mere fact that the visit could take place at all was proof that the political situation in Poland has stabilized. On the other hand it was a defeat for the forces that live for and see their political mission in exploiting every opportunity to spread unrest, quarrels, and even physical violence. The Polish people have shown that they are decisively against this method of solving conflicts and the authorities, having assessed the social mood correctly, have by inviting the pope given proof of their sincere striving for dialogue and renewal. The visit was therefore not forced upon them as some would like to believe. The authorities have authorized the visit not because of fear for their position but because the internal situation has become sufficiently normal to guarantee that meetings with the pope would not become a pretext for disrupting law and order and a threat to the state's security.

2. The call for peace was heard many times all over Poland. Nobody can deny that the People's Poland stands consistently for maintaining and consolidating this priceless value of international life. It was important for the great cause of peace that when the international situation was deteriorating, the call of the Polish pope, here on the Vistula, was added to the general call when the pope renewed his appeals to halt the arms race and save humanity from a nuclear catastrophe. The aims of the Socialist state and of the Roman Catholic Church have come together on this point.

3. The pope's addresses, especially in Wroclaw and on St. Ann's Mountain, carried the loud voice of the head of the Roman Catholic Church and of the Vatican State that the lands on the Oder, Neisse,

and the Baltic are Polish and that the western and northern frontiers of Poland are there to stay. The pope proclaimed that an independent, peaceful, strong, and secure Poland is what the nation, Europe, and the world need.

4. The visit was an opportunity to demonstrate the convergence of views of the state authorities, of the majority of people, and the church on issues that are fundamental to Poland, namely that Poland must live and develop by using its own resources, solve its problem through dialogue and concord, and go toward a better future through moral revival, build its future through work that must enjoy general respect because it increases the volume of material goods and represents the only means by which a human being can show his worth. [The Pope's visit] confirmed the truth that the transition from crisis to normality can be achieved only through concord and work.

During and in connection with the visit there was a great deal of speculation as to who gained most, the church or the state. This question stems from the fact that the Socialist state and the church draw inspiration from different ideological sources. These differences exist and it would be foolish to deny them. But at this point in history, in the very complicated world, they should not be the main object of interest and analysis. And they certainly should not give rise to a question of who has won and who has lost. In the situation when all can be lost, every point of agreement is worth consolidating irrespective of the difference in motivation. In this and in this way alone salvation, revival, and concord may be achieved.

Searching for points of agreement does not mean that the state renounces its secular character. The religious neutrality of the state, and the treatment of all denominations and religious movements as equal are valuable, progressive, and democratic assets. This is in line with the freedom of conscience and religion that are enshrined in the Constitution and represents tolerance that is characteristic of civilized societies. Consolidation of the secular character of the state is therefore in the interest of believers of all denominations, of nonbelievers, and of society as a whole. It is also in the interest of the state and Socialist democracy.

Source: Passages extracted in full from the lead article in Wojsko Ludowe, No. 8, 1983, pp. 3-4.

Appendix I

Name	Military Rank	Academic Title	Main Profile	Last Known Appointment and/or Organization
ANDRACKI, Henryk	Maj.-Gen.		Line Offr.	Commander of Signal Troops MON
ANYSZ, Marian	Colonel		Polit. Offr.	Commandant of CSOP
BADOWSKI, Tadeusz	Colonel	MA	Polit. Offr.	Deputy Chief Editor of Wojsko Ludowe
BANASZCZYK, Eugeniusz	Colonel		Polit. Offr.	Chief Political Directorate
BARSZCZEWSKI, Zdzislaw	Maj.-Gen.			Chief Commandant of OHP
BARYLA, Jozef	General	D.Phil.		Head Chief Political Directorate
BEBEN, Wladyslaw	Colonel	Staff Coll.	Polit. Offr.	Deputy Chairman of CKKP
BEIM, Jozef	Maj.-Gen. (Militia)			Chief Commandant of Citizens' Militia
BIDZINSKI, Adam	Maj.-Gen.	Staff Coll.	Line Offr.	Commandant of WOSL
BIENIASZ, Tadeusz	Colonel			Director of Defense Department in Ministry of Education
BIENIEK, Jerzy	Colonel	D.Phil.		Deputy Head of Political Directorate of SOW
BIERNACZYK, Zdzislaw	Maj.-Gen. (Militia)	D.Phil.	Polit. Offr.	Head Regional Office of Internal Affairs, Wroclaw
BLECHMAN, Zbigniew	Lt.-Gen.		Line Offr.	Commander of POW
BOGUSZ, Jan	Colonel	D.Phil.	Social sci.	Professor at WAP
BORGOSZ, Jozef	Colonel	D.Phil.	Social sci.	Professor at WAP
BRODZINSKI, Stanislaw	Colonel		Polit. Offr.	Political Directorate of WOW
BUDZINSKI, Jan	Colonel	MA		Editor's Office of Zolnierz Wolnosci
BUJAN, Leonid	Colonel	MA		Political Deputy Commandant of WSOWL
BULA, Edmund	Colonel	MA		Army Security Service
CALKA, Stanislaw	Colonel	D.Phil.	Polit. Offr.	Deputy Chief Commandant, OHP
CELEK, Jan	Colonel	D.Phil.		Political Deputy Commander Polish Air Force
CHUDY, Kazimierz	Colonel	Staff Coll.	Polit. Offr.	Commandant of WSOWRiA
CHWILKOWSKI, Simforian	Colonel	MA		Head of Propaganda Department of GZP
CIASTON, Wladyslaw	Lt.-Gen. (Militia)			Ministry of Internal Affairs
CICHOCKI, Leszek	Colonel			Chief Editor of Zolnierz Polski
CYGAN, Mieczyslaw	Maj.-Gen.			Voyevode of Gdansk Region
CYTOWSKI, Jerzy	Colonel	D.Phil.	Milit. sci.	Assistant professor at WAP
CZAJKOWSKI, Stanislaw	Nav. Capt.	MA	Polit. Offr.	Political Deputy Head of Naval Supplies
CZAPLA, Jan	Lt.-Gen.		Polit. Offr.	Deputy Minister of Education

273

*colonel and above level and equivalent; as at end 1983

Name	Military Rank	Academic Title	Main Profile	Last Known Appointment and/or Organization
CZERWINSKI, Jozef	Nav. Capt.	D.Phil.	Polit. Offr.	Staff of WAP
CZERWINSKI, Zdzislaw	Colonel	MA	Polit. Offr.	Chief Editor of Wojsko Ludowe
CZUBINSKI, Lucjan	Maj.-Gen.	D.Phil.	Social Sci.	Deputy Minister of Internal Affairs
CZYZEWSKI, Waclaw	Lt.-Gen.			Deputy Chairman of ZBoWiD
DACHOWSKI, Mieczyslaw	Lt.-Gen.		Line Offr.	Party Committee of Ministry of Defense
DE BICKI, Mieczyslaw	Lt.-Gen.	D.Phil.		President of Warsaw
DEGA, Czeslaw	Maj.-Gen.		Milit. Sci.	Head of Foreign Department of CC PUWP
DMOCHOWSKI, Ryszard	Colonel		Polit. Offr.	Political Deputy Head of Regional Military Staff, Cracow
DOMINIK, Henryk	Colonel	Staff Coll.		Secretary Party Committee 6th Airborne Division
DRZAZGA, Edward	Maj.-Gen.			Head of Chief Inspection Commission of Ministry of Administration
DUDEK, Leslaw	Maj.-Gen.	D.Phil.	Social Sci.	Assistant Professor at ASG
DUDZIAK, Zenon	Nav. Capt.		Polit. Offr.	1st Secretary of Party Committee Polish Navy
DUTKOWSKI, Ludwik	Rear Adm.		Polit. Offr.	Political Deputy Commander Polish Navy
DYSKO, Edward	Maj.-Gen.			Deputy Commandant of WAP
DZIEKAN, Tadeusz	Maj.-Gen.		Polit. Offr.	Head Personnel Dept. of CC PUWP
FIEDOROW, Artur	Colonel	Staff Coll.	Polit. Offr.	1st Secretary of Party Committee POW
FILIPEK, Wiktor Z.	Colonel			Commander of Security Troops of Ministry of Internal Affairs
GAC, Stanislaw	Colonel	D.Phil.	Social Sci.	Military Historical Institute
GARBACIK, Kazimierz	Colonel	Staff Coll.		Member of WRON
GARDY, Mieczyslaw	Colonel			Director of Army Printing Works
GASPEROWICZ, Stefan	Colonel	Staff Coll.		1st Secretary Party Committee of Polish Air Force
GASZCZOLOWSKI, Andrzej	Colonel		Polit. Offr.	Chief Political Directorate
GEBKA, Piotr	Colonel	MA	Polit. Offr.	Secretary in Regional Party Committee, Katowice
GLUSZCZYK, Zdzislaw	Maj.-Gen.			Commandant of WSOWP
GRABOWSKI, Kazimierz	Colonel		Polit. Offr.	Chairman of Party Control Commission WOP
GRABOWSKI, Tadeusz	Colonel	D.Phil.	Social Sci.	Professor at WAP
GROT, Leszek	Colonel	D.Phil.	Polit. Offr.	Chief Editor of Wojskowy Przegląd Historyczny
GRZASKO, Stanislaw	Colonel	Staff Coll.		First Secretary of Party Committee SOW
HERMASZEWSKI, Miroslaw	Colonel	MA		Member of WRON
HOLOWNIA, Kazimierz	Colonel			First Secretary of Party Committee Polish Air Force

Name	Military Rank	Academic Title	Main Profile	Last Known Appointment and/or Organization
HONKISZ, Wladyslaw	Maj.-Gen.		Polit. Offr.	Head Organization Department of GZP
HUCZEK, Josef	Colonel	MA	Polit. Offr.	Chief Political Directorate
HUPALOWSKI, Tadeusz	Lt.-Gen.		Line Offr.	Chairman of Supreme Chamber of Control (former member of WRON) Chairman of Chairman of LOK
HUSZCZA, Zygmunt	Lt.-Gen.	MA		Chief Editor of Zolnierz Polski
IGNACZAK, Jan	Colonel	D.Phil.	Social Sci.	Professor at Military Med. Academy
INDISOW, Longin	Colonel			Deputy Chief Inspector of OTK
JAGAS, Waclaw	Lt.-Gen.		Polit. Offr.	Chief Political Directorate
JAKUBCZYK, Ryszard	Colonel	MA (Eng.)	Polit. Offr.	Railway Troops Command
JAKUBIAK, Stanislaw	Col. (Retd.)	Staff Coll.		Chairman of ex-Ryazan Officer Club
JAMROZINSKI, Antoni				
JANCZYSZYN, Ludwik	Admiral			Chief Polish Navy (former member of WRON)
JANISZEWSKI, Michal	Lt.-Gen.	Staff Coll.		Chief of Office of Council of Ministers (former member of WRON)
JANUSZ, Henryk	Colonel	MA		Political Deputy Commandant of WAP
JAROSZ, Jerzy	Maj.-Gen.			Commander 1st Warsaw Mechanized Division (former member of WRON)
JARUZELSKI, Wojciech	Gen. of Army			Chairman of KOK, Supreme Commander of the Polish Armed Forces, Prime Minister, First Secretary PUWP
JATCZAK, Zdzislaw	Colonel			Secretary of Party Committee of Central Institutions of MON
JAWORSKI, Mieczyslaw	Colonel	D.Phil.	Social Sci.	Assistant Professor at WAP
JEDRYCHOWSKI, Zbigniew	Colonel			Chairman of Party Control Commission, SOW
JEDYNAK, Bonifacy	General (Militia)			Head of Personnel Department, Ministry of Internal Affairs
JERZYK, Stefan	Colonel		Polit. Offr.	1st Secretary of Party Committee, SOW
JURA, Wladyslaw	Maj.-Gen.	D.Phil.	Milit. Sci.	Political Deputy Commander of WOP
KACZMAREK, Julian	Colonel			Professor at ASG
KAMINSKI, Jozef	General			Commandant ASG
KANIA, Stanislaw				Member of Council of State (former 1st Secretary of the PUWP)
KAWULA, Waldemar	Colonel	MA	Polit. Offr.	Deputy Head Political Directorate of POW
KAZMIERCZAK, Ryszard	Colonel	MA	Polit. Offr.	Chief Political Directorate
KISZCZAK, Czeslaw	General			Minister of Internal Affairs (former Head WSW)
KNIAZIEWICZ, Stanislaw	Nav. Capt.			Chairman of Party Control Commission, Navy
KOBAK, Jaroslaw	Colonel	MA	Polit. Offr.	Ideological Training Center, Bydgoszcz
KOCZARA, Henryk	Lt.-Gen.		Polit. Offr.	Attaché (all Arms), Moscow

Name	Military Rank	Academic Title	Main Profile	Last Known Appointment and/or Organization
KOCZWARSKI, Jerzy	Colonel	MA	Polit. Offr.	Chief Political Directorate
KOJDER, Tadeusz	Maj.-Gen.		Polit. Offr.	Political Deputy Commander of WOPK
KOLATKOWSKI, Leon	Maj.-Gen.			Deputy Minister of Communications
KOLODZIEJCZAK, Boguslaw	Colonel	MA	Polit. Offr.	Head of Main Office of CC PUWP
KONDAS, Henryk	Maj.-Gen.	MA	Polit. Offr.	Political Deputy Commander, POW
KORCZAK, Wladyslaw	Colonel	MA	Polit. Offr.	Deputy Chairman of Polish Radio and TV Committee
KORZENIOWSKI, Franciszek	Colonel	MA	Polit. Offr.	Political Deputy Commander of Internal Defense Troops Unit, Warsaw
KOSTRZEWA, Henryk	Maj.-Gen.			Commissary of KOK in Ministry of Justice
KOSTRZEWA, Ryszard	Colonel	MA	Polit. Offr.	Political Deputy Commandant of Military Medical Academy
KOSYRZ, Zdzislaw	Colonel		Social Sci.	Assistant Professor at WAP
KOT, Marian	Colonel			Head of Office of Complaints and Inspections of the CC PUWP
KOZLOWSKI, Eugeniusz	Colonel	D.Phil.		Assistant Professor at WIH
KOZLOWSKI, Wladyslaw	Colonel	D.Phil.	Polit. Offr.	Political Directorate of Polish Air Force
KRAJEWSKI, Zenon	Colonel	MA	Polit. Offr.	Chief Political Directorate
KRAWCZYC, Tytus	Lt.-Gen.			Chief of Polish Air Force
KREPSKI, Tadeusz	Lt.-Gen.			Former Chief of Polish Air Force and member of WRON
KRYNSKI, Henryk	Colonel	MA	Polit. Offr.	1st Secretary Party Committee, GZP
KUBICA, Feliks	Colonel			Assistant Professor, Military Institute of Armored and Motor Vehicles
KUBICZEK, Ryszard	Maj.-Gen.			Commander of Rocket and Artillery Troops
KUCZERA, Stefan	Colonel	MA	Polit. Offr.	Secretary of Party Committee, WSW
KULIK, Kazimierz	Colonel	MA	Polit. Offr.	Chief Political Directorate
KURZEPA, Wladyslaw	Colonel	MA	Polit. Offr.	Secretary Party Committee, WOP
KWASNIEWSKI, Tadeusz	Colonel	MA	Polit. Offr.	Head Regional Military Staffs, Krosno
KWIATEK, Stefan	Colonel	MA	Polit. Offr.	Chief Political Directorate
KWIATKOWSKI, Stanislaw	Colonel	D.Phil.	Polit. Offr.	Complaints Department of GZP
KWIATKOWSKI, Zygmunt	Colonel	MA	Polit. Offr.	Head of Public Opinion Research Center
LASON, Albin	Colonel	MA		Head of Department of Military Schools, GZP
LEBKOWSKI, Wojciech	Colonel	D.Phil.		Deputy Chairman of Main Board of ZOSP
LECZYK, Marian	Colonel	D.Phil.	Social Sci.	Commissary of KOK in Lublin Region / Professor at WAP
LES, Roman	Col. (Retd.)	D.Phil.	Social Sci.	Chairman of ZBZZ

Name	Military Rank	Academic Title	Main Profile	Last Known Appointment and/or Organization
LEWICKI, Jozef	Colonel	MA	Polit. Offr.	Chief Political Directorate
LIPINSKI, Kazimierz	Maj.-Gen.			President of Military Chamber of Supreme Court
LOZOWICKI, Longin	Lt.-Gen.			Commander of WOPK (former member of WRON)
LUDWICZAK, Hieronim	Colonel	MA	Polit. Offr.	Polit. Deputy Commander 1st Warsaw Mechanized Division
LUKASIK, Edward	Maj.-Gen.		Polit. Offr.	1st Secretary of Party Committee of Poznan Region
MAGON, Walerian	Nav. Capt.	D.Phil		Deputy Commandant of WAP
MAKAREWICZ, Tadeusz	Colonel	Staff Coll.		Commander of unspecified Unit, former member of WRON
MAKOWIECKI, Waldemar	Colonel			Head of Section in Editorial Office of Zolnierz Wolnosci
MARCHEWKA, Bernard	Colonel			Former Commissary of KOK in Lenin Shipyard, Gdansk
MARCHEWKA, Brunon	Maj.-Gen. (Retd.)			Deputy Chairman of ZBZZ
MARKIEWICZ, Wieslaw M.	Colonel	MA		Political Deputy Commandant of WOSL
MAZUREK, Bogdan	Colonel	MA	Polit. Offr.	Political Deputy Commandant of Training Center of WOP
MAZURKIEWICZ, Stanislaw	Colonel	Staff Coll.		First Secretary of Party Committee 6th Airborne Division
MAZURKIEWICZ, Zdzislaw	Colonel	Staff Coll.	Social Sci.	Voyevode of Koszalin Region
MICHALIK, Mieczyslaw	Maj.-Gen.	D.Phil.	Polit. Offr.	Deputy Commandant and Prof. of WAP
MICHTA, Norbert	Colonel	D.Phil.		Rector of Higher School of Social Sciences, CC PUWP
MIEKUS, Zbigniew	Colonel			Commissary of KOK for key establishments in Warsaw
MIKOLAJCZAK, Walerian	Colonel		Polit. Offr.	Voyevode Zielona Gora Region
MILCZAREK, Ryszard	Maj.-Gen.		Polit. Offr.	Political Deputy Commander of SOW
MILLER, Henryk	Colonel	MA	Polit. Offr.	Chief Political Directorate
MISZTAL, Zdzislaw	Nav. Capt.	D.Phil.	Social Sci.	Department of Military Schools, GZP
MODRZEWSKI, Jerzy	Lt.-Gen.			Deputy Commandant of WAP
MOLCZYK, Eugeniusz	General			Deputy Minister of Metallurgy and Machine Building
MOLCZYK, Zenon	Colonel	D.Phil		Chief Inspector of Training (former member of WRON)
MROZ, Wladyslaw	Lt.-Gen.	D.Phil		Head Regional Military Staff, Gdansk
MUCHOWIECKI, Piotr	Colonel	MA		Head of Inspection Department, MON
				First Secretary of Party Committee WOPK

277

Name	Military Rank	Academic Title	Main Profile	Last Known Appointment and/or Organization
MUSIAL, Jozef	Colonel	Staff Coll.		Head of Regional Military Staff, Bydgoszcz
MUSZYNSKI, Jerzy	Colonel	D.Phil.	Social Sci.	Professor at WAP
MURASZKIEWICZ, Andrzej	Maj.-Gen.	D.Phil.		Advanced Officer Training Center
NIEDEK, Witold	General			Commandant of WSOWOPi
NOWAK, Zbigniew	General			Chief Inspector of Equipment
OBIEDZINSKI, Mieczyslaw	Lt.-Gen.			Chief Quartermaster of the PPA
OBRONIECKI, Tadeusz	Lt.-Gen.			Commander of WOPK
OCHOCKI, Kazimierz	Colonel	D.Phil.	Polit. Offr.	Secretary of Party Control Commission of the Army
OLIWA, Wlodzimierz	Lt.-Gen.			Minister of Administration (former member of WRON)
OLSZEWSKI, Ignacy	Colonel	MA	Polit. Offr.	Editors' Board of Wojsko Ludowe
OSTROWSKI, Tomasz	General			Commandant of professional Fire-Fighting Service
PACZESNIAK, Jerzy	Colonel			Deputy Chief Editor of Zolnierz Wolnosci
PAJKO, Aleksander	Colonel			1st Secretary of Party Committee, WOW
PALUCH, Edward	Colonel		Polit. Offr.	Director of Military Journals Publishing Agency
PASTERNAK, Marian	Maj.-Gen.			Commander of Communication (Signals) Troops
PASTUSZYN, Leon	Colonel	MA	Polit. Offr.	Chief Political Directorate
PASZKOWSKI, Roman	Lt.-Gen.			Voyevode of Katowice Region
PAWLOWSKI, Wiktor	Colonel	MA		Army Security Service
PECIAK, Roman	Colonel	Staff Coll.		Head of Regional Military Staff, Szczecin
PERCHLAK, Zygmunt	Colonel			Political Officers Training Center, Lodz
PIOTROWSKI, Czeslaw	Lt.-Gen.		Polit. Offr.	Minister for Mines and Power Industry (former member of WRON)
PIROG, Jan	Maj.-Gen.			Head Regional Military Staff, Lublin
PLIKUS, Mikolaj	Colonel	Staff Coll.		Chairman of Defense Knowledge Association
POLANSKI, Wladyslaw	Lt.-Gen.		Polit. Offr.	Commandant of WAP
POPIOLEK, Marian	Colonel	Staff Coll.		Head of Regional Military Staff, Warsaw City & Region
PORADKO, Edward	Maj.-Gen.			Head of Army Security Service
POWALA, Jan	Colonel	D.Phil.	Polit. Offr.	Deputy Commandant of CSOP
POZOGA, Wladyslaw	Lt.-Gen. (Militia)			Deputy Minister of Internal Affairs
PRZYBYSZEWSKI, Piotr	Maj.-Gen.			Commandant of WSOSK
RAPACEWICZ, Henryk	Lt.-Gen.		Social Sci.	Commander of Silesian Military District
RATAJCZYK, Leonard	Colonel	D.Phil.	Polit. Offr.	Assistant Professor at WH
ROSTOWSKI, Adam	Colonel	D.Phil.	Polit. Offr.	Chief Political Directorate
ROZBICKI, Kazimierz	Colonel	MA	Polit. Offr.	Polit Deputy Head Regional Military Staffs, Warsaw
ROZBICKI, Zdzislaw	Colonel	D.Phil.	Polit. Offr.	Head of Political Directorate, SOW
ROZKO, Zenon	Colonel	MA	Polit. Offr.	Deputy Commandant of Military Medical Academy

Name	Military Rank	Academic Title	Main Profile	Last Known Appointment and/or Organization
RUTKOWSKI, Henryk	Colonel	MA	Polit. Offr.	Chief Political Directorate
RUTKOWSKI, Stefan	Colonel	MA	Polit. Offr.	Chairman of Party Control Commission of the PPA
RYBA, Marian	Maj.-Gen.			Gen Director Office of Council of Ministers
RYBARCZYK, Ryszard	Colonel	MA		Army Security Service
SAWCZUK, Wlodzimierz	General		Polit. Offr.	Diplomatic Service (former Head GZP)
SIWICKI, Florian	General		Line Offr.	Minister of Defense
SKALSKI, Jerzy	Lt.-Gen.			Commander Warsaw Military District
SLIWINSKI, Jan	Lt.-Gen.		Social Sci.	Commissary of KOK in Ministry of Foreign Trade
SOBCZAK, Kazimierz	Colonel	D.Phil.		Commandant Military Historical Institute
SOBIERAJ, Ludwik	Colonel			Political Deputy Commandant of ASG
SOCHA, Jan	Maj.-Gen.	D.Phil.		Political Deputy Commander, WOW
SOKOL, Julian	Colonel	MA	Polit. Offr.	Chief Political Directorate
SOKOLOWSKI, Stanislaw	Colonel	D.Phil.	Social Sci.	Assistant Professor at WAP
SOKORSKI, Wlodzimierz	Colonel		Polit. Offr.	Chairman Main Board of ZBoWiD
STACIWA, Czeslaw	Colonel	D.Phil.	Polit. Offr.	Institute of Social Studies (WAP)
STAPOR, Zdzislaw	Colonel	D.Phil.	Social Sci.	Assistant Professor at ASG
STEPNIOWSKI, Franciszek	Colonel	MA		Chief Editor MON Publishing House
STRAMIK, Feliks	Maj.-Gen.			Commander of Frontier Troops
SUWART, Jerzy	Colonel	MA	Polit. Offr.	Civil Defense Organization
SWIATOWIEC, Jan	Maj.-Gen.			First Deputy Chief Inspector OTK and Internal Defense Troops
SWIECICKI, Henryk	Colonel	Staff Coll.		Commissary of KOK for Olsztyn Region
SZACILO, Tadeusz	Lt.-Gen.	D.Phil.	Polit. Offr.	1st Deputy Head of GZP
SZCZEPKOWSKI, Marek	Colonel	D.Phil.	Polit. Offr.	Department of Culture and Education GZP
SZUMSKI, Henryk	Maj.-Gen.	Staff Coll.		Commander 12th Mechanized Division. Szczecin
SZYMANSKI, Henryk	Colonel			Commissary of KOK for Gdansk
TARKIEWICZ, Jan	Colonel	MA		1st Secretary of Party Committee Security Troops of Ministry of Internal Affairs
TORBUS, Janusz	Nav. Capt.			1st Secretary of Party Committee WSMW
TRZYBINSKI, Adam	Colonel			Head Regional Office of Internal Affairs
TUCZAPSKI, Tadeusz	General			Chief Inspector of OTK (former member of WRON)
URBANIAK, Wladyslaw	Colonel			Political Deputy Commandant of WAT
URBANOWICZ, Jozef	General		Polit. Offr.	Deputy Minister of Defense (former Head of GZP)
URBANSKI, Wladyslaw	Colonel	MA (Eng.)		Commandant of WSOWL
URLINSKI, Ryszard	Colonel	D.Phil.		Voyevode Elblag Region
UZYCKI, Jozef	Lt.-Gen.			Chief of General Staff (former member of WRON)
WAGA, Andrzej	Nav. Capt.		Polit. Offr.	Political Apparatus of the Navy

Name	Military Rank	Academic Title	Main Profile	Last Known Appointment and/or Organization
WALICHNOWSKI, Tadeusz	Colonel			Commandant of Academy of Internal Affairs
WAWRZKIEWICZ, Wladyslaw	Colonel			Deputy Commander of Signal Troops
WIECHA, Stanislaw	Colonel	D. Phil.	Social Sci.	Director of WAP Library
WIECZOREK, Mieczyslaw	Colonel	D. Phil.	Social Sci.	Chair of Military History at WAP
WIMMER, Jan	Maj.-Gen.	D. Phil.	Social Sci.	Professor at Military Historical Institute
WLODARCZYK, Edward				Commissary of KOK at Ministry of Science and Technology
WLODARSKI, Mieczyslaw	Maj.-Gen.	D. Phil.	Polit. Offr.	Deputy Head GZP for Military Schools
WLOSINSKI, Jerzy	Colonel			Commander of Mazowsze Unit of Internal Defense Troops (former member of WRON)
WOJCIK, Edward	Colonel	Staff Coll.		Member of Board of Editors of Wojsko Ludowe
WOJTASIK, Leslaw	Colonel		Polit. Offr.	Head of Propaganda Department of GZP
ZACZKOWSKI, Stanislaw	Maj.-Gen. (Militia)			Deputy Minister of Internal Affairs
ZAJKO, Eugeniusz	Colonel	Staff Coll.		Vice-President of Warsaw
ZAMBO, Henryk	Colonel	D. Phil.		Director of Central Army Library
ZARON, Piotr	Colonel	D. Phil.		Commissary of Torun Region
ZBINIEWICZ, Fryderyk	Colonel	D. Phil.	Social Sci.	Assistant Professor at WIH
ZLAJA, Leon	Lt.-Gen.	D. Phil.	Social Sci.	Assistant Professor at WAP
ZIELINSKI, Jan	Colonel			Commissary of KOK at Ministry of Foreign Trade
ZIELINSKI, Wladyslaw	Lt.-Gen.			Head of Foreign Section in Zolnierz Wolnosci
ZIELINSKI, Zygmunt	Colonel	D. Phil.		Head of Personnel Department MON
ZIOLKOWSKI, Stanislaw	Colonel	MA		Political Apparatus of Frontier Troops
ZYTO, Albin	Maj.-Gen.		Polit. Offr.	Head Culture and Education Department, GZP

Index

About the Author

GEORGE C. MALCHER was born in the Upper Silesia region of Poland. He studied law and administration at the Jagiellonian University of Cracow and political science at the School of Political Sciences, Cracow. During World War II he served as an intelligence officer with the Polish forces fighting on the side of the Western allies. After the war, he was prevented from returning to Communist Poland and subsequently worked for over 30 years as a top-grade linguist in the British civil service. This book sprang from a lifelong interest in the "mechanisms of power" and out of concern for the future of Poland.